Data-Intensive Text Processing with MapReduce

Synthesis Lectures on Human Language Technologies

Editor

Graeme Hirst, *University of Toronto*

Synthesis Lectures on Human Language Technologies is edited by Graeme Hirst of the University of Toronto. The series consists of 50- to 150-page monographs on topics relating to natural language processing, computational linguistics, information retrieval, and spoken language understanding. Emphasis is on important new techniques, on new applications, and on topics that combine two or more HLT subfields.

Data-Intensive Text Processing with MapReduce

Jimmy Lin and Chris Dyer

www.morganclaypool.com

ISBN: 9781608453429   paperback
ISBN: 9781608453436   ebook

DOI 10.2200/S00274ED1V01Y201006HLT007

A Publication in the Morgan & Claypool Publishers series
SYNTHESIS LECTURES ON HUMAN LANGUAGE TECHNOLOGIES

Lecture #7
Series Editor: Graeme Hirst, *University of Toronto*
Series ISSN
Synthesis Lectures on Human Language Technologies
Print 1947-4040   Electronic 1947-4059

Data-Intensive Text Processing with MapReduce

Jimmy Lin and Chris Dyer
University of Maryland

SYNTHESIS LECTURES ON HUMAN LANGUAGE TECHNOLOGIES #7

MORGAN & CLAYPOOL PUBLISHERS

ABSTRACT

Our world is being revolutionized by data-driven methods: access to large amounts of data has generated new insights and opened exciting new opportunities in commerce, science, and computing applications. Processing the enormous quantities of data necessary for these advances requires large clusters, making distributed computing paradigms more crucial than ever. MapReduce is a programming model for expressing distributed computations on massive datasets and an execution framework for large-scale data processing on clusters of commodity servers. The programming model provides an easy-to-understand abstraction for designing scalable algorithms, while the execution framework transparently handles many system-level details, ranging from scheduling to synchronization to fault tolerance. This book focuses on MapReduce algorithm design, with an emphasis on text processing algorithms common in natural language processing, information retrieval, and machine learning. We introduce the notion of MapReduce design patterns, which represent general reusable solutions to commonly occurring problems across a variety of problem domains. This book not only intends to help the reader "think in MapReduce", but also discusses limitations of the programming model as well.

KEYWORDS

Hadoop, parallel and distributed programming, algorithm design, text processing, natural language processing, information retrieval, machine learning

Contents

Acknowledgments

The first author is grateful to Esther and Kiri for their loving support. He dedicates this book to Joshua and Jacob, the new joys of his life.

The second author would like to thank Herb for putting up with his disorderly living habits and Philip for being a very indulgent linguistics advisor.

This work was made possible by the Google and IBM Academic Cloud Computing Initiative (ACCI) and the National Science Foundation's Cluster Exploratory (CLuE) program, under award IIS-0836560, and also award IIS-0916043. Any opinions, findings, conclusions, or recommendations expressed in this book are those of the authors and do not necessarily reflect the views of the sponsors.

We are grateful to Jeff Dean, Miles Osborne, Tom White, as well as numerous other individuals who have commented on earlier drafts of this book.

Jimmy Lin and Chris Dyer
May 2010

CHAPTER 1

Introduction

MapReduce [45] is a programming model for expressing distributed computations on massive amounts of data and an execution framework for large-scale data processing on clusters of commodity servers. It was originally developed by Google and built on well-known principles in parallel and distributed processing dating back several decades. MapReduce has since enjoyed widespread adoption via an open-source implementation called Hadoop, whose development was led by Yahoo (now an Apache project). Today, a vibrant software ecosystem has sprung up around Hadoop, with significant activity in both industry and academia.

This book is about scalable approaches to processing large amounts of text with MapReduce. Given this focus, it makes sense to start with the most basic question: Why? There are many answers to this question, but we focus on two. First, "big data" is a fact of the world, and therefore an issue that real-world systems must grapple with. Second, across a wide range of text processing applications, more data translates into more effective algorithms, and thus it makes sense to take advantage of the plentiful amounts of data that surround us.

Modern information societies are defined by vast repositories of data, both public and private. Therefore, any practical application must be able to scale up to datasets of interest. For many, this means scaling up to the web, or at least a non-trivial fraction thereof. Any organization built around gathering, analyzing, monitoring, filtering, searching, or organizing web content must tackle large-data problems: "web-scale" processing is practically synonymous with data-intensive processing. This observation applies not only to well-established internet companies, but also countless startups and niche players as well. Just think, how many companies do you know that start their pitch with "we're going to harvest information on the web and..."?

Another strong area of growth is the analysis of user behavior data. Any operator of a moderately successful website can record user activity and in a matter of weeks (or sooner) be drowning in a torrent of log data. In fact, logging user behavior generates so much data that many organizations simply can't cope with the volume, and either turn the functionality off or throw away data after some time. This represents lost opportunities, as there is a broadly held belief that great value lies in insights derived from mining such data. Knowing what users look at, what they click on, how much time they spend on a web page, etc., leads to better business decisions and competitive advantages. Broadly, this is known as business intelligence, which encompasses a wide range of technologies including data warehousing, data mining, and analytics.

How much data are we talking about? A few examples: Google grew from processing 100 terabytes of data a day with MapReduce in 2004 [45] to processing 20 petabytes a day with MapReduce in 2008 [46]. In April 2009, a blog post[1] was written about eBay's two enormous data warehouses: one with 2 petabytes of user data, and the other with 6.5 petabytes of user data spanning 170 trillion records and growing by 150 billion new records per day. Shortly thereafter, Facebook revealed[2] similarly impressive numbers, boasting of 2.5 petabytes of user data, growing at about 15 terabytes per day. Petabyte datasets are rapidly becoming the norm, and the trends are clear: our ability to store data is fast overwhelming our ability to process what we store. More distressing, increases in capacity are outpacing improvements in bandwidth such that our ability to even *read* back what we store is deteriorating [91]. Disk capacities have grown from tens of megabytes in the mid-1980s to about a couple of terabytes today (several orders of magnitude). On the other hand, latency and bandwidth have improved relatively little: in the case of latency, perhaps $2\times$ improvement during the last quarter century, and in the case of bandwidth, perhaps $50\times$. Given the tendency for individuals and organizations to continuously fill up whatever capacity is available, large-data problems are growing increasingly severe.

Moving beyond the commercial sphere, many have recognized the importance of data management in many scientific disciplines, where petabyte-scale datasets are also becoming increasingly common [21]. For example:

- The high-energy physics community was already describing experiences with petabyte-scale databases back in 2005 [20]. Today, the Large Hadron Collider (LHC) near Geneva is the world's largest particle accelerator, designed to probe the mysteries of the universe, including the fundamental nature of matter, by recreating conditions shortly following the Big Bang. When it becomes fully operational, the LHC will produce roughly 15 petabytes of data a year.[3]

- Astronomers have long recognized the importance of a "digital observatory" that would support the data needs of researchers across the globe—the Sloan Digital Sky Survey [145] is perhaps the most well known of these projects. Looking into the future, the Large Synoptic Survey Telescope (LSST) is a wide-field instrument that is capable of observing the entire sky every few days. When the telescope comes online around 2015 in Chile, its 3.2 gigapixel primary camera will produce approximately half a petabyte of archive images every month [19].

- The advent of next-generation DNA sequencing technology has created a deluge of sequence data that needs to be stored, organized, and delivered to scientists for further study. Given the fundamental tenant in modern genetics that genotypes explain phenotypes, the impact of this technology is nothing less than transformative [103]. The European Bioinformatics Institute (EBI), which hosts a central repository of sequence data called EMBL-bank, has increased storage capacity from 2.5 petabytes in 2008 to 5 petabytes in 2009 [142]. Scientists are predicting that, in the not-so-distant future, sequencing an individual's genome will be no more complex than getting a blood test today—ushering a new era of personalized medicine, where interventions can be specifically targeted for an individual.

---

[1] http://www.dbms2.com/2009/04/30/ebays-two-enormous-data-warehouses/
[2] http://www.dbms2.com/2009/05/11/facebook-hadoop-and-hive/
[3] http://public.web.cern.ch/public/en/LHC/Computing-en.html

Increasingly, scientific breakthroughs will be powered by advanced computing capabilities that help researchers manipulate, explore, and mine massive datasets [72]—this has been hailed as the emerging "fourth paradigm" of science [73] (complementing theory, experiments, and simulations). In other areas of academia, particularly computer science, systems and algorithms incapable of scaling to massive real-world datasets run the danger of being dismissed as "toy systems" with limited utility. Large data is a fact of today's world and data-intensive processing is fast becoming a necessity, not merely a luxury or curiosity.

Although large data comes in a variety of forms, this book is primarily concerned with processing large amounts of text, but touches on other types of data as well (e.g., relational and graph data). The problems and solutions we discuss mostly fall into the disciplinary boundaries of natural language processing (NLP) and information retrieval (IR). Recent work in these fields is dominated by a data-driven, empirical approach, typically involving algorithms that attempt to capture statistical regularities in data for the purposes of some task or application. There are three components to this approach: data, representations of the data, and some method for capturing regularities in the data. Data are called *corpora* (singular, corpus) by NLP researchers and *collections* by those from the IR community. Aspects of the representations of the data are called *features*, which may be "superficial" and easy to extract, such as the words and sequences of words themselves, or "deep" and more difficult to extract, such as the grammatical relationship between words. Finally, algorithms or models are applied to capture regularities in the data in terms of the extracted features for some application. One common application, classification, is to sort text into categories. Examples include: Is this email spam or not spam? Is this word part of an address or a location? The first task is easy to understand, while the second task is an instance of what NLP researchers call named-entity detection [138], which is useful for local search and pinpointing locations on maps. Another common application is to rank texts according to some criteria—search is a good example, which involves ranking documents by relevance to the user's query. Another example is to automatically situate texts along a scale of "happiness", a task known as sentiment analysis or opinion mining [118], which has been applied to everything from understanding political discourse in the blogosphere to predicting the movement of stock prices.

There is a growing body of evidence, at least in text processing, that of the three components discussed above (data, features, algorithms), data probably matters the most. Superficial word-level features coupled with simple models in most cases trump sophisticated models with deeper features and less data. But why can't we have our cake and eat it too? Why not both sophisticated models *and* deep features applied to lots of data? Because inference over sophisticated models and extraction of deep features are often computationally intensive, they don't scale well.

Consider a simple task such as determining the correct usage of easily confusable words such as "than" and "then" in English. One can view this as a supervised machine learning problem: we can train a classifier to disambiguate between the options, and then apply the classifier to new instances of the problem (say, as part of a grammar checker). Training data is fairly easy to come by—we can just gather a large corpus of texts and assume that most writers make correct choices (the training data may be noisy, since people make mistakes, but no matter). In 2001, Banko and Brill [14] published what has become a classic paper in natural language processing exploring the effects of training data size on classification accuracy, using this task as the specific example. They explored several classification algorithms (the exact ones aren't important, as we shall see), and not surprisingly, found that more data led to better accuracy. Across many different algorithms, the increase in accuracy was approximately linear in the log of the size of the training data. Furthermore, with increasing amounts of training data, the accuracy of different algorithms converged, such that pronounced differences in effectiveness observed on smaller datasets basically disappeared at scale. This led to a somewhat controversial conclusion (at least at the time): machine learning algorithms really don't matter, all that matters is the amount of data you have. This resulted in an even more controversial recommendation, delivered somewhat tongue-in-cheek: we should just give up working on algorithms and simply spend our time gathering data (while waiting for computers to become faster so we can process the data).

As another example, consider the problem of answering short, fact-based questions such as "Who shot Abraham Lincoln?" Instead of returning a list of documents that the user would then have to sort through, a question answering (QA) system would directly return the answer: John Wilkes Booth. This problem gained interest in the late 1990s, when natural language processing researchers approached the challenge with sophisticated linguistic processing techniques such as syntactic and semantic analysis. Around 2001, researchers discovered a far simpler approach to answering such questions based on pattern matching [27; 53; 92]. Suppose you wanted the answer to the above question. As it turns out, you can simply search for the phrase "shot Abraham Lincoln" on the web and look for what appears to its left. Or better yet, look through multiple instances of this phrase and tally up the words that appear to the left. This simple strategy works surprisingly well, and has become known as the *redundancy-based approach* to question answering. It capitalizes on the insight that in a very large text collection (i.e., the web), answers to commonly asked questions will be stated in obvious ways, such that pattern-matching techniques suffice to extract answers accurately.

Yet another example concerns smoothing in web-scale language models [25]. A language model is a probability distribution that characterizes the likelihood of observing a particular sequence of words, estimated from a large corpus of texts. They are useful in a variety of applications, such as speech recognition (to determine what the speaker is more likely to have said) and machine translation (to determine which of possible translations is the most fluent, as we will discuss in Section 6.4). Since there are infinitely many possible strings, and probabilities must be assigned to all of them, language modeling is a more challenging task than simply keeping track of which strings were seen how many times: some number of likely strings will never be encountered, even with lots and lots of training data! Most modern language models make the Markov assumption: in a n-gram language model, the conditional probability of a word is given by the $n-1$ previous words. Thus, by the chain rule, the probability of a sequence of words can be decomposed into the product of n-gram probabilities. Nevertheless, an enormous number of parameters must still be estimated from a training corpus: potentially V^n parameters, where V is the number of words in the vocabulary. Even if we treat every word on the web as the training corpus from which to estimate the n-gram probabilities, most n-grams—in any language, even English—will never have been seen. To cope with this sparseness, researchers have developed a number of smoothing techniques [35; 79; 102], which all share the basic idea of moving probability mass from observed to unseen events in a principled manner. Smoothing approaches vary in effectiveness, both in terms of intrinsic and application-specific metrics. In 2007, Brants et al. [25] described language models trained on up to two trillion words.[4] Their experiments compared a state-of-the-art approach known as Kneser-Ney smoothing [35] with another technique the authors affectionately referred to as "stupid backoff".[5] Not surprisingly, stupid backoff didn't work as well as Kneser-Ney smoothing on smaller corpora. However, it was simpler and could be trained on *more* data, which ultimately yielded better language models. That is, a simpler technique on more data beat a more sophisticated technique on less data.

Recently, three Google researchers summarized this data-driven philosophy in an essay titled *The Unreasonable Effectiveness of Data* [65].[6] Why is this so? It boils down to the fact that language *in the wild*, just like human behavior in general, is messy. Unlike, say, the interaction of subatomic particles, human *use* of language is not constrained by succinct, universal "laws of grammar". There are of course rules that govern the formation of words and sentences—for example, that verbs appear before objects in English, and that subjects and verbs must agree in number in many languages—but real-world language is affected by a multitude of other factors as well: people invent new words and phrases all the time, authors occasionally make mistakes, groups of individuals write within a shared context, etc. The Argentine writer Jorge Luis Borges wrote a famous allegorical one-paragraph story about a fictional society in which the art of cartography had gotten so advanced that their maps were as big as the lands they were describing.[7] The world, he would say, is the best description of itself. In the same way, the more observations we gather about language use, the more accurate a description we have of language itself. This, in turn, translates into more effective algorithms and systems.

So, in summary, why large data? In some ways, the first answer is similar to the reason people climb mountains: because they're there. But the second answer is even more compelling. Data represent the rising tide that lifts all boats—more data lead to better algorithms and systems for solving real-world problems. Now that we've addressed the *why*, let's tackle the *how*. Let's start with the obvious observation: data-intensive processing is beyond the capability of any individual machine and requires clusters—which means that large-data problems are fundamentally about organizing computations on dozens, hundreds, or even thousands of machines. This is exactly what MapReduce does, and the rest of this book is about the *how*.

[4]As an aside, it is interesting to observe the evolving definition of *large* over the years. Banko and Brill's paper in 2001 was titled *Scaling to Very Very Large Corpora for Natural Language Disambiguation*, and dealt with a corpus containing a billion words.
[5]As in, so stupid it couldn't possibly work.
[6]This title was inspired by a classic article titled *The Unreasonable Effectiveness of Mathematics in the Natural Sciences* [155]. This is somewhat ironic in that the original article lauded the beauty and elegance of mathematical models in capturing natural phenomena, which is the exact opposite of the data-driven approach.
[7]*On Exactitude in Science* [23]. A similar exchange appears in Chapter XI of *Sylvie and Bruno Concluded* by Lewis Carroll (1893).

1.1 COMPUTING IN THE CLOUDS

For better or for worse, it is often difficult to untangle MapReduce and large-data processing from the broader discourse on cloud computing. True, there is substantial promise in this new paradigm of computing, but unwarranted hype by the media and popular sources threatens its credibility in the long run. In some ways, cloud computing is simply brilliant marketing. Before clouds, there were grids,[8] and before grids, there were vector supercomputers, each having claimed to be the best thing since sliced bread.

So what exactly is cloud computing? This is one of those questions where 10 experts will give 11 different answers; in fact, countless papers have been written simply to attempt to define the term (e.g., [9; 31; 149], just to name a few examples). Here we offer up our own thoughts and attempt to explain how cloud computing relates to MapReduce and data-intensive processing.

At the most superficial level, everything that used to be called web applications has been rebranded to become "cloud applications", which includes what we have previously called "Web 2.0" sites. In fact, anything running inside a browser that gathers and stores user-generated content now qualifies as an example of cloud computing. This includes social-networking services such as Facebook, video-sharing sites such as YouTube, web-based email services such as Gmail, and applications such as Google Docs. In this context, the cloud simply refers to the servers that power these sites, and user data is said to reside "in the cloud". The accumulation of vast quantities of user data creates large-data problems, many of which are suitable for MapReduce. To give two concrete examples: a social-networking site analyzes connections in the enormous globe-spanning graph of friendships to recommend new connections. An online email service analyzes messages and user behavior to optimize ad selection and placement. These are all large-data problems that have been tackled with MapReduce.[9]

Another important facet of cloud computing is what's more precisely known as utility computing [31; 129]. As the name implies, the idea behind utility computing is to treat computing resource as a metered service, like electricity or natural gas. The idea harkens back to the days of time-sharing machines, and in truth isn't very different from this antiquated form of computing. Under this model, a "cloud user" can dynamically provision any amount of computing resources from a "cloud provider" on demand and only pay for what is consumed. In practical terms, the user is paying for access to virtual machine instances that run a standard operating system such as Linux. Virtualization technology (e.g., [15]) is used by the cloud provider to allocate available physical

---

[8]What *is* the difference between cloud computing and grid computing? Although both tackle the fundamental problem of how best to bring computational resources to bear on large and difficult problems, they start with different assumptions. Whereas clouds are assumed to be relatively homogeneous servers that reside in a datacenter or are distributed across a relatively small number of datacenters controlled by a single organization, grids are assumed to be a less tightly-coupled federation of heterogeneous resources under the control of distinct but cooperative organizations. As a result, grid computing tends to deal with tasks that are coarser-grained, and must deal with the practicalities of a federated environment, e.g., verifying credentials across multiple administrative domains. Grid computing has adopted a middleware-based approach for tackling many of these challenges.

[9]The first example is Facebook, a well-known user of Hadoop, in exactly the manner as described [68]. The second is, of course, Google, which uses MapReduce to continuously improve existing algorithms and to devise new algorithms for ad selection and placement.

resources and enforce isolation between multiple users who may be sharing the same hardware. Once one or more virtual machine instances have been provisioned, the user has full control over the resources and can use them for arbitrary computation. Virtual machines that are no longer needed are destroyed, thereby freeing up physical resources that can be redirected to other users. Resource consumption is measured in some equivalent of machine-hours and users are charged in increments thereof.

Both users and providers benefit in the utility computing model. Users are freed from upfront capital investments necessary to build datacenters and substantial reoccurring costs in maintaining them. They also gain the important property of elasticity—as demand for computing resources grow, for example, from an unpredicted spike in customers, more resources can be seamlessly allocated from the cloud without an interruption in service. As demand falls, provisioned resources can be released. Prior to the advent of utility computing, coping with unexpected spikes in demand was fraught with challenges: under-provision and run the risk of service interruptions, or over-provision and tie up precious capital in idle machines that are depreciating.

From the utility provider point of view, this business also makes sense because large datacenters benefit from economies of scale and can be run more efficiently than smaller datacenters. In the same way that insurance works by aggregating risk and redistributing it, utility providers aggregate the computing demands for a large number of users. Although demand may fluctuate significantly for each user, overall trends in aggregate demand should be smooth and predictable, which allows the cloud provider to adjust capacity over time with less risk of either offering too much (resulting in inefficient use of capital) or too little (resulting in unsatisfied customers). In the world of utility computing, Amazon Web Services currently leads the way and remains the dominant player, but a number of other cloud providers populate a market that is becoming increasingly crowded. Most systems are based on proprietary infrastructure, but there is at least one, Eucalyptus [111], that is available open source. Increased competition will benefit cloud users, but what direct relevance does this have for MapReduce? The connection is quite simple: processing large amounts of data with MapReduce requires access to clusters with sufficient capacity. However, not everyone with large-data problems can afford to purchase and maintain clusters. This is where utility computing comes in: clusters of sufficient size can be provisioned only when the need arises, and users pay only as much as is required to solve their problems. This lowers the barrier to entry for data-intensive processing and makes MapReduce much more accessible.

A generalization of the utility computing concept is "everything as a service", which is itself a new take on the age-old idea of outsourcing. A cloud provider offering customers access to virtual machine instances is said to be offering infrastructure as a service, or IaaS for short. However, this may be too low level for many users. Enter platform as a service (PaaS), which is a rebranding of what used to be called hosted services in the "pre-cloud" era. Platform is used generically to refer to any set of well-defined services on top of which users can build applications, deploy content, etc. This class of services is best exemplified by Google App Engine, which provides the backend datastore and API for anyone to build highly scalable web applications. Google maintains the infrastructure, freeing the user from having to backup, upgrade, patch, or otherwise maintain basic services such as the storage layer or the programming environment. At an even higher level, cloud providers can offer software as a service (SaaS), as exemplified by Salesforce, a leader in customer relationship management (CRM) software. Other examples include outsourcing an entire organization's email to a third party, which is commonplace today.

What does this proliferation of services have to do with MapReduce? No doubt that "everything as a service" is driven by desires for greater business efficiencies, but scale and elasticity play important roles as well. The cloud allows seamless expansion of operations without the need for careful planning and supports scales that may otherwise be difficult or cost-prohibitive for an organization to achieve. Cloud services, just like MapReduce, represent the search for an appropriate level of abstraction and beneficial divisions of labor. IaaS is an abstraction over raw physical hardware—an organization might lack the capital, expertise, or interest in running datacenters, and therefore pays a cloud provider to do so on its behalf. The argument applies similarly to PaaS and SaaS. In the same vein, the MapReduce programming model is a powerful abstraction that separates the *what* from the *how* of data-intensive processing.

1.2   BIG IDEAS

Tackling large-data problems requires a distinct approach that sometimes runs counter to traditional models of computing. In this section, we discuss a number of "big ideas" behind MapReduce. To be fair, all of these ideas have been discussed in the computer science literature for some time (some for decades), and MapReduce is certainly not the first to adopt these ideas. Nevertheless, the engineers at Google deserve tremendous credit for pulling these various threads together and demonstrating the power of these ideas on a scale previously unheard of.

Scale "out", not "up".   For data-intensive workloads, a large number of commodity low-end servers (i.e., the scaling "out" approach) is preferred over a small number of high-end servers (i.e., the scaling "up" approach). The latter approach of purchasing symmetric multi-processing (SMP) machines with a large number of processor sockets (dozens, even hundreds) and a large amount of shared memory (hundreds or even thousands of gigabytes) is not cost effective, since the costs of such machines do not scale linearly (i.e., a machine with twice as many processors is often significantly more than twice as expensive). On the other hand, the low-end server market overlaps with the high-volume desktop computing market, which has the effect of keeping prices low due to competition, interchangeable components, and economies of scale.

Barroso and Hölzle's recent treatise of what they dubbed "warehouse-scale computers" [18] contains a thoughtful analysis of the two approaches. The Transaction Processing Council (TPC) is a neutral, non-profit organization whose mission is to establish objective database benchmarks. Benchmark data submitted to that organization are probably the closest one can get to a fair "apples-to-apples" comparison of cost and performance for specific, well-defined relational processing applications. Based on TPC-C benchmark results from late 2007, a low-end server platform is about four times more cost efficient than a high-end shared memory platform from the same vendor. Excluding storage costs, the price/performance advantage of the low-end server increases to about a factor of twelve.

What if we take into account the fact that communication between nodes in a high-end SMP machine is orders of magnitude faster than communication between nodes in a commodity network-based cluster? Since workloads today are beyond the capability of any *single* machine (no matter how powerful), the comparison is more accurately between a smaller cluster of high-end machines and a larger cluster of low-end machines (network communication is unavoidable in both cases). Barroso and Hölzle model these two approaches under workloads that demand more or less communication, and conclude that a cluster of low-end servers approaches the performance of the equivalent cluster of high-end servers—the small performance gap is insufficient to justify the price premium of the high-end servers. For data-intensive applications, the conclusion appears to be clear: scaling "out" is superior to scaling "up", and therefore most existing implementations of the MapReduce programming model are designed around clusters of low-end commodity servers.

Capital costs in acquiring servers is, of course, only one component of the total cost of delivering computing capacity. Operational costs are dominated by the cost of electricity to power the servers as well as other aspects of datacenter operations that are functionally related to power: power distribution, cooling, etc. [18; 67]. As a result, energy efficiency has become a key issue in building warehouse-scale computers for large-data processing. Therefore, it is important to factor in operational costs when deploying a scale-out solution based on large numbers of commodity servers.

Datacenter efficiency is typically factored into three separate components that can be independently measured and optimized [18]. The first component measures how much of a building's incoming power is actually delivered to computing equipment, and correspondingly, how much is lost to the building's mechanical systems (e.g., cooling, air handling) and electrical infrastructure (e.g., power distribution inefficiencies). The second component measures how much of a server's incoming power is lost to the power supply, cooling fans, etc. The third component captures how much of the power delivered to computing components (processor, RAM, disk, etc.) is actually used to perform useful computations.

Of the three components of datacenter efficiency, the first two are relatively straightforward to objectively quantify. Adoption of industry best-practices can help datacenter operators achieve state-of-the-art efficiency. The third component, however, is much more difficult to measure. One important issue that has been identified is the non-linearity between load and power draw. That is, a server at 10% utilization may draw slightly more than half as much power as a server at 100% utilization (which means that a lightly loaded server is much less efficient than a heavily loaded server). A survey of five thousand Google servers over a six-month period shows that servers operate most of the time at between 10% and 50% utilization [17], which is an energy-inefficient operating region. As a result, Barroso and Hölzle have advocated for research and development in energy-proportional machines, where energy consumption would be proportional to load, such that an idle processor would (ideally) consume no power, but yet retain the ability to power up (nearly) instantaneously in response to demand.

Although we have provided a brief overview here, datacenter efficiency is a topic that is beyond the scope of this book. For more details, consult Barroso and Hölzle [18] and Hamilton [67], who provide detailed cost models for typical modern datacenters. However, even factoring in operational costs, evidence suggests that scaling out remains more attractive than scaling up.

Assume failures are common.   At warehouse scale, failures are not only inevitable, but commonplace. A simple calculation suffices to demonstrate: let us suppose that a cluster is built from reliable machines with a mean-time between failures (MTBF) of 1000 days (about three years). Even with these reliable servers, a 10,000-server cluster would still experience roughly 10 failures a day. For the sake of argument, let us suppose that a MTBF of 10,000 days (about 30 years) were achievable at realistic costs (which is unlikely). Even then, a 10,000-server cluster would still experience one failure daily. This means that any large-scale service that is distributed across a large cluster (either a user-facing application or a computing platform like MapReduce) must cope with hardware failures as an intrinsic aspect of its operation [66]. That is, a server may fail at any time, without notice. For example, in large clusters disk failures are common [123] and RAM experiences more errors than one might expect [135]. Datacenters suffer from both planned outages (e.g., system maintenance and hardware upgrades) and unexpected outages (e.g., power failure, connectivity loss, etc.).

A well-designed, fault-tolerant service must cope with failures up to a point without impacting the quality of service—failures should not result in inconsistencies or indeterminism from the user perspective. As servers go down, other cluster nodes should seamlessly step in to handle the load, and overall performance should gracefully degrade as server failures pile up. Just as important, a broken server that has been repaired should be able to seamlessly rejoin the service without manual reconfiguration by the administrator. Mature implementations of the MapReduce programming model are able to robustly cope with failures through a number of mechanisms such as automatic task restarts on different cluster nodes.

Move processing to the data.   In traditional high-performance computing (HPC) applications (e.g., for climate or nuclear simulations), it is commonplace for a supercomputer to have "processing nodes" and "storage nodes" linked together by a high-capacity interconnect. Many data-intensive workloads are not very processor-demanding, which means that the separation of compute and storage creates a bottleneck in the network. As an alternative to moving data around, it is more efficient to move the processing around. That is, MapReduce assumes an architecture where processors and storage (disk) are co-located. In such a setup, we can take advantage of data locality by running code on the processor directly attached to the block of data we need. The distributed file system is responsible for managing the data over which MapReduce operates.

Process data sequentially and avoid random access.   Data-intensive processing by definition means that the relevant datasets are too large to fit in memory and must be held on disk. Seek times for random disk access are fundamentally limited by the mechanical nature of the devices: read heads can only move so fast and platters can only spin so rapidly. As a result, it is desirable to avoid random data access, and instead organize computations so that data are processed sequentially. A simple scenario[10] poignantly illustrates the large performance gap between sequential operations and random seeks: assume a 1 terabyte database containing 10^{10} 100-byte records. Given reasonable assumptions about disk latency and throughput, a back-of-the-envelop calculation will show that updating 1% of the records (by accessing and then mutating each record) will take about a month on a single machine. On the other hand, if one simply reads the entire database and rewrites all the records (mutating those that need updating), the process would finish in under a work day on a single machine. Sequential data access is, literally, orders of magnitude faster than random data access.[11]

The development of solid-state drives is unlikely to change this balance for at least two reasons. First, the cost differential between traditional magnetic disks and solid-state disks remains substantial: large-data will for the most part remain on mechanical drives, at least in the near future. Second, although solid-state disks have substantially faster seek times, order-of-magnitude differences in performance between sequential and random access still remain.

MapReduce is primarily designed for batch processing over large datasets. To the extent possible, all computations are organized into long streaming operations that take advantage of the aggregate bandwidth of many disks in a cluster. Many aspects of MapReduce's design explicitly trade latency for throughput.

Hide system-level details from the application developer.   According to many guides on the practice of software engineering written by experienced industry professionals, one of the key reasons why writing code is difficult is because the programmer must simultaneously keep track of many details in short-term memory—ranging from the mundane (e.g., variable names) to the sophisticated (e.g., a corner case of an algorithm that requires special treatment). This imposes a high cognitive load and requires intense concentration, which leads to a number of recommendations about a programmer's environment (e.g., quiet office, comfortable furniture, large monitors, etc.). The challenges in writing distributed software are greatly compounded—the programmer must manage details across several threads, processes, or machines. Of course, the biggest headache in distributed programming is that code runs concurrently in unpredictable orders, accessing data in unpredictable patterns. This gives rise to race conditions, deadlocks, and other well-known problems. Programmers are taught to use low-level devices such as mutexes and to apply high-level "design patterns" such as producer–consumer queues to tackle these challenges, but the truth remains: concurrent programs are notoriously difficult to reason about and even harder to debug.

MapReduce addresses the challenges of distributed programming by providing an abstraction that isolates the developer from system-level details (e.g., locking of data structures, data starvation issues in the processing pipeline, etc.). The programming model specifies simple and well-defined interfaces between a small number of components, and therefore is easy for the programmer to reason

---

[10]Adapted from a post by Ted Dunning on the Hadoop mailing list.
[11]For more detail, Jacobs [76] provides real-world benchmarks in his discussion of large-data problems.

about. MapReduce maintains a separation of *what* computations are to be performed and *how* those computations are actually carried out on a cluster of machines. The first is under the control of the programmer, while the second is exclusively the responsibility of the execution framework or "runtime". The advantage is that the execution framework only needs to be designed once and verified for correctness—thereafter, as long as the developer expresses computations in the programming model, code is guaranteed to behave as expected. The upshot is that the developer is freed from having to worry about system-level details (e.g., no more debugging race conditions and addressing lock contention) and can instead focus on algorithm or application design.

Seamless scalability.   For data-intensive processing, it goes without saying that scalable algorithms are highly desirable. As an aspiration, let us sketch the behavior of an ideal algorithm. We can define scalability along at least two dimensions.[12] First, in terms of data: given twice the amount of data, the same algorithm should take at most twice as long to run, all else being equal. Second, in terms of resources: given a cluster twice the size, the same algorithm should take no more than half as long to run. Furthermore, an ideal algorithm would maintain these desirable scaling characteristics across a wide range of settings: on data ranging from gigabytes to petabytes, on clusters consisting of a few to a few thousand machines. Finally, the ideal algorithm would exhibit these desired behaviors without requiring any modifications whatsoever, not even tuning of parameters.

Other than for embarrassingly parallel problems, algorithms with the characteristics sketched above are, of course, unobtainable. One of the fundamental assertions in Fred Brook's classic *The Mythical Man-Month* [28] is that adding programmers to a project behind schedule will only make it fall further behind. This is because complex tasks cannot be chopped into smaller pieces and allocated in a linear fashion, and is often illustrated with a cute quote: "nine women cannot have a baby in one month". Although Brook's observations are primarily about software engineers and the software development process, the same is also true of algorithms: increasing the degree of parallelization also increases communication costs. The algorithm designer is faced with diminishing returns, and beyond a certain point, greater efficiencies gained by parallelization are entirely offset by increased communication requirements.

Nevertheless, these fundamental limitations shouldn't prevent us from at least striving for the unobtainable. The truth is that most current algorithms are far from the ideal. In the domain of text processing, for example, most algorithms today assume that data fit in memory on a single machine. For the most part, this is a fair assumption. But what happens when the amount of data doubles in the near future, and then doubles again shortly thereafter? Simply buying more memory is not a viable solution, as the amount of data is growing faster than the price of memory is falling. Furthermore, the price of a machine does not scale linearly with the amount of available memory beyond a certain point (once again, the scaling "up" vs. scaling "out" argument). Quite simply, algorithms that require holding intermediate data in memory on a single machine will break on sufficiently large datasets—moving from a single machine to a cluster architecture requires fundamentally different algorithms (and reimplementations).

---

[12]See also DeWitt and Gray [50] for slightly different definitions in terms of *speedup* and *scaleup*.

Perhaps the most exciting aspect of MapReduce is that it represents a small step toward algorithms that behave in the ideal manner discussed above. Recall that the programming model maintains a clear separation between *what* computations need to occur with *how* those computations are actually orchestrated on a cluster. As a result, a MapReduce algorithm remains fixed, and it is the responsibility of the execution framework to execute the algorithm. Amazingly, the MapReduce programming model is simple enough that it is actually possible, in many circumstances, to *approach* the ideal scaling characteristics discussed above. We introduce the idea of the "tradeable machine hour", as a play on Brook's classic title. If running an algorithm on a particular dataset takes 100 machine hours, then we should be able to finish in an hour on a cluster of 100 machines, or use a cluster of 10 machines to complete the same task in ten hours.[13] With MapReduce, this isn't so far from the truth, at least for some applications.

1.3 WHY IS THIS DIFFERENT?

"Due to the rapidly decreasing cost of processing, memory, and communication, it has appeared inevitable for at least two decades that parallel machines will eventually displace sequential ones in computationally intensive domains. This, however, has not happened."
— Leslie Valiant [148][14]

For several decades, computer scientists have predicted that the dawn of the age of parallel computing was "right around the corner" and that sequential processing would soon fade into obsolescence (consider, for example, the above quote). Yet, until very recently, they have been wrong. The relentless progress of Moore's Law for several decades has ensured that most of the world's problems could be solved by single-processor machines, save the needs of a few (scientists simulating molecular interactions or nuclear reactions, for example). Couple that with the inherent challenges of concurrency, and the result has been that parallel processing and distributed systems have largely been confined to a small segment of the market and esoteric upper-level electives in the computer science curriculum.

However, all of that changed around the middle of the first decade of this century. The manner in which the semiconductor industry had been exploiting Moore's Law simply ran out of opportunities for improvement: faster clocks, deeper pipelines, superscalar architectures, and other tricks of the trade reached a point of diminishing returns that did not justify continued investment. This marked the beginning of an entirely new strategy and the dawn of the multi-core era [115]. Unfortunately, this radical shift in hardware architecture was not matched at that time by corresponding advances in how software could be easily designed for these new processors (but not for lack of trying [104]). Nevertheless, parallel processing became an important issue at the forefront of everyone's mind—it represented the only way forward.

---

[13]Note that this idea meshes well with utility computing, where a 100-machine cluster running for one hour would cost the same as a 10-machine cluster running for ten hours.
[14]Guess when this was written? You may be surprised.

At around the same time, we witnessed the growth of large-data problems. In the late 1990s and even during the beginning of the first decade of this century, relatively few organizations had data-intensive processing needs that required large clusters: a handful of internet companies and perhaps a few dozen large corporations. But then, everything changed. Through a combination of many different factors (falling prices of disks, rise of user-generated web content, etc.), large-data problems began popping up everywhere. Data-intensive processing needs became widespread, which drove innovations in distributed computing such as MapReduce—first by Google, and then by Yahoo and the open source community. This in turn created more demand: when organizations learned about the availability of effective data analysis tools for large datasets, they began instrumenting various business processes to gather even more data—driven by the belief that more data lead to deeper insights and greater competitive advantages. Today, not only are large-data problems ubiquitous, but technological solutions for addressing them are widely accessible. Anyone can download the open-source Hadoop implementation of MapReduce, pay a modest fee to rent a cluster from a utility cloud provider, and be happily processing terabytes upon terabytes of data within the week. Finally, the computer scientists are right—the age of parallel computing has begun, both in terms of multiple cores in a chip and multiple machines in a cluster (each of which often has multiple cores).

Why is MapReduce important? In practical terms, it provides a very effective tool for tackling large-data problems. But beyond that, MapReduce is important in how it has changed the way we organize computations at a massive scale. MapReduce represents the first *widely adopted* step away from the von Neumann model that has served as the foundation of computer science over the last half plus century. Valiant called this a *bridging model* [148], a conceptual bridge between the physical implementation of a machine and the software that is to be executed on that machine. Until recently, the von Neumann model has served us well: Hardware designers focused on efficient implementations of the von Neumann model and didn't have to think much about the actual software that would run on the machines. Similarly, the software industry developed software targeted at the model without worrying about the hardware details. The result was extraordinary growth: chip designers churned out successive generations of increasingly powerful processors, and software engineers were able to develop applications in high-level languages that exploited those processors.

Today, however, the von Neumann model isn't sufficient anymore: we can't treat a multi-core processor or a large cluster as an agglomeration of many von Neumann machine instances communicating over some interconnect. Such a view places too much burden on the software developer to effectively take advantage of available computational resources—it simply is the wrong level of abstraction. MapReduce can be viewed as the first breakthrough in the quest for new abstractions that allow us to organize computations, not over individual machines, but over entire clusters. As Barroso puts it, the datacenter *is* the computer [18; 119].

To be fair, MapReduce is certainly not the first model of parallel computation that has been proposed. The most prevalent model in theoretical computer science, which dates back several decades, is the PRAM [60; 77].[15] In the model, an arbitrary number of processors, sharing an

---

[15]More than a theoretical model, the PRAM has been recently prototyped in hardware [153].

unboundedly large memory, operate synchronously on a shared input to produce some output. Other models include LogP [43] and BSP [148]. For reasons that are beyond the scope of this book, none of these previous models have enjoyed the success that MapReduce has in terms of adoption and in terms of impact on the daily lives of millions of users.[16]

MapReduce is the most successful abstraction over large-scale computational resources we have seen to date. However, as anyone who has taken an introductory computer science course knows, abstractions manage complexity by hiding details and presenting well-defined behaviors to users of those abstractions. They, inevitably, are imperfect—making certain tasks easier but others more difficult, and sometimes, impossible (in the case where the detail suppressed by the abstraction is exactly what the user cares about). This critique applies to MapReduce: it makes certain large-data problems easier, but suffers from limitations as well. This means that MapReduce is not the final word, but rather the first in a new class of programming models that will allow us to more effectively organize computations at a massive scale.

So if MapReduce is only the beginning, what's next beyond MapReduce? We're getting ahead of ourselves, as we can't meaningfully answer this question before thoroughly understanding what MapReduce can and cannot do well. This is exactly the purpose of this book: let us now begin our exploration.

1.4   WHAT THIS BOOK IS NOT

Actually, not quite yet…A final word before we get started. This book is about MapReduce algorithm design, particularly for text processing (and related) applications. Although our presentation most closely follows the Hadoop open-source implementation of MapReduce, this book is explicitly *not* about Hadoop programming. We don't, for example, discuss APIs, command-line invocations for running jobs, etc. For those aspects, we refer the reader to Tom White's excellent book, "Hadoop: The Definitive Guide" [154].

---

[16]Nevertheless, it is important to understand the relationship between MapReduce and existing models so that we can bring to bear accumulated knowledge about parallel algorithms; for example, Karloff et al. [82] demonstrated that a large class of PRAM algorithms can be efficiently simulated via MapReduce.

CHAPTER 2

MapReduce Basics

The only feasible approach to tackling large-data problems today is to divide and conquer, a fundamental concept in computer science that is introduced very early in typical undergraduate curricula. The basic idea is to partition a large problem into smaller sub-problems. To the extent that the sub-problems are independent [5], they can be tackled in parallel by different workers—threads in a processor core, cores in a multi-core processor, multiple processors in a machine, or many machines in a cluster. Intermediate results from each individual worker are then combined to yield the final output.[1]

The general principles behind divide-and-conquer algorithms are broadly applicable to a wide range of problems in many different application domains. However, the details of their implementations are varied and complex. For example, the following are just some of the issues that need to be addressed:

- How do we break up a large problem into smaller tasks? More specifically, how do we decompose the problem so that the smaller tasks can be executed in parallel?

- How do we assign tasks to workers distributed across a potentially large number of machines (while keeping in mind that some workers are better suited to running some tasks than others, e.g., due to available resources, locality constraints, etc.)?

- How do we ensure that the workers get the data they need?

- How do we coordinate synchronization among the different workers?

- How do we share partial results from one worker that is needed by another?

- How do we accomplish all of the above in the face of software errors and hardware faults?

In traditional parallel or distributed programming environments, the developer needs to explicitly address many (and sometimes, all) of the above issues. In shared memory programming, the developer needs to explicitly coordinate access to shared data structures through synchronization primitives such as mutexes, to explicitly handle process synchronization through devices such as barriers, and to remain ever vigilant for common problems such as deadlocks and race conditions. Language extensions, like OpenMP for shared memory parallelism,[2] or libraries implementing the

---

[1]We note that promising technologies such as quantum or biological computing could potentially induce a paradigm shift, but they are far from being sufficiently mature to solve real-world problems.
[2]http://www.openmp.org/

Message Passing Interface (MPI) for cluster-level parallelism,[3] provide logical abstractions that hide details of operating system synchronization and communications primitives. However, even with these extensions, developers are still burdened to keep track of how resources are made available to workers. Additionally, these frameworks are mostly designed to tackle processor-intensive problems and have only rudimentary support for dealing with very large amounts of input data. When using existing parallel computing approaches for large-data computation, the programmer must devote a significant amount of attention to low-level system details, which detracts from higher-level problem solving.

One of the most significant advantages of MapReduce is that it provides an abstraction that hides many system-level details from the programmer. Therefore, a developer can focus on what computations need to be performed, as opposed to how those computations are actually carried out or how to get the data to the processes that depend on them. Like OpenMP and MPI, MapReduce provides a means to distribute computation without burdening the programmer with the details of distributed computing (but at a different level of granularity). However, organizing and coordinating large amounts of computation is only part of the challenge. Large-data processing by definition requires bringing data and code together for computation to occur—no small feat for datasets that are terabytes and perhaps petabytes in size! MapReduce addresses this challenge by providing a simple abstraction for the developer, transparently handling most of the details behind the scenes in a scalable, robust, and efficient manner. As we mentioned in Chapter 1, instead of moving large amounts of data around, it is far more efficient, if possible, to move the code to the data. This is operationally realized by spreading data across the local disks of nodes in a cluster and running processes on nodes that hold the data. The complex task of managing storage in such a processing environment is typically handled by a distributed file system that sits underneath MapReduce.

This chapter introduces the MapReduce programming model and the underlying distributed file system. We start in Section 2.1 with an overview of functional programming, from which MapReduce draws its inspiration. Section 2.2 introduces the basic programming model, focusing on mappers and reducers. Section 2.3 discusses the role of the execution framework in actually running MapReduce programs (called jobs). Section 2.4 fills in additional details by introducing partitioners and combiners, which provide greater control over data flow. MapReduce would not be practical without a tightly-integrated distributed file system that manages the data being processed; Section 2.5 covers this in detail. Tying everything together, a complete cluster architecture is described in Section 2.6 before the chapter ends with a summary.

2.1   FUNCTIONAL PROGRAMMING ROOTS

MapReduce has its roots in functional programming, which is exemplified in languages such as Lisp and ML.[4] A key feature of functional languages is the concept of higher-order functions, or functions

---

[3]http://www.mcs.anl.gov/mpi/

[4]However, there are important characteristics of MapReduce that make it non-functional in nature—this will become apparent later.

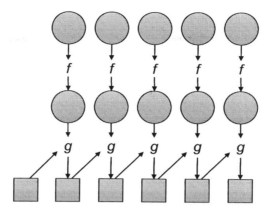

Figure 2.1: Illustration of *map* and *fold*, two higher-order functions commonly used together in functional programming: *map* takes a function f and applies it to every element in a list, while *fold* iteratively applies a function g to aggregate results.

that can accept other functions as arguments. Two common built-in higher order functions are *map* and *fold*, illustrated in Figure 2.1. Given a list, *map* takes as an argument a function f (that takes a single argument) and applies it to all elements in a list (the top part of the diagram). Given a list, *fold* takes as arguments a function g (that takes two arguments) and an initial value: g is first applied to the initial value and the first item in the list, the result of which is stored in an intermediate variable. This intermediate variable and the next item in the list serve as the arguments to a second application of g, the results of which are stored in the intermediate variable. This process repeats until all items in the list have been consumed; *fold* then returns the final value of the intermediate variable. Typically, *map* and *fold* are used in combination. For example, to compute the sum of squares of a list of integers, one could map a function that squares its argument (i.e., $\lambda x.x^2$) over the input list, and then fold the resulting list with the addition function (more precisely, $\lambda x \lambda y.x + y$) using an initial value of zero.

We can view *map* as a concise way to represent the transformation of a dataset (as defined by the function f). In the same vein, we can view *fold* as an aggregation operation, as defined by the function g. One immediate observation is that the application of f to each item in a list (or more generally, to elements in a large dataset) can be parallelized in a straightforward manner, since each functional application happens in isolation. In a cluster, these operations can be distributed across many different machines. The *fold* operation, on the other hand, has more restrictions on data locality—elements in the list must be "brought together" before the function g can be applied. However, many real-world applications do not require g to be applied to *all* elements of the list. To the extent that elements in the list can be divided into groups, the fold aggregations can also proceed in parallel. Furthermore, for operations that are commutative and associative, significant efficiencies can be gained in the *fold* operation through local aggregation and appropriate reordering.

In a nutshell, we have described MapReduce. The map phase in MapReduce roughly corresponds to the *map* operation in functional programming, whereas the reduce phase in MapReduce roughly corresponds to the *fold* operation in functional programming. As we will discuss in detail shortly, the MapReduce execution framework coordinates the map and reduce phases of processing over large amounts of data on large clusters of commodity machines.

Viewed from a slightly different angle, MapReduce codifies a generic "recipe" for processing large datasets that consists of two stages. In the first stage, a user-specified computation is applied over all input records in a dataset. These operations occur in parallel and yield intermediate output that is then aggregated by another user-specified computation. The programmer defines these two types of computations, and the execution framework coordinates the actual processing (very loosely, MapReduce provides a functional abstraction). Although such a two-stage processing structure may appear to be very restrictive, many interesting algorithms can be expressed quite concisely—especially if one decomposes complex algorithms into a sequence of MapReduce jobs. Subsequent chapters in this book focus on how a number of algorithms can be implemented in MapReduce.

To be precise, MapReduce can refer to three distinct but related concepts. First, MapReduce is a programming model, which is the sense discussed above. Second, MapReduce can refer to the execution framework (i.e., the "runtime") that coordinates the execution of programs written in this particular style. Finally, MapReduce can refer to the software implementation of the programming model and the execution framework: for example, Google's proprietary implementation vs. the open-source Hadoop implementation in Java. And, in fact, there are many implementations of MapReduce, e.g., targeted specifically for multi-core processors [127], for GPGPUs [71], for the CELL architecture [126], etc. There are some differences between the MapReduce programming model implemented in Hadoop and Google's proprietary implementation, which we will explicitly discuss throughout the book. However, we take a rather Hadoop-centric view of MapReduce, since Hadoop remains the most mature and accessible implementation to date, and therefore the one most developers are likely to use.

2.2   MAPPERS AND REDUCERS

Key-value pairs form the basic data structure in MapReduce. Keys and values may be primitives such as integers, floating point values, strings, and raw bytes, or they may be arbitrarily complex structures (lists, tuples, associative arrays, etc.). Programmers typically need to define their own custom data types, although a number of libraries such as Protocol Buffers,[5] Thrift,[6] and Avro[7] simplify the task.

Part of the design of MapReduce algorithms involves imposing the key-value structure on arbitrary datasets. For a collection of web pages, keys may be URLs and values may be the actual

---

[5]http://code.google.com/p/protobuf/
[6]http://incubator.apache.org/thrift/
[7]http://hadoop.apache.org/avro/

HTML content. For a graph, keys may represent node ids and values may contain the adjacency lists of those nodes (see Chapter 5 for more details). In some algorithms, input keys are not particularly meaningful and are simply ignored during processing, while in other cases input keys are used to uniquely identify a datum (such as a record id). In Chapter 3, we discuss the role of complex keys and values in the design of various algorithms.

In MapReduce, the programmer defines a mapper and a reducer with the following signatures:

$$\text{map: } (k_1, v_1) \rightarrow [(k_2, v_2)]$$
$$\text{reduce: } (k_2, [v_2]) \rightarrow [(k_3, v_3)]$$

The convention [. . .] is used throughout this book to denote a list. The input to a MapReduce job starts as data stored on the underlying distributed file system (see Section 2.5). The mapper is applied to every input key-value pair (split across an arbitrary number of files) to generate an arbitrary number of intermediate key-value pairs. The reducer is applied to all values associated with the same intermediate key to generate output key-value pairs.[8] Implicit between the map and reduce phases is a distributed "group by" operation on intermediate keys. Intermediate data arrive at each reducer in order, sorted by the key. However, no ordering relationship is guaranteed for keys across different reducers. Output key-value pairs from each reducer are written persistently back onto the distributed file system (whereas intermediate key-value pairs are transient and not preserved). The output ends up in r files on the distributed file system, where r is the number of reducers. For the most part, there is no need to consolidate reducer output, since the r files often serve as input to yet another MapReduce job. Figure 2.2 illustrates this two-stage processing structure.

A simple word count algorithm in MapReduce is shown in Figure 2.3. This algorithm counts the number of occurrences of every word in a text collection, which may be the first step in, for example, building a unigram language model (i.e., probability distribution over words in a collection). Input key-values pairs take the form of (docid, doc) pairs stored on the distributed file system, where the former is a unique identifier for the document, and the latter is the text of the document itself. The mapper takes an input key-value pair, tokenizes the document, and emits an intermediate key-value pair for every word: the word itself serves as the key, and the integer one serves as the value (denoting that we've seen the word once). The MapReduce execution framework guarantees that all values associated with the same key are brought together in the reducer. Therefore, in our word count algorithm, we simply need to sum up all counts (ones) associated with each word. The reducer does exactly this, and emits final key-value pairs with the word as the key, and the count as the value. Final output is written to the distributed file system, one file per reducer. Words within each file will be sorted by alphabetical order, and each file will contain roughly the same number of words. The partitioner, which we discuss later in Section 2.4, controls the assignment of words to reducers. The output can be examined by the programmer or used as input to another MapReduce program.

There are some differences between the Hadoop implementation of MapReduce and Google's implementation.[9] In Hadoop, the reducer is presented with a key and an iterator over all values

---

[8]This characterization, while conceptually accurate, is a slight simplification. See Section 2.6 for more details.
[9]Personal communication, Jeff Dean.

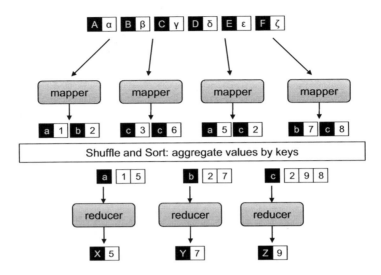

Figure 2.2: Simplified view of MapReduce. Mappers are applied to all input key-value pairs, which generate an arbitrary number of intermediate key-value pairs. Reducers are applied to all values associated with the same key. Between the map and reduce phases lies a barrier that involves a large distributed sort and group by.

1: **class** MAPPER
2:     **method** MAP(docid a, doc d)
3:         **for all** term $t \in$ doc d **do**
4:             EMIT(term t, count 1)

1: **class** REDUCER
2:     **method** REDUCE(term t, counts $[c_1, c_2, \ldots]$)
3:         $sum \leftarrow 0$
4:         **for all** count $c \in$ counts $[c_1, c_2, \ldots]$ **do**
5:             $sum \leftarrow sum + c$
6:         EMIT(term t, count sum)

Figure 2.3: Pseudo-code for the word count algorithm in MapReduce. The mapper emits an intermediate key-value pair for each word in a document. The reducer sums up all counts for each word.

associated with the particular key. The values are arbitrarily ordered. Google's implementation allows the programmer to specify a secondary sort key for ordering the values (if desired)—in which case values associated with each key would be presented to the developer's reduce code in sorted order. Later in Section 3.4 we discuss how to overcome this limitation in Hadoop to perform secondary sorting. Another difference: in Google's implementation the programmer is not allowed to change the key in the reducer. That is, the reducer output key must be exactly the same as the reducer input key. In Hadoop, there is no such restriction, and the reducer can emit an arbitrary number of output key-value pairs (with different keys).

To provide a bit more implementation detail: pseudo-code provided in this book roughly mirrors how MapReduce programs are written in Hadoop. Mappers and reducers are objects that implement the MAP and REDUCE methods, respectively. In Hadoop, a mapper object is initialized for each map task (associated with a particular sequence of key-value pairs called an input split) and the MAP method is called on each key-value pair by the execution framework. In configuring a MapReduce job, the programmer provides a hint on the number of map tasks to run, but the execution framework (see next section) makes the final determination based on the physical layout of the data (more details in Section 2.5 and Section 2.6). The situation is similar for the reduce phase: a reducer object is initialized for each reduce task, and the REDUCE method is called once per intermediate key. In contrast with the number of map tasks, the programmer can precisely specify the number of reduce tasks. We will return to discuss the details of Hadoop job execution in Section 2.6, which is dependent on an understanding of the distributed file system (covered in Section 2.5). To reiterate: although the presentation of algorithms in this book closely mirrors the way they would be implemented in Hadoop, our focus is on algorithm design and conceptual understanding—not actual Hadoop programming. For that, we recommend Tom White's book [154].

What are the restrictions on mappers and reducers? Mappers and reducers can express arbitrary computations over their inputs. However, one must generally be careful about use of external resources since multiple mappers or reducers may be contending for those resources. For example, it may be unwise for a mapper to query an external SQL database, since that would introduce a scalability bottleneck on the number of map tasks that could be run in parallel (since they might all be simultaneously querying the database).[10] In general, mappers can emit an arbitrary number of intermediate key-value pairs, and they need not be of the same type as the input key-value pairs. Similarly, reducers can emit an arbitrary number of final key-value pairs, and they can differ in type from the intermediate key-value pairs. Although not permitted in functional programming, mappers and reducers can have side effects. This is a powerful and useful feature: for example, preserving state across multiple inputs is central to the design of many MapReduce algorithms (see Chapter 3). Such algorithms can be understood as having side effects that only change state that is *internal* to the mapper or reducer. While the correctness of such algorithms may be more difficult to guarantee (since the function's behavior depends not only on the current input but on previous inputs), most potential synchronization problems are avoided since internal state is private only to individual map-

---

[10]Unless, of course, the database itself is highly scalable.

pers and reducers. In other cases (see Sections 4.4 and 6.5), it may be useful for mappers or reducers to have *external* side effects, such as writing files to the distributed file system. Since many mappers and reducers are run in parallel, and the distributed file system is a shared global resource, special care must be taken to ensure that such operations avoid synchronization conflicts. One strategy is to write a temporary file that is renamed upon successful completion of the mapper or reducer [45].

In addition to the "canonical" MapReduce processing flow, other variations are also possible. MapReduce programs can contain no reducers, in which case mapper output is directly written to disk (one file per mapper). For embarrassingly parallel problems, e.g., parse a large text collection or independently analyze a large number of images, this would be a common pattern. The converse—a MapReduce program with no mappers—is not possible, although in some cases it is useful for the mapper to implement the identity function and simply pass input key-value pairs to the reducers. This has the effect of sorting and regrouping the input for reduce-side processing. Similarly, in some cases it is useful for the reducer to implement the identity function, in which case the program simply sorts and groups mapper output. Finally, running identity mappers and reducers has the effect of regrouping and resorting the input data (which is sometimes useful).

Although in the most common case, input to a MapReduce job comes from data stored on the distributed file system and output is written back to the distributed file system, any other system that satisfies the proper abstractions can serve as a data source or sink. With Google's MapReduce implementation, Bigtable [34], a sparse, distributed, persistent multidimensional sorted map, is frequently used as a source of input and as a store of MapReduce output. HBase is an open-source Bigtable clone and has similar capabilities. Also, Hadoop has been integrated with existing MPP (massively parallel processing) relational databases, which allows a programmer to write MapReduce jobs over database rows and dump output into a new database table. Finally, in some cases MapReduce jobs may not consume any input at all (e.g., computing π) or may only consume a small amount of data (e.g., input parameters to many instances of processor-intensive simulations running in parallel).

2.3   THE EXECUTION FRAMEWORK

One of the most important ideas behind MapReduce is separating the *what* of distributed processing from the *how*. A MapReduce program, referred to as a job, consists of code for mappers and reducers (as well as combiners and partitioners to be discussed in the next section) packaged together with configuration parameters (such as where the input lies and where the output should be stored). The developer submits the job to the submission node of a cluster (in Hadoop, this is called the jobtracker) and execution framework (sometimes called the "runtime") takes care of everything else: it transparently handles all other aspects of distributed code execution, on clusters ranging from a single node to a few thousand nodes. Specific responsibilities include:

Scheduling.   Each MapReduce job is divided into smaller units called tasks (see Section 2.6 for more details). For example, a map task may be responsible for processing a certain block of input key-value pairs (called an input split in Hadoop); similarly, a reduce task may handle a portion of the intermediate key space. It is not uncommon for MapReduce jobs to have thousands of individual tasks that need to be assigned to nodes in the cluster. In large jobs, the total number of tasks may exceed the number of tasks that can be run on the cluster concurrently, making it necessary for the scheduler to maintain some sort of a task queue and to track the progress of running tasks so that waiting tasks can be assigned to nodes as they become available. Another aspect of scheduling involves coordination among tasks belonging to different jobs (e.g., from different users). How can a large, shared resource support several users simultaneously in a predictable, transparent, policy-driven fashion? There has been some recent work along these lines in the context of Hadoop [131; 160].

Speculative execution is an optimization that is implemented by both Hadoop and Google's MapReduce implementation (called "backup tasks" [45]). Due to the barrier between the map and reduce tasks, the map phase of a job is only as fast as the slowest map task. Similarly, the completion time of a job is bounded by the running time of the slowest reduce task. As a result, the speed of a MapReduce job is sensitive to what are known as *stragglers*, or tasks that take an usually long time to complete. One cause of stragglers is flaky hardware: for example, a machine that is suffering from recoverable errors may become significantly slower. With speculative execution, an identical copy of the same task is executed on a different machine, and the framework simply uses the result of the first task attempt to finish. Zaharia et al. [161] presented different execution strategies in a recent paper, and Google reported that speculative execution can improve job running times by 44% [45]. Although in Hadoop both map and reduce tasks can be speculatively executed, the common wisdom is that the technique is more helpful for map tasks than reduce tasks, since each copy of the reduce task needs to pull data over the network. Note, however, that speculative execution cannot adequately address another common cause of stragglers: skew in the distribution of values associated with intermediate keys (leading to reduce stragglers). In text processing we often observe Zipfian distributions, which means that the task or tasks responsible for processing the most frequent few elements will run much longer than the typical task. Better local aggregation, discussed in the next chapter, is one possible solution to this problem.

Data/code co-location.   The phrase *data distribution* is misleading, since one of the key ideas behind MapReduce is to move the code, not the data. However, the more general point remains—in order for computation to occur, we need to somehow feed data to the code. In MapReduce, this issue is inextricably intertwined with scheduling and relies heavily on the design of the underlying distributed file system.[11] To achieve data locality, the scheduler starts tasks on the node that holds a particular block of data (i.e., on its local drive) needed by the task. This has the effect of moving code to the data. If this is not possible (e.g., a node is already running too many tasks), new tasks will be started elsewhere, and the necessary data will be streamed over the network. An important optimization here is to prefer nodes that are on the same rack in the datacenter as the node holding the relevant data block, since inter-rack bandwidth is significantly less than intra-rack bandwidth.

---

[11]In the canonical case, that is. Recall that MapReduce may receive its input from other sources.

Synchronization.   In general, synchronization refers to the mechanisms by which multiple concurrently running processes "join up", for example, to share intermediate results or otherwise exchange state information. In MapReduce, synchronization is accomplished by a barrier between the map and reduce phases of processing. Intermediate key-value pairs must be grouped by key, which is accomplished by a large distributed sort involving all the nodes that executed map tasks and all the nodes that will execute reduce tasks. This necessarily involves copying intermediate data over the network, and therefore the process is commonly known as "shuffle and sort". A MapReduce job with m mappers and r reducers involves up to $m \times r$ distinct copy operations, since each mapper may have intermediate output going to every reducer.

Note that the reduce computation cannot start until all the mappers have finished emitting key-value pairs and all intermediate key-value pairs have been shuffled and sorted, since the execution framework cannot otherwise guarantee that all values associated with the same key have been gathered. This is an important departure from functional programming: in a *fold* operation, the aggregation function g is a function of the intermediate value and the next item in the list—which means that values can be lazily generated and aggregation can begin as soon as values are available. In contrast, the reducer in MapReduce receives *all* values associated with the same key at once. However, it is possible to start copying intermediate key-value pairs over the network to the nodes running the reducers as soon as each mapper finishes—this is a common optimization and implemented in Hadoop.

Error and fault handling.   The MapReduce execution framework must accomplish all the tasks above in an environment where errors and faults are the norm, not the exception. Since MapReduce was explicitly designed around low-end commodity servers, the runtime must be especially resilient. In large clusters, disk failures are common [123] and RAM experiences more errors than one might expect [135]. Datacenters suffer from both planned outages (e.g., system maintenance and hardware upgrades) and unexpected outages (e.g., power failure, connectivity loss, etc.).

And that's just hardware. No software is bug free—exceptions must be appropriately trapped, logged, and recovered from. Large-data problems have a penchant for uncovering obscure corner cases in code that is otherwise thought to be bug-free. Furthermore, any sufficiently large dataset will contain corrupted data or records that are mangled beyond a programmer's imagination—resulting in errors that one would never think to check for or trap. The MapReduce execution framework must thrive in this hostile environment.

2.4 PARTITIONERS AND COMBINERS

We have thus far presented a simplified view of MapReduce. There are two additional elements that complete the programming model: partitioners and combiners.

Partitioners are responsible for dividing up the intermediate key space and assigning intermediate key-value pairs to reducers. In other words, the partitioner specifies the task to which an intermediate key-value pair must be copied. Within each reducer, keys are processed in sorted order (which is how the "group by" is implemented). The simplest partitioner involves computing the hash value of the key and then taking the mod of that value with the number of reducers. This assigns approximately the same number of keys to each reducer (dependent on the quality of the hash function). Note, however, that the partitioner only considers the key and ignores the value—therefore, a roughly even partitioning of the key space may nevertheless yield large differences in the number of key-values pairs sent to each reducer (since different keys may have different numbers of associated values). This imbalance in the amount of data associated with each key is relatively common in many text processing applications due to the Zipfian distribution of word occurrences.

Combiners are an optimization in MapReduce that allow for local aggregation before the shuffle and sort phase. We can motivate the need for combiners by considering the word count algorithm in Figure 2.3, which emits a key-value pair for each word in the collection. Furthermore, all these key-value pairs need to be copied across the network, and so the amount of intermediate data will be larger than the input collection itself. This is clearly inefficient. One solution is to perform local aggregation on the output of each mapper, i.e., to compute a local count for a word over all the documents processed by the mapper. With this modification (assuming the maximum amount of local aggregation possible), the number of intermediate key-value pairs will be at most the number of unique words in the collection times the number of mappers (and typically far smaller because each mapper may not encounter every word).

The combiner in MapReduce supports such an optimization. One can think of combiners as "mini-reducers" that take place on the output of the mappers, prior to the shuffle and sort phase. Each combiner operates in isolation and therefore does not have access to intermediate output from other mappers. The combiner is provided keys and values associated with each key (the same types as the mapper output keys and values). Critically, one cannot assume that a combiner will have the opportunity to process *all* values associated with the same key. The combiner can emit any number of key-value pairs, but the keys and values must be of the same type as the mapper output (same as the reducer input).[12] In cases where an operation is both associative and commutative (e.g., addition or multiplication), reducers can directly serve as combiners. In general, however, reducers and combiners are not interchangeable.

In many cases, proper use of combiners can spell the difference between an impractical algorithm and an efficient algorithm. This topic will be discussed in Section 3.1, which focuses on various techniques for local aggregation. It suffices to say for now that a combiner can significantly reduce the amount of data that needs to be copied over the network, resulting in much faster algorithms.

The complete MapReduce model is shown in Figure 2.4. Output of the mappers is processed by the combiners, which perform local aggregation to cut down on the number of intermediate key-value pairs. The partitioner determines which reducer will be responsible for processing a particular

---

[12]A note on the implementation of combiners in Hadoop: by default, the execution framework reserves the right to use combiners at its discretion. In reality, this means that a combiner may be invoked zero, one, or multiple times. In addition, combiners in Hadoop may actually be invoked in the reduce phase, i.e., after key-value pairs have been copied over to the reducer, but before the user reducer code runs. As a result, combiners must be carefully written so that they can be executed in these different environments. Section 3.1.2 discusses this in more detail.

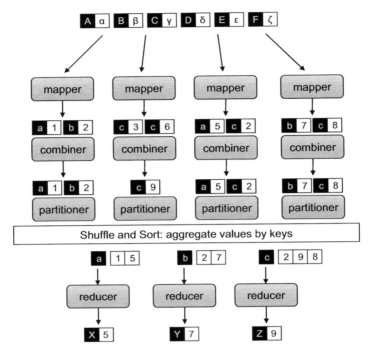

Figure 2.4: Complete view of MapReduce, illustrating combiners and partitioners in addition to mappers and reducers. Combiners can be viewed as "mini-reducers" in the map phase. Partitioners determine which reducer is responsible for a particular key.

key, and the execution framework uses this information to copy the data to the right location during the shuffle and sort phase.[13] Therefore, a complete MapReduce job consists of code for the mapper, reducer, combiner, and partitioner, along with job configuration parameters. The execution framework handles everything else.

2.5 THE DISTRIBUTED FILE SYSTEM

So far, we have mostly focused on the *processing* aspect of data-intensive processing, but it is important to recognize that without data, there is nothing to compute on. In high-performance computing (HPC) and many traditional cluster architectures, storage is viewed as a distinct and separate component from computation. Implementations vary widely, but network-attached storage (NAS) and storage area networks (SAN) are common; supercomputers often have dedicated subsystems for handling storage (separate nodes, and often even separate networks). Regardless of the details, the

[13]In Hadoop, partitioners are actually executed before combiners, so while Figure 2.4 is conceptually accurate, it doesn't precisely describe the Hadoop implementation.

processing cycle remains the same at a high level: the compute nodes fetch input from storage, load the data into memory, process the data, and then write back the results (with perhaps intermediate checkpointing for long-running processes).

As dataset sizes increase, more compute capacity is required for processing. But as compute capacity grows, the link between the compute nodes and the storage becomes a bottleneck. At that point, one could invest in higher performance but more expensive networks (e.g., 10 gigabit Ethernet) or special-purpose interconnects such as InfiniBand (even more expensive). In most cases, this is not a cost-effective solution, as the price of networking equipment increases non-linearly with performance (e.g., a switch with ten times the capacity is usually more than ten times more expensive). Alternatively, one could abandon the separation of computation and storage as distinct components in a cluster. The distributed file system (DFS) that underlies MapReduce adopts exactly this approach. The Google File System (GFS) [57] supports Google's proprietary implementation of MapReduce; in the open-source world, HDFS (Hadoop Distributed File System) is an open-source implementation of GFS that supports Hadoop. Although MapReduce doesn't necessarily require the distributed file system, it is difficult to realize many of the advantages of the programming model without a storage substrate that behaves much like the DFS.[14]

Of course, distributed file systems are not new [7; 32; 74; 133; 147]. The MapReduce distributed file system builds on previous work but is specifically adapted to large-data processing workloads, and therefore departs from previous architectures in certain respects (see discussion by Ghemawat et al. [57] in the original GFS paper.). The main idea is to divide user data into blocks and replicate those blocks across the local disks of nodes in the cluster. Blocking data, of course, is not a new idea, but DFS blocks are significantly larger than block sizes in typical single-machine file systems (64 MB by default). The distributed file system adopts a master–slave architecture in which the master maintains the file namespace (metadata, directory structure, file to block mapping, location of blocks, and access permissions) and the slaves manage the actual data blocks. In GFS, the master is called the GFS master, and the slaves are called GFS chunkservers. In Hadoop, the same roles are filled by the namenode and datanodes, respectively.[15] This book adopts the Hadoop terminology, although for most basic file operations GFS and HDFS work much the same way. The architecture of HDFS is shown in Figure 2.5, redrawn from a similar diagram describing GFS [57].

In HDFS, an application client wishing to read a file (or a portion thereof) must first contact the namenode to determine where the actual data is stored. In response to the client request, the namenode returns the relevant block id and the location where the block is held (i.e., which datanode). The client then contacts the datanode to retrieve the data. Blocks are themselves stored on standard single-machine file systems, so HDFS lies on top of the standard OS stack (e.g., Linux). An important feature of the design is that data is never moved through the namenode. Instead, all data transfer

---

[14]However, there is evidence that existing POSIX-based distributed cluster file systems (e.g., GPFS or PVFS) can serve as a replacement for HDFS, when properly tuned or modified for MapReduce workloads [6; 146]. This, however, remains an experimental use case.

[15]To be precise, namenode and datanode may refer to physical machines in a cluster, or they may refer to daemons running on those machines providing the relevant services.

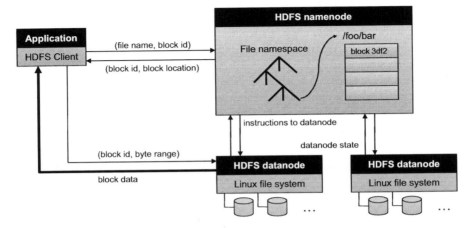

Figure 2.5: The architecture of HDFS. The namenode (master) is responsible for maintaining the file namespace and directing clients to datanodes (slaves) that actually hold data blocks containing user data.

occurs directly between clients and datanodes; communication with the namenode only involves transfer of metadata.

By default, HDFS stores three separate copies of each data block to ensure reliability, availability, and performance. In large clusters, the three replicas are spread across different physical racks, so HDFS is resilient towards two common failure scenarios: individual datanode crashes and failures in networking equipment that bring an entire rack offline. Replicating blocks across physical machines also increases opportunities to co-locate data and processing in the scheduling of MapReduce jobs, since multiple copies yield more opportunities to exploit locality. The namenode is in periodic communication with the datanodes to ensure proper replication of all the blocks: if there aren't enough replicas (e.g., due to disk or machine failures or to connectivity losses due to networking equipment failures), the namenode directs the creation of additional copies;[16] if there are too many replicas (e.g., a repaired node rejoins the cluster), extra copies are discarded.

To create a new file and write data to HDFS, the application client first contacts the namenode, which updates the file namespace after checking permissions and making sure the file doesn't already exist. The namenode allocates a new block on a suitable datanode, and the application is directed to stream data directly to it. From the initial datanode, data is further propagated to additional replicas. In the most recent release of Hadoop as of this writing (release 0.20.2), files are immutable—they cannot be modified after creation. There are current plans to officially support file appends in the near future, which is a feature already present in GFS.

In summary, the HDFS namenode has the following responsibilities:

---

[16]Note that the namenode coordinates the replication process, but data transfer occurs directly from datanode to datanode.

- Namespace management. The namenode is responsible for maintaining the file namespace, which includes metadata, directory structure, file to block mapping, location of blocks, and access permissions. These data are held in memory for fast access and all mutations are persistently logged.

- Coordinating file operations. The namenode directs application clients to datanodes for read operations, and allocates blocks on suitable datanodes for write operations. All data transfers occur directly between clients and datanodes. When a file is deleted, HDFS does not immediately reclaim the available physical storage; rather, blocks are lazily garbage collected.

- Maintaining overall health of the file system. The namenode is in periodic contact with the datanodes via heartbeat messages to ensure the integrity of the system. If the namenode observes that a data block is under-replicated (fewer copies are stored on datanodes than the desired replication factor), it will direct the creation of new replicas. Finally, the namenode is also responsible for rebalancing the file system.[17] During the course of normal operations, certain datanodes may end up holding more blocks than others; rebalancing involves moving blocks from datanodes with more blocks to datanodes with fewer blocks. This leads to better load balancing and more even disk utilization.

Since GFS and HDFS were specifically designed to support Google's proprietary and the open-source implementation of MapReduce, respectively, they were designed with a number of assumptions about the operational environment, which in turn influenced the design of the systems. Understanding these choices is critical to designing effective MapReduce algorithms:

- The file system stores a relatively modest number of large files. The definition of "modest" varies by the size of the deployment, but in HDFS multi-gigabyte files are common (and even encouraged). There are several reasons why lots of small files are to be avoided. Since the namenode must hold all file metadata in memory, this presents an upper bound on both the number of files and blocks that can be supported.[18] Large multi-block files represent a more efficient use of namenode memory than many single-block files (each of which consumes less space than a single block size). In addition, mappers in a MapReduce job use individual files as a basic unit for splitting input data. At present, there is no default mechanism in Hadoop that allows a mapper to process multiple files. As a result, mapping over many small files will yield as many map tasks as there are files. This results in two potential problems: first, the startup costs of mappers may become significant compared to the time spent actually processing input key-value pairs; second, this may result in an excessive number of across-the-network copy operations during the "shuffle and sort" phase (recall that a MapReduce job with m mappers and r reducers involves up to $m \times r$ distinct copy operations).

---

[17]In Hadoop, this is a manually invoked process.
[18]According to Dhruba Borthakur in a post to the Hadoop mailing list on 6/8/2008, each block in HDFS occupies about 150 bytes of memory on the namenode.

- Workloads are batch oriented, dominated by long streaming reads and large sequential writes. As a result, high sustained bandwidth is more important than low latency. This exactly describes the nature of MapReduce jobs, which are batch operations on large amounts of data. Due to the common-case workload, both HDFS and GFS do not implement any form of data caching.[19]

- Applications are aware of the characteristics of the distributed file system. Neither HDFS nor GFS present a general POSIX-compliant API, but rather support only a subset of possible file operations. This simplifies the design of the distributed file system, and in essence pushes part of the data management onto the end application. One rationale for this decision is that each application knows best how to handle data specific to that application, for example, in terms of resolving inconsistent states and optimizing the layout of data structures.

- The file system is deployed in an environment of cooperative users. There is no discussion of security in the original GFS paper, but HDFS explicitly assumes a datacenter environment where only authorized users have access. File permissions in HDFS are only meant to prevent unintended operations and can be easily circumvented.[20]

- The system is built from unreliable but inexpensive commodity components. As a result, failures are the norm rather than the exception. HDFS is designed around a number of self-monitoring and self-healing mechanisms to robustly cope with common failure modes.

Finally, some discussion is necessary to understand the single-master design of HDFS and GFS. It has been demonstrated that in large-scale distributed systems, simultaneously providing consistency, availability, and partition tolerance is impossible—this is Brewer's so-called CAP Theorem [58]. Since partitioning is unavoidable in large-data systems, the real tradeoff is between consistency and availability. A single-master design trades availability for consistency and significantly simplifies implementation. If the master (HDFS namenode or GFS master) goes down, the entire file system becomes unavailable, which trivially guarantees that the file system will never be in an inconsistent state. An alternative design might involve multiple masters that jointly manage the file namespace—such an architecture would increase availability (if one goes down, another can step in) at the cost of consistency, not to mention requiring a more complex implementation (cf. [4; 105]).

The single-master design of GFS and HDFS is a well-known weakness, since if the master goes offline, the entire file system and all MapReduce jobs running on top of it will grind to a halt. This weakness is mitigated in part by the lightweight nature of file system operations. Recall that no data is ever moved through the namenode and that all communication between clients and datanodes involve only metadata. Because of this, the namenode rarely is the bottleneck, and for the most part avoids load-induced crashes. In practice, this single point of failure is not as severe a limitation as it may appear—with diligent monitoring of the namenode, mean time between failure measured in months are not uncommon for production deployments. Furthermore, the Hadoop community is

---

[19]However, since the distributed file system is built on top of a standard operating system such as Linux, there is still OS-level caching.

[20]However, there are existing plans to integrate Kerberos into Hadoop/HDFS.

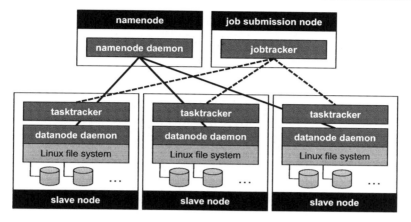

Figure 2.6: Architecture of a complete Hadoop cluster, which consists of three separate components: the HDFS master (called the namenode), the job submission node (called the jobtracker), and many slave nodes (three shown here). Each of the slave nodes runs a tasktracker for executing map and reduce tasks and a datanode daemon for serving HDFS data.

well aware of this problem and has developed several reasonable workarounds—for example, a warm standby namenode that can be quickly switched over when the primary namenode fails. The open source environment and the fact that many organizations already depend on Hadoop for production systems virtually guarantees that more effective solutions will be developed over time.

2.6   HADOOP CLUSTER ARCHITECTURE

Putting everything together, the architecture of a complete Hadoop cluster is shown in Figure 2.6. The HDFS namenode runs the namenode daemon. The job submission node runs the jobtracker, which is the single point of contact for a client wishing to execute a MapReduce job. The jobtracker monitors the progress of running MapReduce jobs and is responsible for coordinating the execution of the mappers and reducers. Typically, these services run on two separate machines, although in smaller clusters they are often co-located. The bulk of a Hadoop cluster consists of slave nodes (only three of which are shown in the figure) that run both a tasktracker, which is responsible for actually running user code, and a datanode daemon, for serving HDFS data.

   A Hadoop MapReduce job is divided up into a number of map tasks and reduce tasks. Tasktrackers periodically send heartbeat messages to the jobtracker that also doubles as a vehicle for task allocation. If a tasktracker is available to run tasks (in Hadoop parlance, has empty task slots), the return acknowledgment of the tasktracker heartbeat contains task allocation information. The number of reduce tasks is equal to the number of reducers specified by the programmer. The number of map tasks, on the other hand, depends on many factors: the number of mappers specified by the programmer serves as a hint to the execution framework, but the actual number of tasks depends on both the number of input files and the number of HDFS data blocks occupied by those files. Each map task is assigned a sequence of input key-value pairs, called an input split in Hadoop. Input splits are computed automatically and the execution framework strives to align them to HDFS block boundaries so that each map task is associated with a single data block. In scheduling map tasks, the jobtracker tries to take advantage of data locality—if possible, map tasks are scheduled on the slave node that holds the input split, so that the mapper will be processing local data. The alignment of input splits with HDFS block boundaries simplifies task scheduling. If it is not possible to run a map task on local data, it becomes necessary to stream input key-value pairs across the network. Since large clusters are organized into racks, with far greater intra-rack bandwidth than inter-rack bandwidth, the execution framework strives to at least place map tasks on a rack which has a copy of the data block.

Although conceptually in MapReduce one can think of the mapper being applied to all input key-value pairs and the reducer being applied to all values associated with the same key, actual job execution is a bit more complex. In Hadoop, mappers are Java objects with a MAP method (among others). A mapper object is instantiated for every map task by the tasktracker. The life-cycle of this object begins with instantiation, where a hook is provided in the API to run programmer-specified code. This means that mappers can read in "side data", providing an opportunity to load state, static data sources, dictionaries, etc. After initialization, the MAP method is called (by the execution framework) on all key-value pairs in the input split. Since these method calls occur in the context of the same Java object, it is possible to preserve state across multiple input key-value pairs within the same map task—this is an important property to exploit in the design of MapReduce algorithms, as we will see in the next chapter. After all key-value pairs in the input split have been processed, the mapper object provides an opportunity to run programmer-specified termination code. This, too, will be important in the design of MapReduce algorithms.

The actual execution of reducers is similar to that of the mappers. Each reducer object is instantiated for every reduce task. The Hadoop API provides hooks for programmer-specified initialization and termination code. After initialization, for each intermediate key in the partition (defined by the partitioner), the execution framework repeatedly calls the REDUCE method with an intermediate key and an iterator over all values associated with that key. The programming model also guarantees that intermediate keys will be presented to the REDUCE method in sorted order. Since this occurs in the context of a single object, it is possible to preserve state across multiple intermediate keys (and associated values) within a single reduce task. Once again, this property is critical in the design of MapReduce algorithms and will be discussed in the next chapter.

2.7   SUMMARY

This chapter provides a basic overview of the MapReduce programming model, starting with its roots in functional programming and continuing with a description of mappers, reducers, partitioners, and combiners. Significant attention is also given to the underlying distributed file system, which is a tightly-integrated component of the MapReduce environment. Given this basic understanding, we now turn our attention to the design of MapReduce algorithms.

CHAPTER 3

MapReduce Algorithm Design

A large part of the power of MapReduce comes from its simplicity: in addition to preparing the input data, the programmer needs only to implement the mapper, the reducer, and optionally, the combiner and the partitioner. All other aspects of execution are handled transparently by the execution framework—on clusters ranging from a single node to a few thousand nodes, over datasets ranging from gigabytes to petabytes. However, this also means that any conceivable algorithm that a programmer wishes to develop must be expressed in terms of a small number of rigidly defined components that must fit together in very specific ways. It may not appear obvious how a multitude of algorithms can be recast into this programming model. The purpose of this chapter is to provide, primarily through examples, a guide to MapReduce algorithm design. These examples illustrate what can be thought of as "design patterns" for MapReduce, which instantiate arrangements of components and specific techniques designed to handle frequently encountered situations across a variety of problem domains. Two of these design patterns are used in the scalable inverted indexing algorithm we'll present later in Chapter 4; concepts presented here will show up again in Chapter 5 (graph processing) and Chapter 6 (expectation-maximization algorithms).

Synchronization is perhaps the most tricky aspect of designing MapReduce algorithms (or for that matter, parallel and distributed algorithms in general). Other than embarrassingly-parallel problems, processes running on separate nodes in a cluster must, at some point in time, come together—for example, to distribute partial results from nodes that produced them to the nodes that will consume them. Within a single MapReduce job, there is only one opportunity for cluster-wide synchronization—during the shuffle and sort stage where intermediate key-value pairs are copied from the mappers to the reducers and grouped by key. Beyond that, mappers and reducers run in isolation without any mechanisms for direct communication. Furthermore, the programmer has little control over many aspects of execution, for example:

- *Where* a mapper or reducer runs (i.e., on which node in the cluster).

- *When* a mapper or reducer begins or finishes.

- *Which* input key-value pairs are processed by a specific mapper.

- *Which* intermediate key-value pairs are processed by a specific reducer.

Nevertheless, the programmer does have a number of techniques for controlling execution and managing the flow of data in MapReduce. In summary, they are:

1. The ability to construct complex data structures as keys and values to store and communicate partial results.

2. The ability to execute user-specified initialization code at the beginning of a map or reduce task, and the ability to execute user-specified termination code at the end of a map or reduce task.

3. The ability to preserve state in both mappers and reducers across multiple input or intermediate keys.

4. The ability to control the sort order of intermediate keys, and therefore the order in which a reducer will encounter particular keys.

5. The ability to control the partitioning of the key space, and therefore the set of keys that will be encountered by a particular reducer.

It is important to realize that many algorithms cannot be easily expressed as a single MapReduce job. One must often decompose complex algorithms into a sequence of jobs, which requires orchestrating data so that the output of one job becomes the input to the next. Many algorithms are iterative in nature, requiring repeated execution until some convergence criteria—graph algorithms in Chapter 5 and expectation-maximization algorithms in Chapter 6 behave in exactly this way. Often, the convergence check itself cannot be easily expressed in MapReduce. The standard solution is an external (non-MapReduce) program that serves as a "driver" to coordinate MapReduce iterations.

This chapter explains how various techniques to control code execution and data flow can be applied to design algorithms in MapReduce. The focus is both on scalability—ensuring that there are no inherent bottlenecks as algorithms are applied to increasingly larger datasets—and efficiency—ensuring that algorithms do not needlessly consume resources and thereby reducing the cost of parallelization. The gold standard, of course, is linear scalability: an algorithm running on twice the amount of data should take only twice as long. Similarly, an algorithm running on twice the number of nodes should only take half as long.

The chapter is organized as follows:

- Section 3.1 introduces the important concept of local aggregation in MapReduce and strategies for designing efficient algorithms that minimize the amount of partial results that need to be copied across the network. The proper use of combiners is discussed in detail, as well as the "in-mapper combining" design pattern.

- Section 3.2 uses the example of building word co-occurrence matrices on large text corpora to illustrate two common design patterns, which we dub "pairs" and "stripes". These two approaches are useful in a large class of problems that require keeping track of joint events across a large number of observations.

- Section 3.3 shows how co-occurrence counts can be converted into relative frequencies using a pattern known as "order inversion". The sequencing of computations in the reducer can be recast as a sorting problem, where pieces of intermediate data are sorted into exactly the order that is required to carry out a series of computations. Often, a reducer needs to compute an aggregate statistic on a set of elements before individual elements can be processed. Normally, this would require two passes over the data, but with the "order inversion" design pattern, the aggregate statistic can be computed in the reducer before the individual elements are encountered. This may seem counter-intuitive: how can we compute an aggregate statistic on a set of elements before encountering elements of that set? As it turns out, clever sorting of special key-value pairs enables exactly this.

- Section 3.4 provides a general solution to secondary sorting, which is the problem of sorting values associated with a key in the reduce phase. We call this technique "value-to-key conversion".

- Section 3.5 covers the topic of performing joins on relational datasets and presents three different approaches: *reduce-side*, *map-side*, and *memory-backed* joins.

3.1 LOCAL AGGREGATION

In the context of data-intensive distributed processing, the single most important aspect of synchronization is the exchange of intermediate results, from the processes that produced them to the processes that will ultimately consume them. In a cluster environment, with the exception of embarrassingly-parallel problems, this necessarily involves transferring data over the network. Furthermore, in Hadoop, intermediate results are written to local disk before being sent over the network. Since network and disk latencies are relatively expensive compared to other operations, reductions in the amount of intermediate data translate into increases in algorithmic efficiency. In MapReduce, local aggregation of intermediate results is one of the keys to efficient algorithms. Through use of the combiner and by taking advantage of the ability to preserve state across multiple inputs, it is often possible to substantially reduce both the number and size of key-value pairs that need to be shuffled from the mappers to the reducers.

3.1.1 COMBINERS AND IN-MAPPER COMBINING

We illustrate various techniques for local aggregation using the simple word count example presented in Section 2.2. For convenience, Figure 3.1 repeats the pseudo-code of the basic algorithm, which is quite simple: the mapper emits an intermediate key-value pair for each term observed, with the term itself as the key and a value of one; reducers sum up the partial counts to arrive at the final count.

The first technique for local aggregation is the combiner, already discussed in Section 2.4. Combiners provide a general mechanism within the MapReduce framework to reduce the amount of intermediate data generated by the mappers—recall that they can be understood as "mini-reducers" that process the output of mappers. In this example, the combiners aggregate term counts across the

```
1: class MAPPER
2:     method MAP(docid a, doc d)
3:         for all term t ∈ doc d do
4:             EMIT(term t, count 1)

1: class REDUCER
2:     method REDUCE(term t, counts [c₁, c₂, . . .])
3:         sum ← 0
4:         for all count c ∈ counts [c₁, c₂, . . .] do
5:             sum ← sum + c
6:         EMIT(term t, count sum)
```

Figure 3.1: Pseudo-code for the basic word count algorithm in MapReduce (repeated from Figure 2.3).

documents processed by each map task. This results in a reduction in the number of intermediate key-value pairs that need to be shuffled across the network—from the order of *total* number of terms in the collection to the order of the number of *unique* terms in the collection.[1]

An improvement on the basic algorithm is shown in Figure 3.2 (the mapper is modified but the reducer remains the same as in Figure 3.1 and therefore is not repeated). An associative array (i.e., Map in Java) is introduced inside the mapper to tally up term counts within a single document: instead of emitting a key-value pair for each term in the document, this version emits a key-value pair for each *unique* term in the document. Given that some words appear frequently within a document (for example, a document about dogs is likely to have many occurrences of the word "dog"), this can yield substantial savings in the number of intermediate key-value pairs emitted, especially for long documents.

This basic idea can be taken one step further, as illustrated in the variant of the word count algorithm in Figure 3.3 (once again, only the mapper is modified). The workings of this algorithm critically depends on the details of how map and reduce tasks in Hadoop are executed, discussed in Section 2.6. Recall, a (Java) mapper object is created for each map task, which is responsible for processing a block of input key-value pairs. Prior to processing any input key-value pairs, the mapper's INITIALIZE method is called, which is an API hook for user-specified code. In this case, we initialize an associative array for holding term counts. Since it is possible to preserve state across multiple calls of the MAP method (for each input key-value pair), we can continue to accumulate partial term counts in the associative array *across* multiple documents, and emit key-value pairs only

[1] More precisely, if the combiners take advantage of all opportunities for local aggregation, the algorithm would generate at most $m \times V$ intermediate key-value pairs, where m is the number of mappers and V is the vocabulary size (number of unique terms in the collection), since every term could have been observed in every mapper. However, there are two additional factors to consider. Due to the Zipfian nature of term distributions, most terms will not be observed by most mappers (for example, terms that occur only once will by definition only be observed by one mapper). On the other hand, combiners in Hadoop are treated as *optional* optimizations, so there is no guarantee that the execution framework will take advantage of all opportunities for partial aggregation.

```
1: class MAPPER
2:     method MAP(docid a, doc d)
3:         H ← new ASSOCIATIVEARRAY
4:         for all term t ∈ doc d do
5:             H{t} ← H{t} + 1                        ▷ Tally counts for entire document
6:         for all term t ∈ H do
7:             EMIT(term t, count H{t})
```

Figure 3.2: Pseudo-code for the improved MapReduce word count algorithm that uses an associative array to aggregate term counts on a per-document basis. Reducer is the same as in Figure 3.1.

```
1: class MAPPER
2:     method INITIALIZE
3:         H ← new ASSOCIATIVEARRAY
4:     method MAP(docid a, doc d)
5:         for all term t ∈ doc d do
6:             H{t} ← H{t} + 1                        ▷ Tally counts across documents
7:     method CLOSE
8:         for all term t ∈ H do
9:             EMIT(term t, count H{t})
```

Figure 3.3: Pseudo-code for the improved MapReduce word count algorithm that demonstrates the "in-mapper combining" design pattern. Reducer is the same as in Figure 3.1.

when the mapper has processed all documents. That is, emission of intermediate data is deferred until the CLOSE method in the pseudo-code. Recall that this API hook provides an opportunity to execute user-specified code *after* the MAP method has been applied to all input key-value pairs of the input data split to which the map task was assigned.

With this technique, we are in essence incorporating combiner functionality directly inside the mapper. There is no need to run a separate combiner, since all opportunities for local aggregation are already exploited.[2] This is a sufficiently common design pattern in MapReduce that it's worth giving it a name, "in-mapper combining", so that we can refer to the pattern more conveniently throughout the book. We'll see later on how this pattern can be applied to a variety of problems. There are two main advantages to using this design pattern:

First, it provides control over when local aggregation occurs and how it exactly takes place. In contrast, the semantics of the combiner is underspecified in MapReduce. For example, Hadoop makes no guarantees on how many times the combiner is applied, or that it is even applied at all. The

---

[2]Leaving aside the minor complication that in Hadoop, combiners can be run in the reduce phase also (when merging intermediate key-value pairs from different map tasks). However, in practice, it makes almost no difference either way.

combiner is provided as a semantics-preserving optimization to the execution framework, which has the *option* of using it, perhaps multiple times, or not at all (or even in the reduce phase). In some cases (although not in this particular example), such indeterminism is unacceptable, which is exactly why programmers often choose to perform their own local aggregation in the mappers.

Second, in-mapper combining will typically be more efficient than using actual combiners. One reason for this is the additional overhead associated with actually materializing the key-value pairs. Combiners reduce the amount of intermediate data that is shuffled across the network, but don't actually reduce the number of key-value pairs that are emitted by the mappers in the first place. With the algorithm in Figure 3.2, intermediate key-value pairs are still generated on a per-document basis, only to be "compacted" by the combiners. This process involves unnecessary object creation and destruction (garbage collection takes time), and furthermore, object serialization and deserialization (when intermediate key-value pairs fill the in-memory buffer holding map outputs and need to be temporarily spilled to disk). In contrast, with in-mapper combining, the mappers will generate only those key-value pairs that need to be shuffled across the network to the reducers.

There are, however, drawbacks to the in-mapper combining pattern. First, it breaks the functional programming underpinnings of MapReduce, since state is being preserved across multiple input key-value pairs. Ultimately, this isn't a big deal, since pragmatic concerns for efficiency often trump theoretical "purity", but there are practical consequences as well. Preserving state across multiple input instances means that algorithmic behavior may depend on the order in which input key-value pairs are encountered. This creates the potential for ordering-dependent bugs, which are difficult to debug on large datasets in the general case (although the correctness of in-mapper combining for word count is easy to demonstrate). Second, there is a fundamental scalability bottleneck associated with the in-mapper combining pattern. It critically depends on having sufficient memory to store intermediate results until the mapper has completely processed all key-value pairs in an input split. In the word count example, the memory footprint is bound by the vocabulary size, since it is theoretically possible that a mapper encounters every term in the collection. Heap's Law, a well-known result in information retrieval, accurately models the growth of vocabulary size as a function of the collection size—the somewhat surprising fact is that the vocabulary size never stops growing.[3] Therefore, the algorithm in Figure 3.3 will scale only up to a point, beyond which the associative array holding the partial term counts will no longer fit in memory.[4]

One common solution to limiting memory usage when using the in-mapper combining technique is to "block" input key-value pairs and "flush" in-memory data structures periodically. The idea is simple: instead of emitting intermediate data only after *every* key-value pair has been processed, emit partial results after processing every *n* key-value pairs. This is straightforwardly implemented with a counter variable that keeps track of the number of input key-value pairs that have been

---

[3]In more detail, Heap's Law relates the vocabulary size V to the collection size as follows: $V = kT^b$, where T is the number of tokens in the collection. Typical values of the parameters k and b are: $30 \leq k \leq 100$ and $b \sim 0.5$ ([101], p. 81).

[4]A few more details: note what matters is that the partial term counts encountered within a particular *input split* fits into memory. However, as collection sizes increase, one will often want to increase the input split size to limit the growth of the number of map tasks (in order to reduce the number of distinct copy operations necessary to shuffle intermediate data over the network).

processed. As an alternative, the mapper could keep track of its own memory footprint and flush intermediate key-value pairs once memory usage has crossed a certain threshold. In both approaches, either the block size or the memory usage threshold needs to be determined empirically: with too large a value, the mapper may run out of memory, but with too small a value, opportunities for local aggregation may be lost. Furthermore, in Hadoop physical memory is split between multiple tasks that may be running on a node concurrently; these tasks are all competing for finite resources, but since the tasks are not aware of each other, it is difficult to coordinate resource consumption effectively. In practice, however, one often encounters diminishing returns in performance gains with increasing buffer sizes, such that it is not worth the effort to search for an *optimal* buffer size (personal communication, Jeff Dean).

In MapReduce algorithms, the extent to which efficiency can be increased through local aggregation depends on the size of the intermediate key space, the distribution of keys themselves, and the number of key-value pairs that are emitted by each individual map task. Opportunities for aggregation, after all, come from having multiple values associated with the same key (whether one uses combiners or employs the in-mapper combining pattern). In the word count example, local aggregation is effective because many words are encountered multiple times within a map task. Local aggregation is also an effective technique for dealing with reduce stragglers (see Section 2.3) that result from a highly skewed (e.g., Zipfian) distribution of values associated with intermediate keys. In our word count example, we do not filter frequently occurring words: therefore, without local aggregation, the reducer that's responsible for computing the count of 'the' will have a lot more work to do than the typical reducer, and therefore will likely be a straggler. With local aggregation (either combiners or in-mapper combining), we substantially reduce the number of values associated with frequently occurring terms, which alleviates the reduce straggler problem.

3.1.2 ALGORITHMIC CORRECTNESS WITH LOCAL AGGREGATION

Although use of combiners can yield dramatic reductions in algorithm running time, care must be taken in applying them. Since combiners in Hadoop are viewed as optional optimizations, the correctness of the algorithm cannot depend on computations performed by the combiner or depend on them even being run at all. In any MapReduce program, the reducer input key-value type must match the mapper output key-value type: this implies that the combiner input *and* output key-value types must match the mapper output key-value type (which is the same as the reducer input key-value type). In cases where the reduce computation is both commutative and associative, the reducer can also be used (unmodified) as the combiner (as is the case with the word count example). In the general case, however, combiners and reducers are not interchangeable.

Consider a simple example: we have a large dataset where input keys are strings and input values are integers, and we wish to compute the mean of all integers associated with the same key (rounded to the nearest integer). A real-world example might be a large user log from a popular website, where keys represent user ids and values represent some measure of activity such as elapsed time for a particular session—the task would correspond to computing the mean session length on

```
1: class MAPPER
2:     method MAP(string t, integer r)
3:         EMIT(string t, integer r)
```

```
1: class REDUCER
2:     method REDUCE(string t, integers [r₁, r₂, . . .])
3:         sum ← 0
4:         cnt ← 0
5:         for all integer r ∈ integers [r₁, r₂, . . .] do
6:             sum ← sum + r
7:             cnt ← cnt + 1
8:         r_avg ← sum/cnt
9:         EMIT(string t, integer r_avg)
```

Figure 3.4: Pseudo-code for the basic MapReduce algorithm that computes the mean of values associated with the same key.

a per-user basis, which would be useful for understanding user demographics. Figure 3.4 shows the pseudo-code of a simple algorithm for accomplishing this task that does not involve combiners. We use an identity mapper, which simply passes all input key-value pairs to the reducers (appropriately grouped and sorted). The reducer keeps track of the running sum and the number of integers encountered. This information is used to compute the mean once all values are processed. The mean is then emitted as the output value in the reducer (with the input string as the key).

This algorithm will indeed work, but suffers from the same drawbacks as the basic word count algorithm in Figure 3.1: it requires shuffling all key-value pairs from mappers to reducers across the network, which is highly inefficient. Unlike in the word count example, the reducer cannot be used as a combiner in this case. Consider what would happen if we did: the combiner would compute the mean of an arbitrary subset of values associated with the same key, and the reducer would compute the mean of those values. As a concrete example, we know that:

$$\text{MEAN}(1, 2, 3, 4, 5) \neq \text{MEAN}(\text{MEAN}(1, 2), \text{MEAN}(3, 4, 5))$$

In general, the mean of means of arbitrary subsets of a set of numbers is not the same as the mean of the set of numbers. Therefore, this approach would not produce the correct result.[5]

So how might we properly take advantage of combiners? An attempt is shown in Figure 3.5. The mapper remains the same, but we have added a combiner that partially aggregates results by computing the numeric components necessary to arrive at the mean. The combiner receives each string and the associated list of integer values, from which it computes the sum of those values and

---

[5]There is, however, one special case in which using reducers as combiners *would* produce the correct result: if each combiner computed the mean of equal-size subsets of the values. However, since such fine-grained control over the combiners is impossible in MapReduce, such a scenario is highly unlikely.

```
1: class MAPPER
2:     method MAP(string t, integer r)
3:         EMIT(string t, integer r)

1: class COMBINER
2:     method COMBINE(string t, integers [r₁, r₂, ...])
3:         sum ← 0
4:         cnt ← 0
5:         for all integer r ∈ integers [r₁, r₂, ...] do
6:             sum ← sum + r
7:             cnt ← cnt + 1
8:         EMIT(string t, pair (sum, cnt))                    ▷ Separate sum and count

1: class REDUCER
2:     method REDUCE(string t, pairs [(s₁, c₁), (s₂, c₂) ...])
3:         sum ← 0
4:         cnt ← 0
5:         for all pair (s, c) ∈ pairs [(s₁, c₁), (s₂, c₂) ...] do
6:             sum ← sum + s
7:             cnt ← cnt + c
8:         r_avg ← sum/cnt
9:         EMIT(string t, integer r_avg)
```

Figure 3.5: Pseudo-code for an incorrect first attempt at introducing combiners to compute the mean of values associated with each key. The mismatch between combiner input and output key-value types violates the MapReduce programming model.

the number of integers encountered (i.e., the count). The sum and count are packaged into a pair, and emitted as the output of the combiner, with the same string as the key. In the reducer, pairs of partial sums and counts can be aggregated to arrive at the mean. Up until now, all keys and values in our algorithms have been primitives (string, integers, etc.). However, there are no prohibitions in MapReduce for more complex types,[6] and, in fact, this represents a key technique in MapReduce algorithm design that we introduced at the beginning of this chapter. We will frequently encounter complex keys and values throughput the rest of this book.

Unfortunately, this algorithm will not work. Recall that combiners must have the same input and output key-value type, which also must be the same as the mapper output type and the reducer input type. This is clearly not the case. To understand why this restriction is necessary in the programming model, remember that combiners are optimizations that cannot change the correctness of the algorithm. So let us remove the combiner and see what happens: the output value type of the

[6]In Hadoop, either custom types or types defined using a library such as Protocol Buffers, Thrift, or Avro.

```
1: class MAPPER
2:     method MAP(string t, integer r)
3:         EMIT(string t, pair (r, 1))
```

```
1: class COMBINER
2:     method COMBINE(string t, pairs [(s_1, c_1), (s_2, c_2) ...])
3:         sum ← 0
4:         cnt ← 0
5:         for all pair (s, c) ∈ pairs [(s_1, c_1), (s_2, c_2) ...] do
6:             sum ← sum + s
7:             cnt ← cnt + c
8:         EMIT(string t, pair (sum, cnt))
```

```
1: class REDUCER
2:     method REDUCE(string t, pairs [(s_1, c_1), (s_2, c_2) ...])
3:         sum ← 0
4:         cnt ← 0
5:         for all pair (s, c) ∈ pairs [(s_1, c_1), (s_2, c_2) ...] do
6:             sum ← sum + s
7:             cnt ← cnt + c
8:         r_avg ← sum/cnt
9:         EMIT(string t, integer r_avg)
```

Figure 3.6: Pseudo-code for a MapReduce algorithm that computes the mean of values associated with each key. This algorithm correctly takes advantage of combiners.

mapper is integer, so the reducer expects to receive a list of integers as values. But the reducer actually expects a list of pairs! The correctness of the algorithm is contingent on the combiner running on the output of the mappers, and more specifically, that the combiner is run exactly once. Recall from our previous discussion that Hadoop makes no guarantees on how many times combiners are called; it could be zero, one, or multiple times. This violates the MapReduce programming model.

Another stab at the algorithm is shown in Figure 3.6, and this time, the algorithm is correct. In the mapper we emit as the value a pair consisting of the integer and one—this corresponds to a partial count over one instance. The combiner separately aggregates the partial sums and the partial counts (as before), and emits pairs with updated sums and counts. The reducer is similar to the combiner, except that the mean is computed at the end. In essence, this algorithm transforms a non-associative operation (mean of numbers) into an associative operation (element-wise sum of a pair of numbers, with an additional division at the very end).

Let us verify the correctness of this algorithm by repeating the previous exercise: What would happen if no combiners were run? With no combiners, the mappers would send pairs (as values)

```
1: class MAPPER
2:     method INITIALIZE
3:         S ← new ASSOCIATIVEARRAY
4:         C ← new ASSOCIATIVEARRAY
5:     method MAP(string t, integer r)
6:         S{t} ← S{t} + r
7:         C{t} ← C{t} + 1
8:     method CLOSE
9:         for all term t ∈ S do
10:            EMIT(term t, pair (S{t}, C{t}))
```

Figure 3.7: Pseudo-code for a MapReduce algorithm that computes the mean of values associated with each key, illustrating the in-mapper combining design pattern. Only the mapper is shown here; the reducer is the same as in Figure 3.6

directly to the reducers. There would be as many intermediate pairs as there were input key-value pairs, and each of those would consist of an integer and one. The reducer would still arrive at the correct sum and count, and hence the mean would be correct. Now add in the combiners: the algorithm would remain correct, no matter how many times they run, since the combiners merely aggregate partial sums and counts to pass along to the reducers. Note that although the output key-value type of the combiner must be the same as the input key-value type of the reducer, the reducer can emit final key-value pairs of a different type.

Finally, in Figure 3.7, we present an even more efficient algorithm that exploits the in-mapper combining pattern. Inside the mapper, the partial sums and counts associated with each string are held in memory across input key-value pairs. Intermediate key-value pairs are emitted only after the entire input split has been processed; similar to before, the value is a pair consisting of the sum and count. The reducer is exactly the same as in Figure 3.6. Moving partial aggregation from the combiner directly into the mapper is subjected to all the trade offs and caveats discussed earlier this section, but in this case the memory footprint of the data structures for holding intermediate data is likely to be modest, making this variant algorithm an attractive option.

3.2   PAIRS AND STRIPES

One common approach for synchronization in MapReduce is to construct complex keys and values in such a way that data necessary for a computation are naturally brought together by the execution framework. We first touched on this technique in the previous section, in the context of "packaging" partial sums and counts in a complex value (i.e., pair) that is passed from mapper to combiner to reducer. Building on previously published work [54; 94], this section introduces two common design patterns we have dubbed "pairs" and "stripes" that exemplify this strategy.

As a running example, we focus on the problem of building word co-occurrence matrices from large corpora, a common task in corpus linguistics and statistical natural language processing. Formally, the co-occurrence matrix of a corpus is a square $n \times n$ matrix where n is the number of unique words in the corpus (i.e., the vocabulary size). A cell m_{ij} contains the number of times word w_i co-occurs with word w_j within a specific context—a natural unit such as a sentence, paragraph, or a document, or a certain window of m words (where m is an application-dependent parameter). Note that the upper and lower triangles of the matrix are identical since co-occurrence is a symmetric relation, though in the general case relations between words need not be symmetric. For example, a co-occurrence matrix M where m_{ij} is the count of how many times word w_i was immediately succeeded by word w_j would usually not be symmetric.

This task is quite common in text processing and provides the starting point to many other algorithms, e.g., for computing statistics such as pointwise mutual information [38], for unsupervised sense clustering [136], and more generally, a large body of work in lexical semantics based on distributional profiles of words, dating back to Firth [55] and Harris [69] in the 1950s and 1960s. The task also has applications in information retrieval (e.g., automatic thesaurus construction [137] and stemming [157]), and other related fields such as text mining. More importantly, this problem represents a specific instance of the task of estimating distributions of discrete joint events from a large number of observations, a very common task in statistical natural language processing for which there are nice MapReduce solutions. Indeed, concepts presented here are also used in Chapter 6 when we discuss expectation-maximization algorithms.

Beyond text processing, problems in many application domains share similar characteristics. For example, a large retailer might analyze point-of-sale transaction records to identify correlated product purchases (e.g., customers who buy *this* tend to also buy *that*), which would assist in inventory management and product placement on store shelves. Similarly, an intelligence analyst might wish to identify associations between re-occurring financial transactions that are otherwise unrelated, which might provide a clue in thwarting terrorist activity. The algorithms discussed in this section could be adapted to tackle these related problems.

It is obvious that the space requirement for the word co-occurrence problem is $O(n^2)$, where n is the size of the vocabulary, which for real-world English corpora can be hundreds of thousands of words, or even billions of words in web-scale collections.[7] The computation of the word co-occurrence matrix is quite simple if the entire matrix fits into memory—however, in the case where the matrix is too big to fit in memory, a naïve implementation on a single machine can be very slow as memory is paged to disk. Although compression techniques can increase the size of corpora for which word co-occurrence matrices can be constructed on a single machine, it is clear that there are inherent scalability limitations. We describe two MapReduce algorithms for this task that can scale to large corpora.

---

[7]The size of the vocabulary depends on the definition of a "word" and techniques (if any) for corpus pre-processing. One common strategy is to replace all rare words (below a certain frequency) with a "special" token such as <UNK> (which stands for "unknown") to model out-of-vocabulary words. Another technique involves replacing numeric digits with #, such that 1.32 and 1.19 both map to the same token (#.##).

Pseudo-code for the first algorithm, dubbed the "pairs" approach, is shown in Figure 3.8. As usual, document ids and the corresponding contents make up the input key-value pairs. The mapper processes each input document and emits intermediate key-value pairs with each co-occurring word pair as the key and the integer one (i.e., the count) as the value. This is straightforwardly accomplished by two nested loops: the outer loop iterates over all words (the left element in the pair), and the inner loop iterates over all neighbors of the first word (the right element in the pair). The neighbors of a word can either be defined in terms of a sliding window or some other contextual unit such as a sentence. The MapReduce execution framework guarantees that all values associated with the same key are brought together in the reducer. Thus, in this case the reducer simply sums up all the values associated with the same co-occurring word pair to arrive at the absolute count of the joint event in the corpus, which is then emitted as the final key-value pair. Each pair corresponds to a cell in the word co-occurrence matrix. This algorithm illustrates the use of complex keys in order to coordinate distributed computations.

An alternative approach, dubbed the "stripes" approach, is presented in Figure 3.9. Like the pairs approach, co-occurring word pairs are generated by two nested loops. However, the major difference is that instead of emitting intermediate key-value pairs for each co-occurring word pair, co-occurrence information is first stored in an associative array, denoted H. The mapper emits key-value pairs with words as keys and corresponding associative arrays as values, where each associative array encodes the co-occurrence counts of the neighbors of a particular word (i.e., its context). The MapReduce execution framework guarantees that all associative arrays with the same key will be brought together in the reduce phase of processing. The reducer performs an element-wise sum of all associative arrays with the same key, accumulating counts that correspond to the same cell in the co-occurrence matrix. The final associative array is emitted with the same word as the key. In contrast to the pairs approach, each final key-value pair encodes a row in the co-occurrence matrix.

It is immediately obvious that the pairs algorithm generates an immense number of key-value pairs compared to the stripes approach. The stripes representation is much more compact, since with pairs the left element is repeated for every co-occurring word pair. The stripes approach also generates fewer and shorter intermediate keys, and therefore the execution framework has less sorting to perform. However, values in the stripes approach are more complex, and come with more serialization and deserialization overhead than with the pairs approach.

Both algorithms can benefit from the use of combiners, since the respective operations in their reducers (addition and element-wise sum of associative arrays) are both commutative and associative. However, combiners with the stripes approach have more opportunities to perform local aggregation because the key space is the vocabulary—associative arrays can be merged whenever a word is encountered multiple times by a mapper. In contrast, the key space in the pairs approach is the cross of the vocabulary with itself, which is far larger—counts can be aggregated only when the same co-occurring word pair is observed multiple times by an individual mapper (which is less likely than observing multiple occurrences of a word, as in the stripes case).

```
1: class MAPPER
2:     method MAP(docid a, doc d)
3:         for all term w ∈ doc d do
4:             for all term u ∈ NEIGHBORS(w) do
5:                 EMIT(pair (w, u), count 1)              ▷ Emit count for each co-occurrence
```

```
1: class REDUCER
2:     method REDUCE(pair p, counts [c_1, c_2, ...])
3:         s ← 0
4:         for all count c ∈ counts [c_1, c_2, ...] do
5:             s ← s + c                                  ▷ Sum co-occurrence counts
6:         EMIT(pair p, count s)
```

Figure 3.8: Pseudo-code for the "pairs" approach for computing word co-occurrence matrices from large corpora.

```
1: class MAPPER
2:     method MAP(docid a, doc d)
3:         for all term w ∈ doc d do
4:             H ← new ASSOCIATIVEARRAY
5:             for all term u ∈ NEIGHBORS(w) do
6:                 H{u} ← H{u} + 1                        ▷ Tally words co-occurring with w
7:             EMIT(Term w, Stripe H)
```

```
1: class REDUCER
2:     method REDUCE(term w, stripes [H_1, H_2, H_3, ...])
3:         H_f ← new ASSOCIATIVEARRAY
4:         for all stripe H ∈ stripes [H_1, H_2, H_3, ...] do
5:             SUM(H_f, H)                                ▷ Element-wise sum
6:         EMIT(term w, stripe H_f)
```

Figure 3.9: Pseudo-code for the "stripes" approach for computing word co-occurrence matrices from large corpora.

For both algorithms, the in-mapper combining optimization discussed in the previous section can also be applied; the modification is sufficiently straightforward that we leave the implementation as an exercise for the reader. However, the above caveats remain: there will be far fewer opportunities for partial aggregation in the pairs approach due to the sparsity of the intermediate key space. The sparsity of the key space also limits the effectiveness of in-memory combining, since the mapper may run out of memory to store partial counts before all documents are processed, necessitating some mechanism to periodically emit key-value pairs (which further limits opportunities to perform partial aggregation). Similarly, for the stripes approach, memory management will also be more complex than in the simple word count example. For common terms, the associative array may grow to be quite large, necessitating some mechanism to periodically flush in-memory structures.

It is important to consider potential scalability bottlenecks of either algorithm. The stripes approach makes the assumption that, at any point in time, each associative array is small enough to fit into memory—otherwise, memory paging will significantly impact performance. The size of the associative array is bounded by the vocabulary size, which is itself unbounded with respect to corpus size (recall the previous discussion of Heap's Law). Therefore, as the sizes of corpora increase, this will become an increasingly pressing issue—perhaps not for gigabyte-sized corpora, but certainly for terabyte-sized and petabyte-sized corpora that will be commonplace tomorrow. The pairs approach, on the other hand, does not suffer from this limitation, since it does not need to hold intermediate data in memory.

Given this discussion, which approach is faster? Here, we present previously published results [94] that empirically answered this question. We implemented both algorithms in Hadoop and applied them to a corpus of 2.27 million documents from the Associated Press Worldstream (APW) totaling 5.7 GB.[8] Prior to working with Hadoop, the corpus was first preprocessed as follows: All XML markup was removed, followed by tokenization and stopword removal using standard tools from the Lucene search engine. All tokens were then replaced with unique integers for a more efficient encoding. Figure 3.10 compares the running time of the pairs and stripes approach on different fractions of the corpus, with a co-occurrence window size of two. These experiments were performed on a Hadoop cluster with 19 slave nodes, each with 2 single-core processors and 2 disks.

Results demonstrate that the stripes approach is much faster than the pairs approach: 666 seconds (~11 minutes) compared to 3758 seconds (~62 minutes) for the entire corpus (improvement by a factor of 5.7). The mappers in the pairs approach generated 2.6 billion intermediate key-value pairs totaling 31.2 GB. After the combiners, this was reduced to 1.1 billion key-value pairs, which quantifies the amount of intermediate data transferred across the network. In the end, the reducers emitted a total of 142 million final key-value pairs (the number of non-zero cells in the co-occurrence matrix). On the other hand, the mappers in the stripes approach generated 653 million intermediate key-value pairs totaling 48.1 GB. After the combiners, only 28.8 million key-value pairs remained. The reducers emitted a total of 1.69 million final key-value pairs (the number of rows in the co-

[8]This was a subset of the English Gigaword corpus (version 3) distributed by the Linguistic Data Consortium (LDC catalog number LDC2007T07).

occurrence matrix). As expected, the stripes approach provided more opportunities for combiners to aggregate intermediate results, thus greatly reducing network traffic in the shuffle and sort phase. Figure 3.10 also shows that both algorithms exhibit highly desirable scaling characteristics—linear in the amount of input data. This is confirmed by a linear regression applied to the running time data, which yields an R^2 value close to one.

An additional series of experiments explored the scalability of the stripes approach along another dimension: the size of the cluster. These experiments were made possible by Amazon's EC2 service, which allows users to rapidly provision clusters of varying sizes for limited durations (for more information, refer back to our discussion of utility computing in Section 1.1). Virtualized computational units in EC2 are called instances, and the user is charged only for the instance-hours consumed. Figure 3.11 (left) shows the running time of the stripes algorithm (on the same corpus, with same setup as before), on varying cluster sizes, from 20 slave "small" instances all the way up to 80 slave "small" instances (along the x-axis). Running times are shown with solid squares. Figure 3.11 (right) recasts the same results to illustrate scaling characteristics. The circles plot the relative size and speedup of the EC2 experiments, with respect to the 20-instance cluster. These results show highly desirable linear scaling characteristics (i.e., doubling the cluster size makes the job twice as fast). This is confirmed by a linear regression with an R^2 value close to one.

Viewed abstractly, the pairs and stripes algorithms represent two different approaches to counting co-occurring events from a large number of observations. This general description captures the gist of many algorithms in fields as diverse as text processing, data mining, and bioinformatics. For this reason, these two design patterns are broadly useful and frequently observed in a variety of applications.

To conclude, it is worth noting that the pairs and stripes approaches represent endpoints along a continuum of possibilities. The pairs approach individually records *each* co-occurring event, while the stripes approach records *all* co-occurring events with respect a conditioning event. A middle ground might be to record a subset of the co-occurring events with respect to a conditioning event. We might divide up the entire vocabulary into b buckets (e.g., via hashing), so that words co-occurring with w_i would be divided into b smaller "sub-stripes", associated with ten separate keys, $(w_i, 1), (w_i, 2) \ldots (w_i, b)$. This would be a reasonable solution to the memory limitations of the stripes approach, since each of the sub-stripes would be smaller. In the case of $b = |V|$, where $|V|$ is the vocabulary size, this is equivalent to the pairs approach. In the case of $b = 1$, this is equivalent to the standard stripes approach.

3.3   COMPUTING RELATIVE FREQUENCIES

Let us build on the pairs and stripes algorithms presented in the previous section and continue with our running example of constructing the word co-occurrence matrix M for a large corpus. Recall that in this large square $n \times n$ matrix, where $n = |V|$ (the vocabulary size), cell m_{ij} contains the number of times word w_i co-occurs with word w_j within a specific context. The drawback of absolute counts is that it doesn't take into account the fact that some words appear more frequently than others. Word

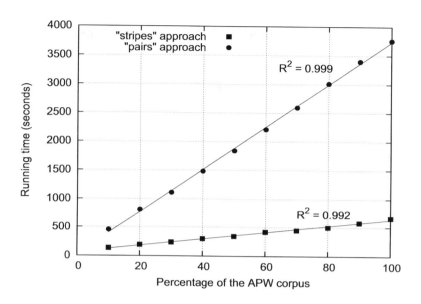

Figure 3.10: Running time of the "pairs" and "stripes" algorithms for computing word co-occurrence matrices on different fractions of the APW corpus. These experiments were performed on a Hadoop cluster with 19 slaves, each with 2 single-core processors and 2 disks.

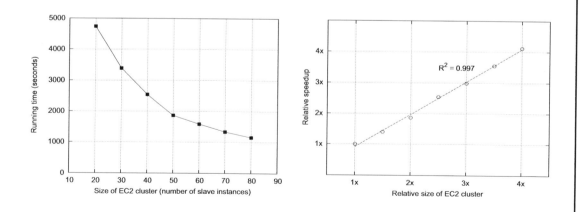

Figure 3.11: Running time of the stripes algorithm on the APW corpus with Hadoop clusters of different sizes from EC2 (left). Scaling characteristics (relative speedup) in terms of increasing Hadoop cluster size (right).

w_i may co-occur frequently with w_j simply because one of the words is very common. A simple remedy is to convert absolute counts into relative frequencies, $f(w_j|w_i)$. That is, what proportion of the time does w_j appear in the context of w_i? This can be computed using the following equation:

$$f(w_j|w_i) = \frac{N(w_i, w_j)}{\sum_{w'} N(w_i, w')} \tag{3.1}$$

Here, $N(\cdot, \cdot)$ indicates the number of times a particular co-occurring word pair is observed in the corpus. We need the count of the joint event (word co-occurrence), divided by what is known as the marginal (the sum of the counts of the conditioning variable co-occurring with anything else).

Computing relative frequencies with the stripes approach is straightforward. In the reducer, counts of all words that co-occur with the conditioning variable (w_i in the above example) are available in the associative array. Therefore, it suffices to sum all those counts to arrive at the marginal (i.e., $\sum_{w'} N(w_i, w')$), and then divide all the joint counts by the marginal to arrive at the relative frequency for all words. This implementation requires minimal modification to the original stripes algorithm in Figure 3.9, and illustrates the use of complex data structures to coordinate distributed computations in MapReduce. Through appropriate structuring of keys and values, one can use the MapReduce execution framework to bring together all the pieces of data required to perform a computation. Note that, as before, this algorithm also assumes that each associative array fits into memory.

How might one compute relative frequencies with the pairs approach? In the pairs approach, the reducer receives (w_i, w_j) as the key and the count as the value. From this alone it is not possible to compute $f(w_j|w_i)$ since we do not have the marginal. Fortunately, as in the mapper, the reducer can preserve state across multiple keys. Inside the reducer, we can buffer in memory all the words that co-occur with w_i and their counts, in essence building the associative array in the stripes approach. To make this work, we must define the sort order of the pair so that keys are first sorted by the left word, and then by the right word. Given this ordering, we can easily detect if all pairs associated with the word we are conditioning on (w_i) have been encountered. At that point we can go back through the in-memory buffer, compute the relative frequencies, and then emit those results in the final key-value pairs.

There is one more modification necessary to make this algorithm work. We must ensure that all pairs with the same left word are sent to the same reducer. This, unfortunately, does not happen automatically: recall that the default partitioner is based on the hash value of the intermediate key, modulo the number of reducers. For a complex key, the raw byte representation is used to compute the hash value. As a result, there is no guarantee that, for example, (dog, aardvark) and (dog, zebra) are assigned to the same reducer. To produce the desired behavior, we must define a custom partitioner that only pays attention to the left word. That is, the partitioner should partition based on the hash of the left word only.

This algorithm will indeed work, but it suffers from the same drawback as the stripes approach: as the size of the corpus grows, so does that vocabulary size, and at some point there will not be sufficient memory to store all co-occurring words and their counts for the word we are conditioning

key	values	
(dog, *)	[6327, 8514, . . .]	compute marginal: $\sum_{w'} N(\text{dog}, w') = 42908$
(dog, aardvark)	[2,1]	$f(\text{aardvark}|\text{dog}) = 3/42908$
(dog, aardwolf)	[1]	$f(\text{aardwolf}|\text{dog}) = 1/42908$
...		
(dog, zebra)	[2,1,1,1]	$f(\text{zebra}|\text{dog}) = 5/42908$
(doge, *)	[682, . . .]	compute marginal: $\sum_{w'} N(\text{doge}, w') = 1267$
...		

Figure 3.12: Example of the sequence of key-value pairs presented to the reducer in the pairs algorithm for computing relative frequencies. This illustrates the application of the order inversion design pattern.

on. For computing the co-occurrence matrix, the advantage of the pairs approach is that it doesn't suffer from any memory bottlenecks. Is there a way to modify the basic pairs approach so that this advantage is retained?

As it turns out, such an algorithm is indeed possible, although it requires the coordination of several mechanisms in MapReduce. The insight lies in properly sequencing data presented to the reducer. If it were possible to somehow compute (or otherwise obtain access to) the marginal in the reducer before processing the joint counts, the reducer could simply divide the joint counts by the marginal to compute the relative frequencies. The notion of "before" and "after" can be captured in the ordering of key-value pairs, which can be explicitly controlled by the programmer. That is, the programmer can define the sort order of keys so that data needed earlier is presented to the reducer before data that is needed later. However, we still need to compute the marginal counts. Recall that in the basic pairs algorithm, each mapper emits a key-value pair with the co-occurring word pair as the key. To compute relative frequencies, we modify the mapper so that it additionally emits a "special" key of the form $(w_i, *)$, with a value of one, that represents the contribution of the word pair to the marginal. Through use of combiners, these partial marginal counts will be aggregated before being sent to the reducers. Alternatively, the in-mapper combining pattern can be used to even more efficiently aggregate marginal counts.

In the reducer, we must make sure that the special key-value pairs representing the partial marginal contributions are processed before the normal key-value pairs representing the joint counts. This is accomplished by defining the sort order of the keys so that pairs with the special symbol of the form $(w_i, *)$ are ordered before any other key-value pairs where the left word is w_i. In addition, as before we must also properly define the partitioner to pay attention to only the left word in each pair. With the data properly sequenced, the reducer can directly compute the relative frequencies.

A concrete example is shown in Figure 3.12, which lists the sequence of key-value pairs that a reducer might encounter. First, the reducer is presented with the special key (dog, *) and a number of values, each of which represents a partial marginal contribution from the map phase (assume here either combiners or in-mapper combining, so the values represent partially aggregated counts). The reducer accumulates these counts to arrive at the marginal, $\sum_{w'} N(\text{dog}, w')$. The reducer holds on to this value as it processes subsequent keys. After (dog, *), the reducer will encounter a series of keys representing joint counts; let's say the first of these is the key (dog, aardvark). Associated with this key will be a list of values representing partial joint counts from the map phase (two separate values in this case). Summing these counts will yield the final joint count, i.e., the number of times dog and aardvark co-occur in the entire collection. At this point, since the reducer already knows the marginal, simple arithmetic suffices to compute the relative frequency. All subsequent joint counts are processed in exactly the same manner. When the reducer encounters the next special key-value pair (doge, *), the reducer resets its internal state and starts to accumulate the marginal all over again. Observe that the memory requirement for this algorithm is minimal, since only the marginal (an integer) needs to be stored. No buffering of individual co-occurring word counts is necessary, and therefore we have eliminated the scalability bottleneck of the previous algorithm.

This design pattern, which we call "order inversion", occurs surprisingly often and across applications in many domains. It is so named because through proper coordination, we can access the result of a computation in the reducer (for example, an aggregate statistic) before processing the data needed for that computation. The key insight is to convert the sequencing of computations into a sorting problem. In most cases, an algorithm requires data in some fixed order: by controlling how keys are sorted and how the key space is partitioned, we can present data to the reducer in the order necessary to perform the proper computations. This greatly cuts down on the amount of partial results that the reducer needs to hold in memory.

To summarize, the specific application of the order inversion design pattern for computing relative frequencies requires the following:

- Emitting a special key-value pair for each co-occurring word pair in the mapper to capture its contribution to the marginal.

- Controlling the sort order of the intermediate key so that the key-value pairs representing the marginal contributions are processed by the reducer before any of the pairs representing the joint word co-occurrence counts.

- Defining a custom partitioner to ensure that all pairs with the same left word are shuffled to the same reducer.

- Preserving state across multiple keys in the reducer to first compute the marginal based on the special key-value pairs and then dividing the joint counts by the marginals to arrive at the relative frequencies.

As we will see in Chapter 4, this design pattern is also used in inverted index construction to properly set compression parameters for postings lists.

3.4   SECONDARY SORTING

MapReduce sorts intermediate key-value pairs by the keys during the shuffle and sort phase, which is very convenient if computations inside the reducer rely on sort order (e.g., the order inversion design pattern described in the previous section). However, what if in addition to sorting by key, we also need to sort by value? Google's MapReduce implementation provides built-in functionality for (optional) secondary sorting, which guarantees that values arrive in sorted order. Hadoop, unfortunately, does not have this capability built in.

Consider the example of sensor data from a scientific experiment: there are m sensors each taking readings on a continuous basis, where m is potentially a large number. A dump of the sensor data might look something like the following, where r_x after each timestamp represents the actual sensor reading (unimportant for this discussion, but may be a series of values, one or more complex records, or even raw bytes of images).

(t_1, m_1, r_{80521})
(t_1, m_2, r_{14209})
(t_1, m_3, r_{76042})
...
(t_2, m_1, r_{21823})
(t_2, m_2, r_{66508})
(t_2, m_3, r_{98347})

Suppose we wish to reconstruct the activity at each individual sensor over time. A MapReduce program to accomplish this might map over the raw data and emit the sensor id as the intermediate key, with the rest of each record as the value:

$$m_1 \rightarrow (t_1, r_{80521})$$

This would bring all readings from the same sensor together in the reducer. However, since Map-Reduce makes no guarantees about the ordering of values associated with the same key, the sensor readings will not likely be in temporal order. The most obvious solution is to buffer all the readings in memory and then sort by timestamp before additional processing. However, it should be apparent by now that any in-memory buffering of data introduces a potential scalability bottleneck. What if we are working with a high frequency sensor or sensor readings over a long period of time? What if the sensor readings themselves are large complex objects? This approach may not scale in these cases—the reducer would run out of memory trying to buffer all values associated with the same key.

This is a common problem, since in many applications we wish to first group together data one way (e.g., by sensor id), and then sort within the groupings another way (e.g., by time). Fortunately, there is a general purpose solution, which we call the "value-to-key conversion" design pattern. The basic idea is to move part of the value into the intermediate key to form a composite key, and let the MapReduce execution framework handle the sorting. In the above example, instead of emitting the sensor id as the key, we would emit the sensor id and the timestamp as a composite key:

$$(m_1, t_1) \rightarrow (r_{80521})$$

The sensor reading itself now occupies the value. We must define the intermediate key sort order to first sort by the sensor id (the left element in the pair) and then by the timestamp (the right element in the pair). We must also implement a custom partitioner so that all pairs associated with the same sensor are shuffled to the same reducer.

Properly orchestrated, the key-value pairs will be presented to the reducer in the correct sorted order:

$$(m_1, t_1) \rightarrow [(r_{80521})]$$
$$(m_1, t_2) \rightarrow [(r_{21823})]$$
$$(m_1, t_3) \rightarrow [(r_{146925})]$$
$$\ldots$$

However, note that sensor readings are now split across multiple keys. The reducer will need to preserve state and keep track of when readings associated with the current sensor end and the next sensor begin.[9]

The basic tradeoff between the two approaches discussed above (buffer and in-memory sort vs. value-to-key conversion) is where sorting is performed. One can explicitly implement secondary sorting in the reducer, which is likely to be faster but suffers from a scalability bottleneck.[10] With value-to-key conversion, sorting is offloaded to the MapReduce execution framework. Note that this approach can be arbitrarily extended to tertiary, quaternary, etc. sorting. This pattern results in many more keys for the framework to sort, but distributed sorting is a task that the MapReduce runtime excels at since it lies at the heart of the programming model.

3.5   RELATIONAL JOINS

One popular application of Hadoop is data-warehousing. In an enterprise setting, a data warehouse serves as a vast repository of data, holding everything from sales transactions to product inventories. Typically, the data is relational in nature, but increasingly data warehouses are used to store semi-structured data (e.g., query logs) as well as unstructured data. Data warehouses form a foundation for business intelligence applications designed to provide decision support. It is widely believed that insights gained by mining historical, current, and prospective data can yield competitive advantages in the marketplace.

Traditionally, data warehouses have been implemented through relational databases, particularly those optimized for a specific workload known as online analytical processing (OLAP). A number of vendors offer parallel databases, but customers find that they often cannot cost-effectively scale to the crushing amounts of data an organization needs to deal with today. Parallel databases

---

[9] Alternatively, Hadoop provides API hooks to define "groups" of intermediate keys that should be processed together in the reducer.
[10] Note that, in principle, this need not be an in-memory sort. It is entirely possible to implement a disk-based sort within the reducer, although one would be duplicating functionality that is already present in the MapReduce execution framework. It makes more sense to take advantage of functionality that is already present with value-to-key conversion.

are often quite expensive—on the order of tens of thousands of dollars per terabyte of user data. Over the past few years, Hadoop has gained popularity as a platform for data-warehousing. Hammerbacher [68], for example, discussed Facebook's experiences with scaling up business intelligence applications with Oracle databases, which they ultimately abandoned in favor of a Hadoop-based solution developed in-house called Hive (which is now an open-source project). Pig [114] is a platform for massive data analytics built on Hadoop and capable of handling structured as well as semi-structured data. It was originally developed by Yahoo, but is now also an open-source project.

Given successful applications of Hadoop to data-warehousing and complex analytical queries that are prevalent in such an environment, it makes sense to examine MapReduce algorithms for manipulating relational data. This section focuses specifically on performing relational joins in MapReduce. We should stress here that even though Hadoop has been applied to process relational data, Hadoop *is not a database*. There is an ongoing debate between advocates of parallel databases and proponents of MapReduce regarding the merits of both approaches for OLAP-type workloads. Dewitt and Stonebraker, two well-known figures in the database community, famously decried MapReduce as "a major step backwards" in a controversial blog post.[11] With colleagues, they ran a series of benchmarks that demonstrated the supposed superiority of column-oriented parallel databases over Hadoop [120; 144]. However, see Dean and Ghemawat's counterarguments [47] and recent attempts at hybrid architectures [1].

We shall refrain here from participating in this lively debate, and instead focus on discussing algorithms. From an application point of view, it is highly unlikely that an analyst interacting with a data warehouse would ever be called upon to write MapReduce programs (and indeed, Hadoop-based systems such as Hive and Pig present a much higher-level language for interacting with large amounts of data). Nevertheless, it is instructive to understand the algorithms that underlie basic relational operations.

This section presents three different strategies for performing relational joins on two datasets (relations), generically named S and T. Let us suppose that relation S looks something like the following:

$$(k_1, s_1, \mathbf{S}_1)$$
$$(k_2, s_2, \mathbf{S}_2)$$
$$(k_3, s_3, \mathbf{S}_3)$$
$$\ldots$$

where k is the key we would like to join on, s_n is a unique id for the tuple, and the $\mathbf{S}_n$ after s_n denotes other attributes in the tuple (unimportant for the purposes of the join). Similarly, suppose relation T looks something like this:

$$(k_1, t_1, \mathbf{T}_1)$$
$$(k_3, t_2, \mathbf{T}_2)$$

---

[11] http://databasecolumn.vertica.com/database-innovation/mapreduce-a-major-step-backwards/

$(k_8, t_3, \mathbf{T}_3)$

$\cdots$

where k is the join key, t_n is a unique id for the tuple, and the $\mathbf{T}_n$ after t_n denotes other attributes in the tuple.

To make this task more concrete, we present one realistic scenario: S might represent a collection of user profiles, in which case k could be interpreted as the primary key (i.e., user id). The tuples might contain demographic information such as age, gender, income, etc. The other dataset, T, might represent logs of online activity. Each tuple might correspond to a page view of a particular URL and may contain additional information such as time spent on the page, ad revenue generated, etc. The k in these tuples could be interpreted as the foreign key that associates each individual page view with a user. Joining these two datasets would allow an analyst, for example, to break down online activity in terms of demographics.

3.5.1   REDUCE-SIDE JOIN

The first approach to relational joins is what's known as a *reduce-side* join. The idea is quite simple: we map over both datasets and emit the join key as the intermediate key, and the tuple itself as the intermediate value. Since MapReduce guarantees that all values with the same key are brought together, all tuples will be grouped by the join key—which is exactly what we need to perform the join operation. This approach is known as a parallel sort-merge join in the database community [134]. In more detail, there are three different cases to consider.

The first and simplest is a *one-to-one* join, where at most one tuple from S and one tuple from T share the same join key (but it may be the case that no tuple from S shares the join key with a tuple from T, or vice versa). In this case, the algorithm sketched above will work fine. The reducer will be presented keys and lists of values along the lines of the following:

$k_{23} \rightarrow [(s_{64}, \mathbf{S}_{64}), (t_{84}, \mathbf{T}_{84})]$
$k_{37} \rightarrow [(s_{68}, \mathbf{S}_{68})]$
$k_{59} \rightarrow [(t_{97}, \mathbf{T}_{97}), (s_{81}, \mathbf{S}_{81})]$
$k_{61} \rightarrow [(t_{99}, \mathbf{T}_{99})]$

$\cdots$

Since we've emitted the join key as the intermediate key, we can remove it from the value to save a bit of space.[12] If there are two values associated with a key, then we know that one must be from S and the other must be from T. However, recall that in the basic MapReduce programming model, no guarantees are made about value ordering, so the first value might be from S or from T. We can proceed to join the two tuples and perform additional computations (e.g., filter by some other attribute, compute aggregates, etc.). If there is only one value associated with a key, this means that no tuple in the other dataset shares the join key, so the reducer does nothing.

---

[12]Not very important if the intermediate data is compressed.

Let us now consider the *one-to-many* join. Assume that tuples in S have unique join keys (i.e., k is the primary key in S), so that S is the "one" and T is the "many". The above algorithm will still work, but when processing each key in the reducer, we have no idea when the value corresponding to the tuple from S will be encountered, since values are arbitrarily ordered. The easiest solution is to buffer all values in memory, pick out the tuple from S, and then cross it with every tuple from T to perform the join. However, as we have seen several times already, this creates a scalability bottleneck since we may not have sufficient memory to hold all the tuples with the same join key.

This is a problem that requires a secondary sort, and the solution lies in the value-to-key conversion design pattern we just presented. In the mapper, instead of simply emitting the join key as the intermediate key, we instead create a composite key consisting of the join key and the tuple id (from either S or T). Two additional changes are required: First, we must define the sort order of the keys to first sort by the join key, and then sort all tuple ids from S before all tuple ids from T. Second, we must define the partitioner to pay attention to only the join key, so that all composite keys with the same join key arrive at the same reducer.

After applying the value-to-key conversion design pattern, the reducer will be presented with keys and values along the lines of the following:

$$(k_{82}, s_{105}) \rightarrow [(\mathbf{S}_{105})]$$
$$(k_{82}, t_{98}) \rightarrow [(\mathbf{T}_{98})]$$
$$(k_{82}, t_{101}) \rightarrow [(\mathbf{T}_{101})]$$
$$(k_{82}, t_{137}) \rightarrow [(\mathbf{T}_{137})]$$
$$\ldots$$

Since both the join key and the tuple id are present in the intermediate key, we can remove them from the value to save a bit of space.[13] Whenever the reducer encounters a new join key, it is guaranteed that the associated value will be the relevant tuple from S. The reducer can hold this tuple in memory and then proceed to cross it with tuples from T in subsequent steps (until a new join key is encountered). Since the MapReduce execution framework performs the sorting, there is no need to buffer tuples (other than the single one from S). Thus, we have eliminated the scalability bottleneck.

Finally, let us consider the *many-to-many* join case. Assuming that S is the smaller dataset, the above algorithm works as well. Consider what happens at the reducer:

$$(k_{82}, s_{105}) \rightarrow [(\mathbf{S}_{105})]$$
$$(k_{82}, s_{124}) \rightarrow [(\mathbf{S}_{124})]$$
$$\ldots$$
$$(k_{82}, t_{98}) \rightarrow [(\mathbf{T}_{98})]$$
$$(k_{82}, t_{101}) \rightarrow [(\mathbf{T}_{101})]$$
$$(k_{82}, t_{137}) \rightarrow [(\mathbf{T}_{137})]$$
$$\ldots$$

---

[13]Once again, not very important if the intermediate data is compressed.

All the tuples from S with the same join key will be encountered first, which the reducer can buffer in memory. As the reducer processes each tuple from T, it is crossed with all the tuples from S. Of course, we are assuming that the tuples from S (with the same join key) will fit into memory, which is a limitation of this algorithm (and why we want to control the sort order so that the smaller dataset comes first).

The basic idea behind the reduce-side join is to repartition the two datasets by the join key. The approach isn't particularly efficient since it requires shuffling both datasets across the network. This leads us to the *map-side* join.

3.5.2   MAP-SIDE JOIN

Suppose we have two datasets that are both sorted by the join key. We can perform a join by scanning through both datasets simultaneously—this is known as a merge join in the database community. We can parallelize this by partitioning and sorting *both* datasets in the same way. For example, suppose S and T were both divided into ten files, partitioned in the same manner by the join key. Further suppose that in each file, the tuples were sorted by the join key. In this case, we simply need to merge join the first file of S with the first file of T, the second file with S with the second file of T, etc. This can be accomplished in parallel, in the map phase of a MapReduce job—hence, a *map-side* join. In practice, we map over one of the datasets (the larger one) and inside the mapper read the corresponding part of the other dataset to perform the merge join.[14] No reducer is required, unless the programmer wishes to repartition the output or perform further processing.

A map-side join is far more efficient than a reduce-side join since there is no need to shuffle the datasets over the network. But is it realistic to expect that the stringent conditions required for map-side joins are satisfied? In many cases, *yes*. The reason is that relational joins happen within the broader context of a workflow, which may include multiple steps. Therefore, the datasets that are to be joined may be the output of previous processes (either MapReduce jobs or other code). If the workflow is known in advance and relatively static (both reasonable assumptions in a mature workflow), we can engineer the previous processes to generate output sorted and partitioned in a way that makes efficient map-side joins possible (in MapReduce, by using a custom partitioner and controlling the sort order of key-value pairs). For *ad hoc* data analysis, reduce-side joins are a more general, albeit less efficient, solution. Consider the case where datasets have multiple keys that one might wish to join on—then no matter how the data is organized, map-side joins will require repartitioning of the data. Alternatively, it is always possible to repartition a dataset using an identity mapper and reducer. But of course, this incurs the cost of shuffling data over the network.

There is a final restriction to bear in mind when using map-side joins with the Hadoop implementation of MapReduce. We assume here that the datasets to be joined were produced by previous MapReduce jobs, so this restriction applies to keys the reducers in those jobs may emit. Hadoop permits reducers to emit keys that are different from the input key whose values they are

---

[14]Note that this almost always implies a non-local read.

processing (that is, input and output keys need not be the same, nor even the same type).[15] However, if the output key of a reducer is different from the input key, then the output dataset from the reducer will not necessarily be partitioned in a manner consistent with the specified partitioner (because the partitioner applies to the *input* keys rather than the *output* keys). Since map-side joins depend on consistent partitioning and sorting of keys, the reducers used to generate data that will participate in a later map-side join *must not* emit any key but the one they are currently processing.

3.5.3   MEMORY-BACKED JOIN

In addition to the two previous approaches to joining relational data that leverage the MapReduce framework to bring together tuples that share a common join key, there is a family of approaches we call *memory-backed* joins based on random access probes. The simplest version is applicable when one of the two datasets completely fits in memory on each node. In this situation, we can load the smaller dataset into memory in every mapper, populating an associative array to facilitate random access to tuples based on the join key. The mapper initialization API hook (see Section 3.1.1) can be used for this purpose. Mappers are then applied to the other (larger) dataset, and for each input key-value pair, the mapper probes the in-memory dataset to see if there is a tuple with the same join key. If there is, the join is performed. This is known as a simple hash join by the database community [51].

What if neither dataset fits in memory? The simplest solution is to divide the smaller dataset, let's say S, into n partitions, such that $S = S_1 \cup S_2 \cup \ldots \cup S_n$. We can choose n so that each partition is small enough to fit in memory, and then run n memory-backed hash joins. This, of course, requires streaming through the other dataset n times.

There is an alternative approach to memory-backed joins for cases where neither datasets fit into memory. A distributed key-value store can be used to hold one dataset in memory across multiple machines while mapping over the other. The mappers would then query this distributed key-value store in parallel and perform joins if the join keys match.[16] The open-source caching system memcached can be used for exactly this purpose, and therefore we've dubbed this approach *memcached* join. For more information, this approach is detailed in a technical report [95].

3.6   SUMMARY

This chapter provides a guide on the design of MapReduce algorithms. In particular, we present a number of "design patterns" that capture effective solutions to common problems. In summary, they are:

- "In-mapper combining", where the functionality of the combiner is moved into the mapper. Instead of emitting intermediate output for every input key-value pair, the mapper aggregates

---

[15]In contrast, recall from Section 2.2 that in Google's implementation, reducers' output keys must be exactly same as their input keys.

[16]In order to achieve good performance in accessing distributed key-value stores, it is often necessary to batch queries before making synchronous requests (to amortize latency over many requests) or to rely on asynchronous requests.

partial results across multiple input records and only emits intermediate key-value pairs after some amount of local aggregation is performed.

- The related patterns "pairs" and "stripes" for keeping track of joint events from a large number of observations. In the pairs approach, we keep track of each joint event separately, whereas in the stripes approach we keep track of all events that co-occur with the same event. Although the stripes approach is significantly more efficient, it requires memory on the order of the size of the event space, which presents a scalability bottleneck.

- "Order inversion", where the main idea is to convert the sequencing of computations into a sorting problem. Through careful orchestration, we can send the reducer the result of a computation (e.g., an aggregate statistic) before it encounters the data necessary to produce that computation.

- "Value-to-key conversion", which provides a scalable solution for secondary sorting. By moving part of the value into the key, we can exploit the MapReduce execution framework itself for sorting.

Ultimately, controlling synchronization in the MapReduce programming model boils down to effective use of the following techniques:

1. Constructing complex keys and values that bring together data necessary for a computation. This is used in all of the above design patterns.

2. Executing user-specified initialization and termination code in either the mapper or reducer. For example, in-mapper combining depends on emission of intermediate key-value pairs in the map task termination code.

3. Preserving state across multiple inputs in the mapper and reducer. This is used in in-mapper combining, order inversion, and value-to-key conversion.

4. Controlling the sort order of intermediate keys. This is used in order inversion and value-to-key conversion.

5. Controlling the partitioning of the intermediate key space. This is used in order inversion and value-to-key conversion.

This concludes our overview of MapReduce algorithm design. It should be clear by now that although the programming model forces one to express algorithms in terms of a small set of rigidly defined components, there are many tools at one's disposal to shape the flow of computation. In the next few chapters, we will focus on specific classes of MapReduce algorithms: for inverted indexing in Chapter 4, for graph processing in Chapter 5, and for expectation-maximization in Chapter 6.

CHAPTER 4

Inverted Indexing for Text Retrieval

Web search is the quintessential large-data problem. Given an information need expressed as a short query consisting of a few terms, the system's task is to retrieve relevant web objects (web pages, PDF documents, PowerPoint slides, etc.) and present them to the user. How large is the web? It is difficult to compute exactly, but even a conservative estimate would place the size at several tens of billions of pages, totaling hundreds of terabytes (considering text alone). In real-world applications, users demand results quickly from a search engine—query latencies longer than a few hundred milliseconds will try a user's patience. Fulfilling these requirements is quite an engineering feat, considering the amounts of data involved!

Nearly all retrieval engines for full-text search today rely on a data structure called an inverted index, which given a term provides access to the list of documents that contain the term. In information retrieval parlance, objects to be retrieved are generically called "documents" even though in actuality they may be web pages, PDFs, or even fragments of code. Given a user query, the retrieval engine uses the inverted index to score documents that contain the query terms with respect to some ranking model, taking into account features such as term matches, term proximity, attributes of the terms in the document (e.g., bold, appears in title, etc.), as well as the hyperlink structure of the documents (e.g., PageRank [117], which we'll discuss in Chapter 5, or related metrics such as HITS [84] and SALSA [88]).

The web search problem decomposes into three components: gathering web content (crawling), construction of the inverted index (indexing) and ranking documents given a query (retrieval). Crawling and indexing share similar characteristics and requirements, but these are very different from retrieval. Gathering web content and building inverted indexes are for the most part offline problems. Both need to be scalable and efficient, but they do not need to operate in real time. Indexing is usually a batch process that runs periodically: the frequency of refreshes and updates is usually dependent on the design of the crawler. Some sites (e.g., news organizations) update their content quite frequently and need to be visited often; other sites (e.g., government regulations) are relatively static. However, even for rapidly changing sites, it is usually tolerable to have a delay of a few minutes until content is searchable. Furthermore, since the amount of content that changes rapidly is relatively small, running smaller-scale index updates at greater frequencies is usually an adequate solution.[1] Retrieval, on the other hand, is an online problem that demands sub-second

---

[1] Leaving aside the problem of searching live data streams such a tweets, which requires different techniques and algorithms.

response time. Individual users expect low query latencies, but query throughput is equally important since a retrieval engine must usually serve many users concurrently. Furthermore, query loads are highly variable, depending on the time of day, and can exhibit "spikey" behavior due to special circumstances (e.g., a breaking news event triggers a large number of searches on the same topic). On the other hand, resource consumption for the indexing problem is more predictable.

A comprehensive treatment of web search is beyond the scope of this chapter, and even this entire book. Explicitly recognizing this, we mostly focus on the problem of inverted indexing, the task most amenable to solutions in MapReduce. This chapter begins by first providing an overview of web crawling (Section 4.1) and introducing the basic structure of an inverted index (Section 4.2). A baseline inverted indexing algorithm in MapReduce is presented in Section 4.3. We point out a scalability bottleneck in that algorithm, which leads to a revised version presented in Section 4.4. Index compression is discussed in Section 4.5, which fills in missing details on building compact index structures. Since MapReduce is primarily designed for batch-oriented processing, it does not provide an adequate solution for the retrieval problem, an issue we discuss in Section 4.6. The chapter concludes with a summary and pointers to additional readings.

4.1   WEB CRAWLING

Before building inverted indexes, we must first acquire the document collection over which these indexes are to be built. In academia and for research purposes, this can be relatively straightforward. Standard collections for information retrieval research are widely available for a variety of genres ranging from blogs to newswire text. For researchers who wish to explore web-scale retrieval, there is the ClueWeb09 collection that contains one billion web pages in ten languages (totaling 25 terabytes) crawled by Carnegie Mellon University in early 2009.[2] Obtaining access to these standard collections is usually as simple as signing an appropriate data license from the distributor of the collection, paying a reasonable fee, and arranging for receipt of the data.[3]

For real-world web search, however, one cannot simply assume that the collection is already available. Acquiring web content requires crawling, which is the process of traversing the web by repeatedly following hyperlinks and storing downloaded pages for subsequent processing. Conceptually, the process is quite simple to understand: we start by populating a queue with a "seed" list of pages. The crawler downloads pages in the queue, extracts links from those pages to add to the queue, stores the pages for further processing, and repeats. In fact, rudimentary web crawlers can be written in a few hundred lines of code.

However, effective and efficient web crawling is far more complex. The following lists a number of issues that real-world crawlers must contend with:

---

[2]http://boston.lti.cs.cmu.edu/Data/clueweb09/

[3]As an interesting side note, in the 1990s, research collections were distributed via postal mail on CD-ROMs, and later, on DVDs. Electronic distribution became common earlier this decade for collections below a certain size. However, many collections today are so large that the only practical method of distribution is shipping hard drives via postal mail.

- A web crawler must practice good "etiquette" and not overload web servers. For example, it is common practice to wait a fixed amount of time before repeated requests to the same server. In order to respect these constraints while maintaining good throughput, a crawler typically keeps many execution threads running in parallel and maintains many TCP connections (perhaps hundreds) open at the same time.

- Since a crawler has finite bandwidth and resources, it must prioritize the order in which unvisited pages are downloaded. Such decisions must be made online and in an adversarial environment, in the sense that spammers actively create "link farms" and "spider traps" full of spam pages to trick a crawler into overrepresenting content from a particular site.

- Most real-world web crawlers are distributed systems that run on clusters of machines, often geographically distributed. To avoid downloading a page multiple times and to ensure data consistency, the crawler as a whole needs mechanisms for coordination and load-balancing. It also needs to be robust with respect to machine failures, network outages, and errors of various types.

- Web content changes, but with different frequency depending on both the site and the nature of the content. A web crawler needs to learn these update patterns to ensure that content is reasonably current. Getting the right recrawl frequency is tricky: too frequent means wasted resources, but not frequent enough leads to stale content.

- The web is full of duplicate content. Examples include multiple copies of a popular conference paper, mirrors of frequently accessed sites such as Wikipedia, and newswire content that is often duplicated. The problem is compounded by the fact that most repetitious pages are not exact duplicates but near duplicates (that is, basically the same page but with different ads, navigation bars, etc.) It is desirable during the crawling process to identify near duplicates and select the best exemplar to index.

- The web is multilingual. There is no guarantee that pages in one language only link to pages in the same language. For example, a professor in Asia may maintain her website in the local language, but link to her publications in English. Furthermore, many pages contain a mix of text in different languages. Since document processing techniques (e.g., tokenization, stemming) differ by language, it is important to identify the (dominant) language on a page.

The above discussion is not meant to be an exhaustive enumeration of issues, but rather to give the reader an appreciation of the complexities involved in this intuitively simple task. For more information, see a recent survey on web crawling [113]. Section 4.7 provides suggestions for additional readings.

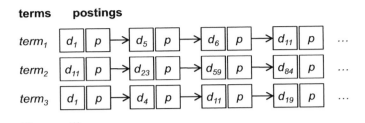

Figure 4.1: Simple illustration of an inverted index. Each term is associated with a list of postings. Each posting is comprised of a document id and a payload, denoted by p in this case. An inverted index provides quick access to documents ids that contain a term.

4.2   INVERTED INDEXES

In its basic form, an inverted index consists of postings lists, one associated with each term that appears in the collection.[4] The structure of an inverted index is illustrated in Figure 4.1. A postings list is comprised of individual postings, each of which consists of a document id and a *payload*—information about occurrences of the term in the document. The simplest payload is...nothing! For simple boolean retrieval, no additional information is needed in the posting other than the document id; the existence of the posting itself indicates the presence of the term in the document. The most common payload, however, is term frequency (*tf*), or the number of times the term occurs in the document. More complex payloads include positions of every occurrence of the term in the document (to support phrase queries and document scoring based on term proximity), properties of the term (such as if it occurred in the page title or not, to support document ranking based on notions of importance), or even the results of additional linguistic processing (for example, indicating that the term is part of a place name, to support address searches). In the web context, anchor text information (text associated with hyperlinks from other pages to the page in question) is useful in enriching the representation of document content (e.g., [107]); this information is often stored in the index as well.

In the example shown in Figure 4.1, we see that $term_1$ occurs in $\{d_1, d_5, d_6, d_{11}, \ldots\}$, $term_2$ occurs in $\{d_{11}, d_{23}, d_{59}, d_{84}, \ldots\}$, and $term_3$ occurs in $\{d_1, d_4, d_{11}, d_{19}, \ldots\}$. In an actual implementation, we assume that documents can be identified by a unique integer ranging from 1 to n, where n is the total number of documents.[5] Generally, postings are sorted by document id, although other sort orders are possible as well. The document ids have no inherent semantic meaning, although assignment of numeric ids to documents need not be arbitrary. For example, pages from the same

---

[4]In information retrieval parlance, *term* is preferred over *word* since documents are processed (e.g., tokenization and stemming) into basic units that are often not words in the linguistic sense.

[5]It is preferable to start numbering the documents at one since it is not possible to code zero with many common compression schemes used in information retrieval; see Section 4.5.

domain may be consecutively numbered. Or, alternatively, pages that are higher in quality (based, for example, on PageRank values) might be assigned smaller numeric values so that they appear toward the front of a postings list. Either way, an auxiliary data structure is necessary to maintain the mapping from integer document ids to some other more meaningful handle, such as a URL.

Given a query, retrieval involves fetching postings lists associated with query terms and traversing the postings to compute the result set. In the simplest case, boolean retrieval involves set operations (union for boolean OR and intersection for boolean AND) on postings lists, which can be accomplished very efficiently since the postings are sorted by document id. In the general case, however, query–document scores must be computed. Partial document scores are stored in structures called *accumulators*. At the end (i.e., once all postings have been processed), the top k documents are then extracted to yield a ranked list of results for the user. Of course, there are many optimization strategies for query evaluation (both approximate and exact) that reduce the number of postings a retrieval engine must examine.

The size of an inverted index varies, depending on the payload stored in each posting. If only term frequency is stored, a well-optimized inverted index can be a tenth of the size of the original document collection. An inverted index that stores positional information would easily be several times larger than one that does not. Generally, it is possible to hold the entire vocabulary (i.e., dictionary of all the terms) in memory, especially with techniques such as front-coding [156]. However, with the exception of well-resourced, commercial web search engines,[6] postings lists are usually too large to store in memory and must be held on disk, usually in compressed form (more details in Section 4.5). Query evaluation, therefore, necessarily involves random disk access and "decoding" of the postings. One important aspect of the retrieval problem is to organize disk operations such that random seeks are minimized.

Once again, this brief discussion glosses over many complexities and does a huge injustice to the tremendous amount of research in information retrieval. However, our goal is to provide the reader with an overview of the important issues; Section 4.7 provides references to additional readings.

4.3 INVERTED INDEXING: BASELINE IMPLEMENTATION

MapReduce was designed from the very beginning to produce the various data structures involved in web search, including inverted indexes and the web graph. We begin with the basic inverted indexing algorithm shown in Figure 4.2.

Input to the mapper consists of document ids (keys) paired with the actual content (values). Individual documents are processed in parallel by the mappers. First, each document is analyzed and broken down into its component terms. The processing pipeline differs depending on the application and type of document, but for web pages typically involves stripping out HTML tags and other elements such as JavaScript code, tokenizing, case folding, removing stopwords (common words such as 'the', 'a', 'of', etc.), and stemming (removing affixes from words so that 'dogs' becomes 'dog').

---

[6]Google keeps indexes in memory.

```
1: class MAPPER
2:     procedure MAP(docid n, doc d)
3:         H ← new ASSOCIATIVEARRAY
4:         for all term t ∈ doc d do
5:             H{t} ← H{t} + 1
6:         for all term t ∈ H do
7:             EMIT(term t, posting ⟨n, H{t}⟩)
```

```
1: class REDUCER
2:     procedure REDUCE(term t, postings [⟨n₁, f₁⟩, ⟨n₂, f₂⟩ ...])
3:         P ← new LIST
4:         for all posting ⟨a, f⟩ ∈ postings [⟨n₁, f₁⟩, ⟨n₂, f₂⟩ ...] do
5:             P.ADD(⟨a, f⟩)
6:         P.SORT()
7:         EMIT(term t, postings P)
```

Figure 4.2: Pseudo-code of the baseline inverted indexing algorithm in MapReduce. Mappers emit postings keyed by terms, the execution framework groups postings by term, and the reducers write postings lists to disk.

Once the document has been analyzed, term frequencies are computed by iterating over all the terms and keeping track of counts. Lines 4 and 5 in the pseudo-code reflect the process of computing term frequencies, but hides the details of document processing. After this histogram has been built, the mapper then iterates over all terms. For each term, a pair consisting of the document id and the term frequency is created. Each pair, denoted by $\langle n, H\{t\}\rangle$ in the pseudo-code, represents an individual posting. The mapper then emits an intermediate key-value pair with the term as the key and the posting as the value, in line 7 of the mapper pseudo-code. Although as presented here only the term frequency is stored in the posting, this algorithm can be easily augmented to store additional information (e.g., term positions) in the payload.

In the shuffle and sort phase, the MapReduce runtime essentially performs a large, distributed group by of the postings by term. Without any additional effort by the programmer, the execution framework brings together all the postings that belong in the same postings list. This tremendously simplifies the task of the reducer, which simply needs to gather together all the postings and write them to disk. The reducer begins by initializing an empty list and then appends all postings associated with the same key (term) to the list. The postings are then sorted by document id, and the entire postings list is emitted as a value, with the term as the key. Typically, the postings list is first compressed, but we leave this aside for now (see Section 4.4 for more details). The final key-value pairs are written to disk and comprise the inverted index. Since each reducer writes its output in a separate file in the distributed file system, our final index will be split across r files, where r is

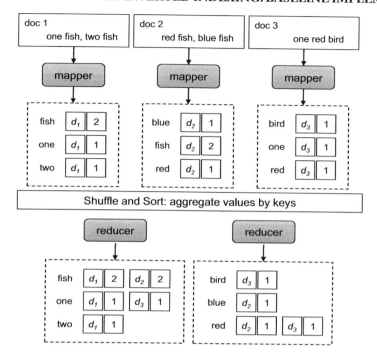

Figure 4.3: Simple illustration of the baseline inverted indexing algorithm in MapReduce with three mappers and two reducers. Postings are shown as pairs of boxes (*docid, tf*).

the number of reducers. There is no need to further consolidate these files. Separately, we must also build an index to the postings lists themselves for the retrieval engine: this is typically in the form of mappings from term to (file, byte offset) pairs, so that given a term, the retrieval engine can fetch its postings list by opening the appropriate file and seeking to the correct byte offset position in that file.

Execution of the complete algorithm is illustrated in Figure 4.3 with a toy example consisting of three documents, three mappers, and two reducers. Intermediate key-value pairs (from the mappers) and the final key-value pairs comprising the inverted index (from the reducers) are shown in the boxes with dotted lines. Postings are shown as pairs of boxes, with the document id on the left and the term frequency on the right.

The MapReduce programming model provides a very concise expression of the inverted indexing algorithm. Its implementation is similarly concise: the basic algorithm can be implemented in as few as a couple dozen lines of code in Hadoop (with minimal document processing). Such an implementation can be completed as a week-long programming assignment in a course for advanced undergraduates or first-year graduate students [83; 93]. In a non-MapReduce indexer, a significant fraction of the code is devoted to grouping postings by term, given constraints imposed by memory and disk (e.g., memory capacity is limited, disk seeks are slow, etc.). In MapReduce, the programmer does not need to worry about any of these issues—most of the heavy lifting is performed by the execution framework.

4.4   INVERTED INDEXING: REVISED IMPLEMENTATION

The inverted indexing algorithm presented in the previous section serves as a reasonable baseline. However, there is a significant scalability bottleneck: the algorithm assumes that there is sufficient memory to hold all postings associated with the same term. Since the basic MapReduce execution framework makes no guarantees about the ordering of values associated with the same key, the reducer first buffers all postings (line 5 of the reducer pseudo-code in Figure 4.2) and then performs an in-memory sort before writing the postings to disk.[7] For efficient retrieval, postings need to be sorted by document id. However, as collections become larger, postings lists grow longer, and at some point in time, reducers will run out of memory.

There is a simple solution to this problem. Since the execution framework guarantees that keys arrive at each reducer in sorted order, one way to overcome the scalability bottleneck is to let the MapReduce runtime do the sorting for us. Instead of emitting key-value pairs of the following type:

(term t, posting $\langle docid, f \rangle$)

We emit intermediate key-value pairs of this type instead:

(tuple $\langle t, docid \rangle$, tf f)

In other words, the key is a tuple containing the term and the document id, while the value is the term frequency. This is exactly the value-to-key conversion design pattern introduced in Section 3.4. With this modification, the programming model ensures that the postings arrive in the correct order. This, combined with the fact that reducers can hold state across multiple keys, allows postings lists to be created with minimal memory usage. As a detail, remember that we must define a custom partitioner to ensure that all tuples with the same term are shuffled to the same reducer.

The revised MapReduce inverted indexing algorithm is shown in Figure 4.4. The mapper remains unchanged for the most part, other than differences in the intermediate key-value pairs. The REDUCE method is called for each key (i.e., $\langle t, n \rangle$), and by design, there will only be one value associated with each key. For each key-value pair, a posting can be directly added to the postings list. Since the postings are guaranteed to arrive in sorted order by document id, they can be incrementally coded in compressed form—thus ensuring a small memory footprint. Finally, when all postings associated with the same term have been processed (i.e., $t \neq t_{prev}$), the entire postings list is emitted. The final postings list must be written out in the CLOSE method. As with the baseline

---

[7]See similar discussion in Section 3.4: in principle, this need not be an in-memory sort. It is entirely possible to implement a disk-based sort within the reducer.

```
1:  class MAPPER
2:      method MAP(docid n, doc d)
3:          H ← new ASSOCIATIVEARRAY
4:          for all term t ∈ doc d do
5:              H{t} ← H{t} + 1
6:          for all term t ∈ H do
7:              EMIT(tuple ⟨t, n⟩, tf H{t})

1:  class REDUCER
2:      method INITIALIZE
3:          t_prev ← ∅
4:          P ← new POSTINGSLIST
5:      method REDUCE(tuple ⟨t, n⟩, tf [f])
6:          if t ≠ t_prev ∧ t_prev ≠ ∅ then
7:              EMIT(term t, postings P)
8:              P.RESET()
9:          P.ADD(⟨n, f⟩)
10:         t_prev ← t
11:     method CLOSE
12:         EMIT(term t, postings P)
```

Figure 4.4: Pseudo-code of a scalable inverted indexing algorithm in MapReduce. By applying the value-to-key conversion design pattern, the execution framework is exploited to sort postings so that they arrive sorted by document id in the reducer.

algorithm, payloads can be easily changed: by simply replacing the intermediate value f (term frequency) with whatever else is desired (e.g., term positional information).

There is one more detail we must address when building inverted indexes. Since almost all retrieval models take into account document length when computing query–document scores, this information must also be extracted. Although it is straightforward to express this computation as another MapReduce job, this task can actually be folded into the inverted indexing process. When processing the terms in each document, the document length is known, and can be written out as "side data" directly to HDFS. We can take advantage of the ability for a mapper to hold state across the processing of multiple documents in the following manner: an in-memory associative array is created to store document lengths, which is populated as each document is processed.[8] When the mapper finishes processing input records, document lengths are written out to HDFS (i.e., in the CLOSE method). This approach is essentially a variant of the in-mapper combining pattern. Document length data end up in m different files, where m is the number of mappers; these files are

---

[8]In general, there is no worry about insufficient memory to hold these data.

then consolidated into a more compact representation. Alternatively, document length information can be emitted in special key-value pairs by the mapper. One must then write a custom partitioner so that these special key-value pairs are shuffled to a single reducer, which will be responsible for writing out the length data separate from the postings lists.

4.5 INDEX COMPRESSION

We return to the question of how postings are actually compressed and stored on disk. This chapter devotes a substantial amount of space to this topic because index compression is one of the main differences between a "toy" indexer and one that works on real-world collections. Otherwise, MapReduce inverted indexing algorithms are pretty straightforward.

Let us consider the canonical case where each posting consists of a document id and the term frequency. A naïve implementation might represent the first as a 32-bit integer[9] and the second as a 16-bit integer. Thus, a postings list might be encoded as follows:

$$[(5, 2), (7, 3), (12, 1), (49, 1), (51, 2), \ldots]$$

where each posting is represented by a pair in parentheses. Note that all brackets, parentheses, and commas are only included to enhance readability; in reality, the postings would be represented as a long stream of integers. This naïve implementation would require six bytes per posting. Using this scheme, the entire inverted index would be about as large as the collection itself. Fortunately, we can do significantly better.

The first trick is to encode *differences* between document ids as opposed to the document ids themselves. Since the postings are sorted by document ids, the differences (called *d*-gaps) must be positive integers greater than zero. The above postings list, represented with *d*-gaps, would be:

$$[(5, 2), (2, 3), (5, 1), (37, 1), (2, 2), \ldots]$$

Of course, we must actually encode the first document id. We haven't lost any information, since the original document ids can be easily reconstructed from the *d*-gaps. However, it's not obvious that we've reduced the space requirements either, since the largest possible *d*-gap is one less than the number of documents in the collection.

This is where the second trick comes in, which is to represent the *d*-gaps in a way such that it takes less space for smaller numbers. Similarly, we want to apply the same techniques to compress the term frequencies, since for the most part they are also small values. But to understand how this is done, we need to take a slight detour into compression techniques, particularly for coding integers.

Compression, in general, can be characterized as either *lossless* or *lossy*: it's fairly obvious that loseless compression is required in this context. To start, it is important to understand that all compression techniques represent a time–space tradeoff. That is, we reduce the amount of space on disk necessary to store data, but at the cost of extra processor cycles that must be spent coding

---

[9]However, note that $2^{32} - 1$ is "only" 4,294,967,295, which is much less than even the most conservative estimate of the size of the web.

and decoding data. Therefore, it is possible that compression reduces size but also slows processing. However, if the two factors are properly balanced (i.e., decoding speed can keep up with disk bandwidth), we can achieve the best of both worlds: smaller *and* faster.

4.5.1 BYTE-ALIGNED AND WORD-ALIGNED CODES

In most programming languages, an integer is encoded in four bytes and holds a value between 0 and $2^{32} - 1$, inclusive. We limit our discussion to *unsigned* integers, since *d*-gaps are always positive (and greater than zero). This means that 1 and 4,294,967,295 both occupy four bytes. Obviously, encoding *d*-gaps this way doesn't yield any reductions in size.

A simple approach to compression is to only use as many bytes as is necessary to represent the integer. This is known as variable-length integer coding (varInt for short) and accomplished by using the high order bit of every byte as the *continuation bit*, which is set to one in the last byte and zero elsewhere. As a result, we have 7 bits per byte for coding the value, which means that $0 \leq n < 2^7$ can be expressed with 1 byte, $2^7 \leq n < 2^{14}$ with 2 bytes, $2^{14} \leq n < 2^{21}$ with 3, and $2^{21} \leq n < 2^{28}$ with 4 bytes. This scheme can be extended to code arbitrarily large integers (i.e., beyond 4 bytes). As a concrete example, the two numbers:

127, 128

would be coded as such:

1 1111111, 0 0000001 1 0000000

The above code contains two code words, the first consisting of 1 byte, and the second consisting of 2 bytes. Of course, the comma and the spaces are there only for readability. Variable-length integers are byte-aligned because the code words always fall along byte boundaries. As a result, there is never any ambiguity about where one code word ends and the next begins. However, the downside of varInt coding is that decoding involves lots of bit operations (masks, shifts). Furthermore, the continuation bit sometimes results in frequent branch mispredicts (depending on the actual distribution of *d*-gaps), which slows down processing.

A variant of the varInt scheme was described by Jeff Dean in a keynote talk at the WSDM 2009 conference.[10] The insight is to code groups of four integers at a time. Each group begins with a prefix byte, divided into four 2-bit values that specify the byte length of each of the following integers. For example, the following prefix byte:

00,00,01,10

indicates that the following four integers are one byte, one byte, two bytes, and three bytes, respectively. Therefore, each group of four integers would consume anywhere between 5 and 17 bytes. A simple lookup table based on the prefix byte directs the decoder on how to process subsequent bytes to recover the coded integers. The advantage of this group varInt coding scheme is that values can

[10]http://research.google.com/people/jeff/WSDM09-keynote.pdf

be decoded with fewer branch mispredicts and bitwise operations. Experiments reported by Dean suggest that decoding integers with this scheme is more than twice as fast as the basic varInt scheme.

In most architectures, accessing entire machine words is more efficient than fetching all its bytes separately. Therefore, it makes sense to store postings in increments of 16-bit, 32-bit, or 64-bit machine words. Anh and Moffat [8] presented several word-aligned coding methods, one of which is called Simple-9, based on 32-bit words. In this coding scheme, four bits in each 32-bit word are reserved as a *selector*. The remaining 28 bits are used to code actual integer values. Now, there are a variety of ways these 28 bits can be divided to code one or more integers: 28 bits can be used to code one 28-bit integer, two 14-bit integers, three 9-bit integers (with one bit unused), etc., all the way up to twenty-eight 1-bit integers. In fact, there are nine different ways the 28 bits can be divided into equal parts (hence the name of the technique), some with leftover unused bits. This is stored in the selector bits. Therefore, decoding involves reading a 32-bit word, examining the selector to see how the remaining 28 bits are packed, and then appropriately decoding each integer. Coding works in the opposite way: the algorithm scans ahead to see how many integers can be squeezed into 28 bits, packs those integers, and sets the selector bits appropriately.

4.5.2   BIT-ALIGNED CODES

The advantage of byte-aligned and word-aligned codes is that they can be coded and decoded quickly. The downside, however, is that they *must* consume multiples of eight bits, even when fewer bits might suffice (the Simple-9 scheme gets around this by packing multiple integers into a 32-bit word, but even then, bits are often wasted). In bit-aligned codes, on the other hand, code words can occupy any number of bits, meaning that boundaries can fall anywhere. In practice, coding and decoding bit-aligned codes require processing bytes and appropriately shifting or masking bits (usually more involved than varInt and group varInt coding).

One additional challenge with bit-aligned codes is that we need a mechanism to delimit code words, i.e., tell where the last ends and the next begins, since there are no byte boundaries to guide us. To address this issue, most bit-aligned codes are so-called prefix codes (confusingly, they are also called prefix-free codes), in which no valid code word is a prefix of any other valid code word. For example, coding $0 \leq x < 3$ with $\{0, 1, 01\}$ is not a valid prefix code, since 0 is a prefix of 01, and so we can't tell if 01 is two code words or one. On the other hand, $\{00, 01, 1\}$ is a valid prefix code, such that a sequence of bits:

0001101001010100

can be unambiguously segmented into:

00 01 1 01 00 1 01 01 00

and decoded without any additional delimiters.

One of the simplest prefix codes is the unary code. An integer $x > 0$ is coded as $x - 1$ one bits followed by a zero bit. Note that unary codes do not allow the representation of zero, which

x	unary	γ	Golomb $b = 5$	Golomb $b = 10$
1	0	0	0:00	0:000
2	10	10:0	0:01	0:001
3	110	10:1	0:10	0:010
4	1110	110:00	0:110	0:011
5	11110	110:01	0:111	0:100
6	111110	110:10	10:00	0:101
7	1111110	110:11	10:01	0:1100
8	11111110	1110:000	10:10	0:1101
9	111111110	1110:001	10:110	0:1110
10	1111111110	1110:010	10:111	0:1111

Figure 4.5: The first ten positive integers in unary, γ, and Golomb ($b = 5, 10$) codes.

is fine since d-gaps and term frequencies should never be zero.[11] As an example, 4 in unary code is 1110. With unary code we can code x in x bits, which although economical for small values, becomes inefficient for even moderately large values. Unary codes are rarely used by themselves, but form a component of other coding schemes. Unary codes of the first ten positive integers are shown in Figure 4.5.

Elias γ code is an efficient coding scheme that is widely used in practice. An integer $x > 0$ is broken into two components, $1 + \lfloor \log_2 x \rfloor$ ($= n$, the length), which is coded in unary code, and $x - 2^{\lfloor \log_2 x \rfloor}$ ($= r$, the remainder), which is in binary.[12] The unary component n specifies the number of bits required to code x, and the binary component codes the remainder r in $n - 1$ bits. As an example, consider $x = 10$: $1 + \lfloor \log_2 10 \rfloor = 4$, which is 1110. The binary component codes $x - 2^3 = 2$ in $4 - 1 = 3$ bits, which is 010. Putting both together, we arrive at 1110:010. The extra colon is inserted only for readability; it's not part of the final code, of course.

Working in reverse, it is easy to unambiguously decode a bit stream of γ codes: First, we read a unary code c_u, which is a prefix code. This tells us that the binary portion is written in $c_u - 1$ bits, which we then read as c_b. We can then reconstruct x as $2^{c_u - 1} + c_b$. For $x < 16$, γ codes occupy less than a full byte, which makes them more compact than variable-length integer codes. Since term frequencies for the most part are relatively small, γ codes make sense for them and can yield substantial space savings. For reference, the γ codes of the first ten positive integers are shown in Figure 4.5. A variation on γ code is δ code, where the n portion of the γ code is coded in γ code itself (as opposed to unary code). For smaller values γ codes are more compact, but for larger values, δ codes take less space.

---

[11] As a note, some sources describe slightly different formulations of the same coding scheme. Here, we adopt the conventions used in the classic IR text *Managing Gigabytes* [156].

[12] Note that $\lfloor x \rfloor$ is the floor function, which maps x to the largest integer not greater than x, so, e.g., $\lfloor 3.8 \rfloor = 3$. This is the default behavior in many programming languages when casting from a floating-point type to an integer type.

Unary and γ codes are parameterless, but even better compression can be achieved with parameterized codes. A good example of this is Golomb code. For some parameter b, an integer $x > 0$ is coded in two parts: first, we compute $q = \lfloor (x - 1)/b \rfloor$ and code $q + 1$ in unary; then, we code the remainder $r = x - qb - 1$ in truncated binary. This is accomplished as follows: if b is a power of two, then truncated binary is exactly the same as normal binary, requiring $\log_2 b$ bits. Otherwise, we code the first $2^{\lfloor \log_2 b \rfloor + 1} - b$ values of r in $\lfloor \log_2 b \rfloor$ bits and code the rest of the values of r by coding $r + 2^{\lfloor \log_2 b \rfloor + 1} - b$ in ordinary binary representation using $\lfloor \log_2 b \rfloor + 1$ bits. In this case, the r is coded in either $\lfloor \log_2 b \rfloor$ or $\lfloor \log_2 b \rfloor + 1$ bits, and unlike ordinary binary coding, truncated binary codes are prefix codes. As an example, if $b = 5$, then r can take the values $\{0, 1, 2, 3, 4\}$, which would be coded with the following code words: $\{00, 01, 10, 110, 111\}$. For reference, Golomb codes of the first ten positive integers are shown in Figure 4.5 for $b = 5$ and $b = 10$. A special case of Golomb code is worth noting: if b is a power of two, then coding and decoding can be handled more efficiently (needing only bit shifts and bit masks, as opposed to multiplication and division). These are known as Rice codes.

Researchers have shown that Golomb compression works well for d-gaps, and is optimal with the following parameter setting:

$$b \approx 0.69 \times \frac{N}{df} \tag{4.1}$$

where df is the document frequency of the term, and N is the number of documents in the collection.[13]

Putting everything together, one popular approach for postings compression is to represent d-gaps with Golomb codes and term frequencies with γ codes [156; 162]. If positional information is desired, we can use the same trick to code differences between term positions using γ codes.

4.5.3   POSTINGS COMPRESSION

Having completed our slight detour into integer compression techniques, we can now return to the scalable inverted indexing algorithm shown in Figure 4.4 and discuss how postings lists can be properly compressed. As we can see from the previous section, there is a wide range of choices that represent different trade offs between compression ratio and decoding speed. Actual performance also depends on characteristics of the collection, which, among other factors, determine the distribution of d-gaps. Büttcher et al. [30] recently compared the performance of various compression techniques on coding document ids. In terms of the amount of compression that can be obtained (measured in bits per *docid*), Golomb and Rice codes performed the best, followed by γ codes, Simple-9, varInt, and group varInt (the least space efficient). In terms of raw decoding speed, the order was almost

---

[13]For details as to why this is the case, we refer the reader elsewhere [156], but here's the intuition: under reasonable assumptions, the appearance of postings can be modeled as a sequence of independent Bernoulli trials, which implies a certain distribution of d-gaps. From this we can derive an optimal setting of b.

the reverse: group varInt was the fastest, followed by varInt.[14] Simple-9 was substantially slower, and the bit-aligned codes were even slower than that. Within the bit-aligned codes, Rice codes were the fastest, followed by γ, with Golomb codes being the slowest (about ten times slower than group varInt).

Let us discuss what modifications are necessary to our inverted indexing algorithm if we were to adopt Golomb compression for d-gaps and represent term frequencies with γ codes. Note that this represents a space-efficient encoding, at the cost of slower decoding compared to alternatives. Whether or not this is actually a worthwhile tradeoff in practice is not important here: use of Golomb codes serves a pedagogical purpose, to illustrate how one might set compression parameters.

Coding term frequencies with γ codes is easy since they are parameterless. Compressing d-gaps with Golomb codes, however, is a bit tricky, since two parameters are required: the size of the document collection and the number of postings for a particular postings list (i.e., the document frequency, or df). The first is easy to obtain and can be passed into the reducer as a constant. The df of a term, however, is not known until all the postings have been processed—and unfortunately, the parameter must be known before any posting is coded. At first glance, this seems like a chicken-and-egg problem. A two-pass solution that involves first buffering the postings (in memory) would suffer from the memory bottleneck we've been trying to avoid in the first place.

To get around this problem, we need to somehow inform the reducer of a term's df before any of its postings arrive. This can be solved with the order inversion design pattern introduced in Section 3.3 to compute relative frequencies. The solution is to have the mapper emit special keys of the form $\langle t, * \rangle$ to communicate partial document frequencies. That is, inside the mapper, in addition to emitting intermediate key-value pairs of the following form:

(tuple $\langle t, docid \rangle$, tf f)

we also emit special intermediate key-value pairs like this:

(tuple $\langle t, * \rangle$, df e)

to keep track of document frequencies associated with each term. In practice, we can accomplish this by applying the in-mapper combining design pattern (see Section 3.1). The mapper holds an in-memory associative array that keeps track of how many documents a term has been observed in (i.e., the local document frequency of the term for the subset of documents processed by the mapper). Once the mapper has processed all input records, special keys of the form $\langle t, * \rangle$ are emitted with the partial df as the value.

To ensure that these special keys arrive first, we define the sort order of the tuple so that the special symbol $*$ precedes all documents (part of the order inversion design pattern). Thus, for each term, the reducer will first encounter the $\langle t, * \rangle$ key, associated with a list of values representing partial df values originating from each mapper. Summing all these partial contributions will yield the term's

---

[14]However, this study found less speed difference between group varInt and basic varInt than Dean's analysis, presumably due to the different distribution of d-gaps in the collections they were examining.

df, which can then be used to set the Golomb compression parameter *b*. This allows the postings to be incrementally compressed as they are encountered in the reducer—memory bottlenecks are eliminated since we do not need to buffer postings in memory.

Once again, the order inversion design pattern comes to the rescue. Recall that the pattern is useful when a reducer needs to access the result of a computation (e.g., an aggregate statistic) before it encounters the data necessary to produce that computation. For computing relative frequencies, that bit of information was the marginal. In this case, it's the document frequency.

4.6   WHAT ABOUT RETRIEVAL?

Thus far, we have briefly discussed web crawling and focused mostly on MapReduce algorithms for inverted indexing. What about retrieval? It should be fairly obvious that MapReduce, which was designed for large batch operations, is a poor solution for retrieval. Since users demand sub-second response times, every aspect of retrieval must be optimized for low latency, which is exactly the opposite tradeoff made in MapReduce. Recall the basic retrieval problem: we must look up postings lists corresponding to query terms, systematically traverse those postings lists to compute query–document scores, and then return the top *k* results to the user. Looking up postings implies random disk seeks, since for the most part postings are too large to fit into memory (leaving aside caching and other special cases for now). Unfortunately, random access is not a forte of the distributed file system underlying MapReduce—such operations require multiple round-trip network exchanges (and associated latencies). In HDFS, a client must first obtain the location of the desired data block from the namenode before the appropriate datanode can be contacted for the actual data. Of course, access will typically require a random disk seek on the datanode itself.

It should be fairly obvious that serving the search needs of a large number of users, each of whom demand sub-second response times, is beyond the capabilities of any single machine. The only solution is to distribute retrieval across a large number of machines, which necessitates breaking up the index in some manner. There are two main partitioning strategies for distributed retrieval: *document partitioning* and *term partitioning*. Under document partitioning, the entire collection is broken up into multiple smaller sub-collections, each of which is assigned to a server. In other words, each server holds the complete index for a subset of the entire collection. This corresponds to partitioning vertically in Figure 4.6. With term partitioning, on the other hand, each server is responsible for a subset of the terms for the entire collection. That is, a server holds the postings for all documents in the collection for a subset of terms. This corresponds to partitioning horizontally in Figure 4.6.

Document and term partitioning require different retrieval strategies and represent different trade offs. Retrieval under document partitioning involves a query broker, which forwards the user's query to all partition servers, merges partial results from each, and then returns the final results to the user. With this architecture, searching the entire collection requires that the query be processed by every partition server. However, since each partition operates independently and traverses postings

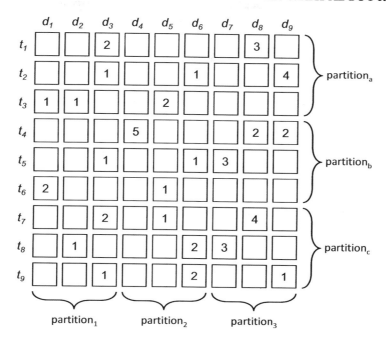

Figure 4.6: Term–document matrix for a toy collection (nine documents, nine terms) illustrating different partitioning strategies: partitioning vertically $(1, 2, 3)$ corresponds to document partitioning, whereas partitioning horizontally (a, b, c) corresponds to term partitioning.

in parallel, document partitioning typically yields shorter query latencies (compared to a single monolithic index with much longer postings lists).

Retrieval under term partitioning, on the other hand, requires a very different strategy. Suppose the user's query Q contains three terms, q_1, q_2, and q_3. Under the pipelined query evaluation strategy, the broker begins by forwarding the query to the server that holds the postings for q_1 (usually the least frequent term). The server traverses the appropriate postings list and computes partial query–document scores, stored in the accumulators. The accumulators are then passed to the server that holds the postings associated with q_2 for additional processing, and then to the server for q_3, before final results are passed back to the broker and returned to the user. Although this query evaluation strategy may not substantially reduce the latency of any particular query, it can theoretically increase a system's throughput due to the far smaller number of total disk seeks required for each user query (compared to document partitioning). However, load-balancing is tricky in a pipelined term-partitioned architecture due to skew in the distribution of query terms, which can create "hot spots" on servers that hold the postings for frequently occurring query terms.

In general, studies have shown that document partitioning is a better strategy overall [109], and this is the strategy adopted by Google [16]. Furthermore, it is known that Google maintains its indexes in memory (although this is certainly not the common case for search engines in general). One key advantage of document partitioning is that result quality degrades gracefully with machine failures. Partition servers that are offline will simply fail to deliver results for their subsets of the collection. With sufficient partitions, users might not even be aware that documents are missing. For most queries, the web contains more relevant documents than any user has time to digest: users of course care about getting relevant documents (sometimes, they are happy with a single relevant document), but they are generally less discriminating when it comes to *which* relevant documents appear in their results (out of the set of *all* relevant documents). Note that partitions may be unavailable due to reasons other than machine failure: cycling through different partitions is a very simple and non-disruptive strategy for index updates.

Working in a document-partitioned architecture, there are a variety of approaches to dividing up the web into smaller pieces. Proper partitioning of the collection can address one major weakness of this architecture, which is that every partition server is involved in every user query. Along one dimension, it is desirable to partition by document quality using one or more classifiers; see [124] for a recent survey on web page classification. Partitioning by document quality supports a multi-phase search strategy: the system examines partitions containing high quality documents first, and only backs off to partitions containing lower quality documents if necessary. This reduces the number of servers that need to be contacted for a user query. Along an orthogonal dimension, it is desirable to partition documents by content (perhaps also guided by the distribution of user queries from logs), so that each partition is "well separated" from the others in terms of topical coverage. This also reduces the number of machines that need to be involved in serving a user's query: the broker can direct queries only to the partitions that are likely to contain relevant documents, as opposed to forwarding the user query to all the partitions.

On a large scale, reliability of service is provided by replication, both in terms of multiple machines serving the same partition within a single datacenter, but also replication across geographically distributed datacenters. This creates at least two query routing problems: since it makes sense to serve clients from the closest datacenter, a service must route queries to the appropriate location. Within a single datacenter, the system needs to properly balance load across replicas.

There are two final components of real-world search engines that are worth discussing. First, recall that postings only store document ids. Therefore, raw retrieval results consist of a ranked list of semantically meaningless document ids. It is typically the responsibility of document servers, functionally distinct from the partition servers holding the indexes, to generate meaningful output for user presentation. Abstractly, a document server takes as input a query and a document id, and computes an appropriate result entry, typically comprising the title and URL of the page, a snippet of the source document showing the user's query terms in context, and additional metadata about the document. Second, query evaluation can benefit immensely from caching, of individual postings (assuming that the index is not already in memory) and even results of entire queries [13]. This is made possible by the Zipfian distribution of queries, with very frequent queries at the head of the distribution dominating the total number of queries. Search engines take advantage of this with cache servers, which are functionally distinct from all of the components discussed above.

4.7 SUMMARY AND ADDITIONAL READINGS

Web search is a complex problem that breaks down into three conceptually distinct components. First, the documents collection must be gathered (by crawling the web). Next, inverted indexes and other auxiliary data structures must be built from the documents. Both of these can be considered offline problems. Finally, index structures must be accessed and processed in response to user queries to generate search results. This last task is an online problem that demands both low latency and high throughput.

This chapter primarily focused on building inverted indexes, the problem most suitable for MapReduce. After all, inverted indexing is nothing but a very large distributed sort and group by operation! We began with a baseline implementation of an inverted indexing algorithm, but quickly noticed a scalability bottleneck that stemmed from having to buffer postings in memory. Application of the value-to-key conversion design pattern (Section 3.4) addressed the issue by offloading the task of sorting postings by document id to the MapReduce execution framework. We also surveyed various techniques for integer compression, which yield postings lists that are both more compact and faster to process. As a specific example, one could use Golomb codes for compressing d-gaps and γ codes for term frequencies. We showed how the order inversion design pattern introduced in Section 3.3 for computing relative frequencies can be used to properly set compression parameters.

Additional Readings.   Our brief discussion of web search glosses over many complexities and does a huge injustice to the tremendous amount of research in information retrieval. Here, however, we provide a few entry points into the literature. A survey article by Zobel and Moffat [162] is an excellent starting point on indexing and retrieval algorithms. Another by Baeza-Yates et al. [11] overviews many important issues in distributed retrieval. A keynote talk at the WSDM 2009 conference by Jeff Dean revealed a lot of information about the evolution of the Google search architecture.[15] Finally, a number of general information retrieval textbooks have been recently published [30; 42; 101]. Of these three, the one by Büttcher et al. [30] is noteworthy in having detailed experimental evaluations that compare the performance (both effectiveness and efficiency) of a wide range of algorithms and techniques. While outdated in many other respects, the textbook *Managing Gigabytes* [156] remains an excellent source for index compression techniques. Finally, ACM SIGIR is an annual conference and the most prestigious venue for academic information retrieval research; proceedings from those events are perhaps the best starting point for those wishing to keep abreast of publicly documented developments in the field.

---

[15]http://research.google.com/people/jeff/WSDM09-keynote.pdf

CHAPTER 5

Graph Algorithms

Graphs are ubiquitous in modern society: examples encountered by almost everyone on a daily basis include the hyperlink structure of the web (simply known as the web graph), social networks (manifest in the flow of email, phone call patterns, connections on social networking sites, etc.), and transportation networks (roads, bus routes, flights, etc.). Our very own existence is dependent on an intricate metabolic and regulatory network, which can be characterized as a large, complex graph involving interactions between genes, proteins, and other cellular products. This chapter focuses on graph algorithms in MapReduce. Although most of the content has nothing to do with text processing *per se*, documents frequently exist in the context of some underlying network, making graph analysis an important component of many text processing applications. Perhaps the best known example is PageRank, a measure of web page quality based on the structure of hyperlinks, which is used in ranking results for web search. As one of the first applications of MapReduce, PageRank exemplifies a large class of graph algorithms that can be concisely captured in the programming model. We will discuss PageRank in detail later this chapter.

In general, graphs can be characterized by nodes (or vertices) and links (or edges) that connect pairs of nodes.[1] These connections can be directed or undirected. In some graphs, there may be an edge from a node to itself, resulting in a self loop; in others, such edges are disallowed. We assume that both nodes and links may be annotated with additional metadata: as a simple example, in a social network where nodes represent individuals, there might be demographic information (e.g., age, gender, location) attached to the nodes and type information attached to the links (e.g., indicating type of relationship such as "friend" or "spouse").

Mathematicians have always been fascinated with graphs, dating back to Euler's paper on the *Seven Bridges of Königsberg* in 1736. Over the past few centuries, graphs have been extensively studied, and today much is known about their properties. Far more than theoretical curiosities, theorems and algorithms on graphs can be applied to solve many real-world problems:

- Graph search and path planning. Search algorithms on graphs are invoked millions of times a day, whenever anyone searches for directions on the web. Similar algorithms are also involved in friend recommendations and expert-finding in social networks. Path planning problems involving everything from network packets to delivery trucks represent another large class of graph search problems.

- Graph clustering. Can a large graph be divided into components that are relatively disjoint (for example, as measured by inter-component links [59])? Among other applications, this task is

---

[1]Throughout this chapter, we use *node* interchangeably with *vertex* and similarly with *link* and *edge*.

useful for identifying communities in social networks (of interest to sociologists who wish to understand how human relationships form and evolve) and for partitioning large graphs (of interest to computer scientists who seek to better parallelize graph processing). See [158] for a survey.

- Minimum spanning trees. A minimum spanning tree for a graph G with weighted edges is a tree that contains all vertices of the graph and a subset of edges connecting all the vertices together that minimizes the sum of edge weights. A real-world example of this problem is a telecommunications company that wishes to lay optical fiber to span a number of destinations at the lowest possible cost (where weights denote costs). This approach has also been applied to wide variety of problems, including social networks and the migration of Polynesian islanders [64].

- Bipartite graph matching. A bipartite graph is one whose vertices can be divided into two disjoint sets. Matching problems on such graphs can be used to model job seekers looking for employment or singles looking for dates.

- Maximum flow. In a weighted directed graph with two special nodes called the source and the sink, the max flow problem involves computing the amount of "traffic" that can be sent from source to sink given various flow capacities defined by edge weights. Transportation companies (airlines, shipping, etc.) and network operators grapple with complex versions of these problems on a daily basis.

- Identifying "special" nodes. There are many ways to define what special means, including metrics based on node in-degree, average distance to other nodes, and relationship to cluster structure. These special nodes are important to investigators attempting to break up terrorist cells, epidemiologists modeling the spread of diseases, advertisers trying to promote products, and many others.

A common feature of these problems is the scale of the datasets on which the algorithms must operate: for example, the hyperlink structure of the web, which contains billions of pages, or social networks that contain hundreds of millions of individuals. Clearly, algorithms that run on a single machine and depend on the entire graph residing in memory are not scalable. We'd like to put MapReduce to work on these challenges.[2]

This chapter is organized as follows: we begin in Section 5.1 with an introduction to graph representations, and then explore two classic graph algorithms in MapReduce: parallel breadth-first search (Section 5.2) and PageRank (Section 5.3). Before concluding with a summary and pointing out additional readings, Section 5.4 discusses a number of general issue that affect graph processing with MapReduce.

---

[2]As a side note, Google recently published a short description of a system called Pregel [98], based on Valiant's Bulk Synchronous Parallel model [148], for large-scale graph algorithms; a longer description is anticipated in a forthcoming paper [99].

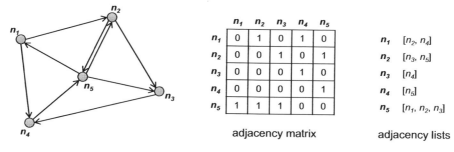

	n_1	n_2	n_3	n_4	n_5
n_1	0	1	0	1	0
n_2	0	0	1	0	1
n_3	0	0	0	1	0
n_4	0	0	0	0	1
n_5	1	1	1	0	0

n_1 $[n_2, n_4]$
n_2 $[n_3, n_5]$
n_3 $[n_4]$
n_4 $[n_5]$
n_5 $[n_1, n_2, n_3]$

adjacency matrix   adjacency lists

Figure 5.1: A simple directed graph (left) represented as an adjacency matrix (middle) and with adjacency lists (right).

5.1 GRAPH REPRESENTATIONS

One common way to represent a graph is with an adjacency matrix. A graph with n nodes can be represented as an $n \times n$ square matrix M, where a value in cell m_{ij} indicates an edge from node n_i to node n_j. In the case of graphs with weighted edges, the matrix cells contain edge weights; otherwise, each cell contains either a one (indicating an edge), or a zero (indicating none). With undirected graphs, only half the matrix is used (e.g., cells above the diagonal). For graphs that allow self loops (a directed edge from a node to itself), the diagonal might be populated; otherwise, the diagonal remains empty. Figure 5.1 provides an example of a simple directed graph (left) and its adjacency matrix representation (middle).

Although mathematicians prefer the adjacency matrix representation of graphs for easy manipulation with linear algebra, such a representation is far from ideal for computer scientists concerned with efficient algorithmic implementations. Most of the applications discussed in the chapter introduction involve *sparse* graphs, where the number of *actual* edges is far smaller than the number of *possible* edges.[3] For example, in a social network of n individuals, there are $n(n-1)/2$ possible "friendships" (where n may be on the order of hundreds of millions). However, even the most gregarious will have relatively few friends compared to the size of the network (thousands, perhaps, but still far smaller than hundreds of millions). The same is true for the hyperlink structure of the web: each individual web page links to a minuscule portion of all the pages on the web. In this chapter, we assume processing of sparse graphs, although we will return to this issue in Section 5.4.

The major problem with an adjacency matrix representation for sparse graphs is its $O(n^2)$ space requirement. Furthermore, most of the cells are zero, by definition. As a result, most computational implementations of graph algorithms operate over adjacency lists, in which a node is associated with neighbors that can be reached via outgoing edges. Figure 5.1 also shows the adjacency list representation of the graph under consideration (on the right). For example, since n_1 is connected

[3]Unfortunately, there is no precise definition of sparseness agreed upon by all, but one common definition is that a sparse graph has $O(n)$ edges, where n is the number of vertices.

by directed edges to n_2 and n_4, those two nodes will be on the adjacency list of n_1. There are two options for encoding undirected graphs: one could simply encode each edge twice (if n_i and n_j are connected, each appears on each other's adjacency list). Alternatively, one could order the nodes (arbitrarily or otherwise) and encode edges only on the adjacency list of the node that comes first in the ordering (i.e., if $i < j$, then n_j is on the adjacency list of n_i, but not the other way around).

Note that certain graph operations are easier on adjacency matrices than on adjacency lists. In the first, operations on incoming links for each node translate into a column scan on the matrix, whereas operations on outgoing links for each node translate into a row scan. With adjacency lists, it is natural to operate on outgoing links, but computing anything that requires knowledge of the incoming links of a node is difficult. However, as we shall see, the shuffle and sort mechanism in MapReduce provides an easy way to group edges by their destination nodes, thus allowing us to compute over incoming edges in the reducer. This property of the execution framework can also be used to invert the edges of a directed graph, by mapping over the nodes' adjacency lists and emitting key–value pairs with the destination node id as the key and the source node id as the value.[4]

5.2   PARALLEL BREADTH-FIRST SEARCH

One of the most common and well-studied problems in graph theory is the *single-source shortest path* problem, where the task is to find shortest paths from a source node to all other nodes in the graph (or alternatively, edges can be associated with costs or weights, in which case the task is to compute lowest-cost or lowest-weight paths). Such problems are a staple in undergraduate algorithm courses, where students are taught the solution using Dijkstra's algorithm. However, this famous algorithm assumes sequential processing—how would we solve this problem in parallel, and more specifically, with MapReduce?

As a refresher and also to serve as a point of comparison, Dijkstra's algorithm is shown in Figure 5.2, adapted from Cormen, Leiserson, and Rivest's classic algorithms textbook [41] (often simply known as *CLR*). The input to the algorithm is a directed, connected graph $G = (V, E)$ represented with adjacency lists, w containing edge distances such that $w(u, v) \geq 0$, and the source node s. The algorithm begins by first setting distances to all vertices $d[v]$, $v \in V$ to ∞, except for the source node, whose distance to itself is zero. The algorithm maintains Q, a global priority queue of vertices with priorities equal to their distance values d.

Dijkstra's algorithm operates by iteratively selecting the node with the lowest current distance from the priority queue (initially, this is the source node). At each iteration, the algorithm "expands" that node by traversing the adjacency list of the selected node to see if any of those nodes can be reached with a path of a shorter distance. The algorithm terminates when the priority queue Q is empty, or equivalently, when all nodes have been considered. Note that the algorithm as presented

---

[4]This technique is used in *anchor text inversion*, where one gathers the anchor text of hyperlinks pointing to a particular page. It is common practice to enrich a web page's standard textual representation with all of the anchor texts associated with its incoming hyperlinks (e.g., [107]).

```
1:  DIJKSTRA(G, w, s)
2:     d[s] ← 0
3:     for all vertex v ∈ V do
4:        d[v] ← ∞
5:     Q ← {V}
6:     while Q ≠ ∅ do
7:        u ← EXTRACTMIN(Q)
8:        for all vertex v ∈ u.ADJACENCYLIST do
9:           if d[v] > d[u] + w(u, v) then
10:             d[v] ← d[u] + w(u, v)
```

Figure 5.2: Pseudo-code for Dijkstra's algorithm, which is based on maintaining a global priority queue of nodes with priorities equal to their distances from the source node. At each iteration, the algorithm expands the node with the shortest distance and updates distances to all reachable nodes.

in Figure 5.2 only computes the shortest distances. The actual paths can be recovered by storing "backpointers" for every node indicating a fragment of the shortest path.

A sample trace of the algorithm running on a simple graph is shown in Figure 5.3 (example also adapted from *CLR*). We start out in (a) with n_1 having a distance of zero (since it's the source) and all other nodes having a distance of ∞. In the first iteration (a), n_1 is selected as the node to expand (indicated by the thicker border). After the expansion, we see in (b) that n_2 and n_3 can be reached at a distance of 10 and 5, respectively. Also, we see in (b) that n_3 is the next node selected for expansion. Nodes we have already considered for expansion are shown in black. Expanding n_3, we see in (c) that the distance to n_2 has decreased because we've found a shorter path. The nodes that will be expanded next, in order, are n_5, n_2, and n_4. The algorithm terminates with the end state shown in (f), where we've discovered the shortest distance to all nodes.

The key to Dijkstra's algorithm is the priority queue that maintains a globally sorted list of nodes by current distance. This is not possible in MapReduce, as the programming model does not provide a mechanism for exchanging global data. Instead, we adopt a brute force approach known as parallel breadth-first search. First, as a simplification let us assume that all edges have unit distance (modeling, for example, hyperlinks on the web). This makes the algorithm easier to understand, but we'll relax this restriction later.

The intuition behind the algorithm is this: the distance of all nodes connected directly to the source node is one; the distance of all nodes directly connected to those is two; and so on. Imagine water rippling away from a rock dropped into a pond—that's a good image of how parallel breadth-first search works. However, what if there are multiple paths to the same node? Suppose we wish to compute the shortest distance to node n. The shortest path must go through one of the nodes in M that contains an outgoing edge to n: we need to examine all $m \in M$ to find m_s, the node with the shortest distance. The shortest distance to n is the distance to m_s plus one.

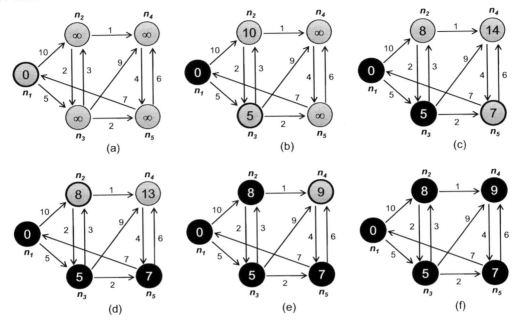

Figure 5.3: Example of Dijkstra's algorithm applied to a simple graph with five nodes, with n_1 as the source and edge distances as indicated. Parts (a)–(e) show the running of the algorithm at each iteration, with the current distance inside the node. Nodes with thicker borders are those being expanded; nodes that have already been expanded are shown in black.

Pseudo-code for the implementation of the parallel breadth-first search algorithm is provided in Figure 5.4. As with Dijkstra's algorithm, we assume a connected, directed graph represented as adjacency lists. Distance to each node is directly stored alongside the adjacency list of that node, and initialized to ∞ for all nodes except for the source node. In the pseudo-code, we use n to denote the node id (an integer) and N to denote the node's corresponding data structure (adjacency list and current distance). The algorithm works by mapping over all nodes and emitting a key-value pair for each neighbor on the node's adjacency list. The key contains the node id of the neighbor, and the value is the current distance to the node plus one. This says: if we can reach node n with a distance d, then we must be able to reach all the nodes that are connected to n with distance $d + 1$. After shuffle and sort, reducers will receive keys corresponding to the destination node ids and distances corresponding to all paths leading to that node. The reducer will select the shortest of these distances and then update the distance in the node data structure.

It is apparent that parallel breadth-first search is an iterative algorithm, where each iteration corresponds to a MapReduce job. The first time we run the algorithm, we "discover" all nodes that are connected to the source. The second iteration, we discover all nodes connected to those, and

```
1: class MAPPER
2:     method MAP(nid n, node N)
3:         d ← N.DISTANCE
4:         EMIT(nid n, N)                              ▷ Pass along graph structure
5:         for all nodeid m ∈ N.ADJACENCYLIST do
6:             EMIT(nid m, d + 1)                      ▷ Emit distances to reachable nodes

1: class REDUCER
2:     method REDUCE(nid m, [d₁, d₂, . . .])
3:         d_min ← ∞
4:         M ← ∅
5:         for all d ∈ counts [d₁, d₂, . . .] do
6:             if ISNODE(d) then
7:                 M ← d                               ▷ Recover graph structure
8:             else if d < d_min then                  ▷ Look for shorter distance
9:                 d_min ← d
10:        M.DISTANCE ← d_min                          ▷ Update shortest distance
11:        EMIT(nid m, node M)
```

Figure 5.4: Pseudo-code for parallel breath-first search in MapReduce: the mappers emit distances to reachable nodes, while the reducers select the minimum of those distances for each destination node. Each iteration (one MapReduce job) of the algorithm expands the "search frontier" by one hop.

so on. Each iteration of the algorithm expands the "search frontier" by one hop, and, eventually, all nodes will be discovered with their shortest distances (assuming a fully-connected graph). Before we discuss termination of the algorithm, there is one more detail required to make the parallel breadth-first search algorithm work. We need to "pass along" the graph structure from one iteration to the next. This is accomplished by emitting the node data structure itself, with the node id as a key (Figure 5.4, line 4 in the mapper). In the reducer, we must distinguish the node data structure from distance values (Figure 5.4, lines 5–6 in the reducer), and update the minimum distance in the node data structure before emitting it as the final value. The final output is now ready to serve as input to the next iteration.[5]

So how many iterations are necessary to compute the shortest distance to all nodes? The answer is the diameter of the graph, or the greatest distance between any pair of nodes. This number is surprisingly small for many real-world problems: the saying "six degrees of separation" suggests that everyone on the planet is connected to everyone else by at most six steps (the people a person knows are one step away, people that they know are two steps away, etc.). If this is indeed true,

---

[5]Note that in this algorithm we are overloading the value type, which can either be a distance (integer) or a complex data structure representing a node. The best way to achieve this in Hadoop is to create a wrapper object with an indicator variable specifying what the content is.

then parallel breadth-first search on the global social network would take at most six MapReduce iterations. For more serious academic studies of "small world" phenomena in networks, we refer the reader to a number of publications [2; 61; 62; 152]. In practical terms, we iterate the algorithm until there are no more node distances that are ∞. Since the graph is connected, all nodes are reachable, and since all edge distances are one, all discovered nodes are guaranteed to have the shortest distances (i.e., there is not a shorter path that goes through a node that hasn't been discovered).

The actual checking of the termination condition must occur outside of MapReduce. Typically, execution of an iterative MapReduce algorithm requires a non-MapReduce "driver" program, which submits a MapReduce job to iterate the algorithm, checks to see if a termination condition has been met, and if not, repeats. Hadoop provides a lightweight API for constructs called "counters", which, as the name suggests, can be used for counting events that occur during execution, e.g., number of corrupt records, number of times a certain condition is met, or anything that the programmer desires. Counters can be defined to count the number of nodes that have distances of ∞: at the end of the job, the driver program can access the final counter value and check to see if another iteration is necessary.

Finally, as with Dijkstra's algorithm in the form presented earlier, the parallel breadth-first search algorithm only finds the shortest distances, not the actual shortest paths. However, the path can be straightforwardly recovered. Storing "backpointers" at each node, as with Dijkstra's algorithm, will work, but may not be efficient since the graph needs to be traversed again to reconstruct the path segments. A simpler approach is to emit paths along with distances in the mapper, so that each node will have its shortest path easily accessible at all times. The additional space requirements for shuffling these data from mappers to reducers are relatively modest, since for the most part paths (i.e., sequence of node ids) are relatively short.

Up until now, we have been assuming that all edges are unit distance. Let us relax that restriction and see what changes are required in the parallel breadth-first search algorithm. The adjacency lists, which were previously lists of node ids, must now encode the edge distances as well. In line 6 of the mapper code in Figure 5.4, instead of emitting $d + 1$ as the value, we must now emit $d + w$ where w is the edge distance. No other changes to the algorithm are required, but the termination behavior is very different. To illustrate, consider the graph fragment in Figure 5.5, where s is the source node, and in this iteration, we just "discovered" node r for the very first time. Assume for the sake of argument that we've already discovered the shortest distance to node p, and that the shortest distance to r so far goes through p. This, however, does not guarantee that we've discovered the shortest distance to r, since there may exist a path going through q that we haven't encountered yet (because it lies outside the search frontier).[6] However, as the search frontier expands, we'll eventually cover q and all other nodes along the path from p to q to r—which means that with sufficient iterations, we will discover the shortest distance to r. But how do we know that we've found the shortest distance to p? Well, if the shortest path to p lies within the search frontier,

---

[6] Note that the same argument does not apply to the unit edge distance case: the shortest path cannot lie outside the search frontier since any such path would necessarily be longer.

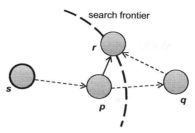

Figure 5.5: In the single-source shortest path problem with arbitrary edge distances, the shortest path from source s to node r may go outside the current search frontier, in which case we will not find the shortest distance to r until the search frontier expands to cover q.

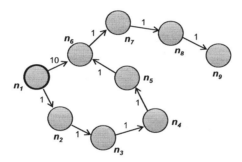

Figure 5.6: A sample graph that elicits worst-case behavior for parallel breadth-first search. Eight iterations are required to discover shortest distances to all nodes from n_1.

we would have already discovered it. And if it doesn't, the above argument applies. Similarly, we can repeat the same argument for all nodes on the path from s to p. The conclusion is that, with sufficient iterations, we'll eventually discover all the shortest distances.

So exactly how many iterations does "eventually" mean? In the worst case, we might need as many iterations as there are nodes in the graph minus one. In fact, it is not difficult to construct graphs that will elicit this worse-case behavior: Figure 5.6 provides an example, with n_1 as the source. The parallel breadth-first search algorithm would not discover that the shortest path from n_1 to n_6 goes through n_3, n_4, and n_5 until the fifth iteration. Three more iterations are necessary to cover the rest of the graph. Fortunately, for most real-world graphs, such extreme cases are rare, and the number of iterations necessary to discover all shortest distances is quite close to the diameter of the graph, as in the unit edge distance case.

In practical terms, how do we know when to stop iterating in the case of arbitrary edge distances? The algorithm can terminate when shortest distances at every node no longer change.

Once again, we can use counters to keep track of such events. Every time we encounter a shorter distance in the reducer, we increment a counter. At the end of each MapReduce iteration, the driver program reads the counter value and determines if another iteration is necessary.

Compared to Dijkstra's algorithm on a single processor, parallel breadth-first search in Map-Reduce can be characterized as a brute force approach that "wastes" a lot of time performing computations whose results are discarded. At each iteration, the algorithm attempts to recompute distances to all nodes, but in reality only useful work is done along the search frontier: inside the search frontier, the algorithm is simply repeating previous computations.[7] Outside the search frontier, the algorithm hasn't discovered any paths to nodes there yet, so no meaningful work is done. Dijkstra's algorithm, on the other hand, is far more efficient. Every time a node is explored, we're guaranteed to have already found the shortest path to it. However, this is made possible by maintaining a global data structure (a priority queue) that holds nodes sorted by distance—this is not possible in MapReduce because the programming model does not provide support for global data that is mutable and accessible by the mappers and reducers. These inefficiencies represent the cost of parallelization.

The parallel breadth-first search algorithm is instructive in that it represents the prototypical structure of a large class of graph algorithms in MapReduce. They share in the following character-istics:

- The graph structure is represented with adjacency lists, which is part of some larger node data structure that may contain additional information (variables to store intermediate output, features of the nodes). In many cases, features are attached to edges as well (e.g., edge weights).

- The MapReduce algorithm maps over the node data structures and performs a computation that is a function of features of the node, intermediate state attached to each node, and features of the adjacency list (outgoing edges and their features). In other words, computations can only involve a node's internal state and its local graph structure. The results of these computations are emitted as values, keyed with the node ids of the neighbors (i.e., those nodes on the adjacency lists). Conceptually, we can think of this as "passing" the results of the computation along outgoing edges. In the reducer, the algorithm receives all partial results that have the same destination node, and performs another computation (usually, some form of aggregation).

- In addition to computations, the graph itself is also passed from the mapper to the reducer. In the reducer, the data structure corresponding to each node is updated and written back to disk.

- Graph algorithms in MapReduce are generally iterative, where the output of the previous iteration serves as input to the next iteration. The process is controlled by a non-MapReduce driver program that checks for termination.

---

[7]Unless the algorithm discovers an instance of the situation described in Figure 5.5, in which case, updated distances will propagate inside the search frontier.

For parallel breadth-first search, the mapper computation is the current distance plus edge distance (emitting distances to neighbors), while the reducer computation is the MIN function (selecting the shortest path). As we will see in the next section, the MapReduce algorithm for PageRank works in much the same way.

5.3   PAGERANK

PageRank [117] is a measure of web page quality based on the structure of the hyperlink graph. Although it is only one of thousands of features that is taken into account in Google's search algorithm, it is perhaps one of the best known and most studied.

A vivid way to illustrate PageRank is to imagine a random web surfer: the surfer visits a page, randomly clicks a link on that page, and repeats ad infinitum. PageRank is a measure of how frequently a page would be encountered by our tireless web surfer. More precisely, PageRank is a probability distribution over nodes in the graph representing the likelihood that a random walk over the link structure will arrive at a particular node. Nodes that have high in-degrees tend to have high PageRank values, as well as nodes that are linked to by other nodes with high PageRank values. This behavior makes intuitive sense: if PageRank is a measure of page quality, we would expect high-quality pages to contain "endorsements" from many other pages in the form of hyperlinks. Similarly, if a high-quality page links to another page, then the second page is likely to be high quality also. PageRank represents one particular approach to inferring the quality of a web page based on hyperlink structure; two other popular algorithms, not covered here, are SALSA [88] and HITS [84] (also known as "hubs and authorities").

The complete formulation of PageRank includes an additional component. As it turns out, our web surfer doesn't just randomly click links. Before the surfer decides where to go next, a biased coin is flipped—heads, the surfer clicks on a random link on the page as usual. Tails, however, the surfer ignores the links on the page and randomly "jumps" or "teleports" to a completely different page.

But enough about random web surfing. Formally, the PageRank P of a page n is defined as follows:

$$P(n) = \alpha \left(\frac{1}{|G|} \right) + (1 - \alpha) \sum_{m \in L(n)} \frac{P(m)}{C(m)} \tag{5.1}$$

where $|G|$ is the total number of nodes (pages) in the graph, α is the random jump factor, $L(n)$ is the set of pages that link to n, and $C(m)$ is the out-degree of node m (the number of links on page m). The random jump factor α is sometimes called the "teleportation" factor; alternatively, $(1 - \alpha)$ is referred to as the "damping" factor.

Let us break down each component of the formula in detail. First, note that PageRank is defined recursively—this gives rise to an iterative algorithm we will detail in a bit. A web page n receives PageRank "contributions" from all pages that link to it, $L(n)$. Let us consider a page m from the set of pages $L(n)$: a random surfer at m will arrive at n with probability $1/C(m)$ since a link is selected at random from all outgoing links. Since the PageRank value of m is the probability that the random surfer will be at m, the probability of arriving at n from m is $P(m)/C(m)$. To compute the PageRank of n, we need to sum contributions from all pages that link to n. This is the summation in the second half of the equation. However, we also need to take into account the random jump: there is a $1/|G|$ chance of landing at any particular page, where $|G|$ is the number of nodes in the graph. Of course, the two contributions need to be combined: with probability α the random surfer executes a random jump, and with probability $1 - \alpha$ the random surfer follows a hyperlink.

Note that PageRank assumes a community of honest users who are not trying to "game" the measure. This is, of course, not true in the real world, where an adversarial relationship exists between search engine companies and a host of other organizations and individuals (marketers, spammers, activists, etc.) who are trying to manipulate search results—to promote a cause, product, or service, or in some cases, to trap and intentionally deceive users (see, for example, [12; 63]). A simple example is a so-called "spider trap", a infinite chain of pages (e.g., generated by CGI) that all link to a single page (thereby artificially inflating its PageRank). For this reason, PageRank is only one of thousands of features used in ranking web pages.

The fact that PageRank is recursively defined translates into an iterative algorithm which is quite similar in basic structure to parallel breadth-first search. We start by presenting an informal sketch. At the beginning of each iteration, a node passes its PageRank contributions to other nodes that it is connected to. Since PageRank is a probability distribution, we can think of this as spreading probability mass to neighbors via outgoing links. To conclude the iteration, each node sums up all PageRank contributions that have been passed to it and computes an updated PageRank score. We can think of this as gathering probability mass passed to a node via its incoming links. This algorithm iterates until PageRank values don't change anymore.

Figure 5.7 shows a toy example that illustrates two iterations of the algorithm. As a simplification, we ignore the random jump factor for now (i.e., $\alpha = 0$) and further assume that there are no dangling nodes (i.e., nodes with no outgoing edges). The algorithm begins by initializing a uniform distribution of PageRank values across nodes. In the beginning of the first iteration (top, left), partial PageRank contributions are sent from each node to its neighbors connected via outgoing links. For example, n_1 sends 0.1 PageRank mass to n_2 and 0.1 PageRank mass to n_4. This makes sense in terms of the random surfer model: if the surfer is at n_1 with a probability of 0.2, then the surfer could end up either in n_2 or n_4 with a probability of 0.1 each. The same occurs for all the other nodes in the graph: note that n_5 must split its PageRank mass three ways, since it has three neighbors, and n_4 receives all the mass belonging to n_3 because n_3 isn't connected to any other node. The end of the first iteration is shown in the top right: each node sums up PageRank contributions from its neighbors. Note that since n_1 has only one incoming link, from n_3, its updated PageRank value is smaller than before, i.e., it "passed along" more PageRank mass than it received. The exact same process repeats, and the second iteration in our toy example is illustrated by the bottom two graphs. At the beginning of each iteration, the PageRank values of all nodes sum to one. PageRank mass is

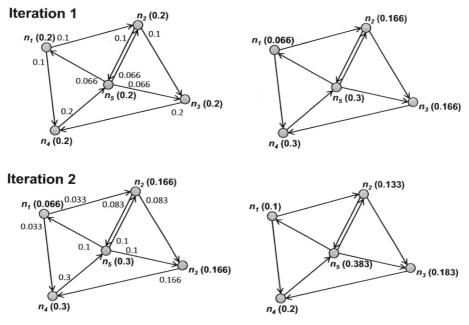

Figure 5.7: PageRank toy example showing two iterations, top and bottom. Left graphs show PageRank values at the beginning of each iteration and how much PageRank mass is passed to each neighbor. Right graphs show updated PageRank values at the end of each iteration.

preserved by the algorithm, guaranteeing that we continue to have a valid probability distribution at the end of each iteration.

Pseudo-code of the MapReduce PageRank algorithm is shown in Figure 5.8; it is simplified in that we continue to ignore the random jump factor and assume no dangling nodes (complications that we will return to later). An illustration of the running algorithm is shown in Figure 5.9 for the first iteration of the toy graph in Figure 5.7. The algorithm maps over the nodes, and for each node computes how much PageRank mass needs to be distributed to its neighbors (i.e., nodes on the adjacency list). Each piece of the PageRank mass is emitted as the value, keyed by the node ids of the neighbors. Conceptually, we can think of this as passing PageRank mass along outgoing edges.

In the shuffle and sort phase, the MapReduce execution framework groups values (piece of PageRank mass) passed along the graph edges by destination node (i.e., all edges that point to the same node). In the reducer, PageRank mass contributions from all incoming edges are summed to arrive at the updated PageRank value for each node. As with the parallel breadth-first search algorithm, the graph structure itself must be passed from iteration to iteration. Each node data structure is emitted in the mapper and written back out to disk in the reducer. All PageRank mass

```
1:  class MAPPER
2:      method MAP(nid n, node N)
3:          p ← N.PAGERANK/|N.ADJACENCYLIST|
4:          EMIT(nid n, N)                                  ▷ Pass along graph structure
5:          for all nodeid m ∈ N.ADJACENCYLIST do
6:              EMIT(nid m, p)                              ▷ Pass PageRank mass to neighbors

1:  class REDUCER
2:      method REDUCE(nid m, [p₁, p₂, . . .])
3:          M ← ∅
4:          for all p ∈ counts [p₁, p₂, . . .] do
5:              if ISNODE(p) then
6:                  M ← p                                  ▷ Recover graph structure
7:              else
8:                  s ← s + p                              ▷ Sum incoming PageRank contributions
9:          M.PAGERANK ← s
10:         EMIT(nid m, node M)
```

Figure 5.8: Pseudo-code for PageRank in MapReduce (leaving aside dangling nodes and the random jump factor). In the map phase we evenly divide up each node's PageRank mass and pass each piece along outgoing edges to neighbors. In the reduce phase PageRank contributions are summed up at each destination node. Each MapReduce job corresponds to one iteration of the algorithm.

emitted by the mappers is accounted for in the reducer: since we begin with the sum of PageRank values across all nodes equal to one, the sum of all the updated PageRank values should remain a valid probability distribution.

Having discussed the simplified PageRank algorithm in MapReduce, let us now take into account the random jump factor and dangling nodes: as it turns out both are treated similarly. Dangling nodes are nodes in the graph that have no outgoing edges, i.e., their adjacency lists are empty. In the hyperlink graph of the web, these might correspond to pages in a crawl that have not been downloaded yet. If we simply run the algorithm in Figure 5.8 on graphs with dangling nodes, the total PageRank mass will not be conserved, since no key-value pairs will be emitted when a dangling node is encountered in the mappers.

The proper treatment of PageRank mass "lost" at the dangling nodes is to redistribute it across all nodes in the graph evenly (cf. [22]). There are many ways to determine the missing PageRank mass. One simple approach is by instrumenting the algorithm in Figure 5.8 with counters: whenever the mapper processes a node with an empty adjacency list, it keeps track of the node's PageRank value in the counter. At the end of the iteration, we can access the counter to find out how much

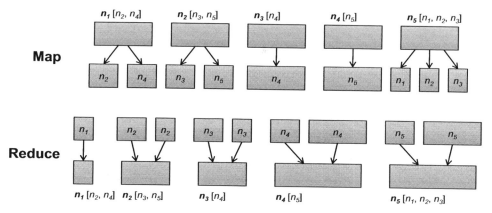

Figure 5.9: Illustration of the MapReduce PageRank algorithm corresponding to the first iteration in Figure 5.7. The size of each box is proportion to its PageRank value. During the map phase, PageRank mass is distributed evenly to nodes on each node's adjacency list (shown at the very top). Intermediate values are keyed by node (shown inside the boxes). In the reduce phase, all partial PageRank contributions are summed together to arrive at updated values.

PageRank mass was lost at the dangling nodes.[8] Another approach is to reserve a special key for storing PageRank mass from dangling nodes. When the mapper encounters a dangling node, its PageRank mass is emitted with the special key; the reducer must be modified to contain special logic for handling the missing PageRank mass. Yet another approach is to write out the missing PageRank mass as "side data" for each map task (using the in-mapper combining technique for aggregation); a final pass in the driver program is needed to sum the mass across all map tasks. Either way, we arrive at the amount of PageRank mass lost at the dangling nodes—this then must be redistribute evenly across all nodes.

This redistribution process can be accomplished by mapping over all nodes again. At the same time, we can take into account the random jump factor. For each node, its current PageRank value p is updated to the final PageRank value p' according to the following formula:

$$p' = \alpha \left(\frac{1}{|G|} \right) + (1 - \alpha) \left(\frac{m}{|G|} + p \right) \tag{5.2}$$

where m is the missing PageRank mass, and $|G|$ is the number of nodes in the entire graph. We add the PageRank mass from link traversal (p, computed from before) to the share of the lost PageRank mass that is distributed to each node ($m/|G|$). Finally, we take into account the random jump factor:

[8]In Hadoop, counters are 8-byte integers: a simple workaround is to multiply PageRank values by a large constant, and then cast as an integer.

with probability α the random surfer arrives via jumping, and with probability $1 - \alpha$ the random surfer arrives via incoming links. Note that this MapReduce job requires no reducers.

Putting everything together, one iteration of PageRank requires two MapReduce jobs: the first to distribute PageRank mass along graph edges, and the second to take care of dangling nodes and the random jump factor. At the end of each iteration, we end up with exactly the same data structure as the beginning, which is a requirement for the iterative algorithm to work. Also, the PageRank values of all nodes sum up to one, which ensures a valid probability distribution.

Typically, PageRank is iterated until convergence, i.e., when the PageRank values of nodes no longer change (within some tolerance, to take into account, for example, floating point precision errors). Therefore, at the end of each iteration, the PageRank driver program must check to see if convergence has been reached. Alternative stopping criteria include running a fixed number of iterations (useful if one wishes to bound algorithm running time) or stopping when the *ranks* of PageRank values no longer change. The latter is useful for some applications that only care about comparing the PageRank of two arbitrary pages and do not need the actual PageRank values. Rank stability is obtained faster than the actual convergence of values.

In absolute terms, how many iterations are necessary for PageRank to converge? This is a difficult question to *precisely* answer since it depends on many factors, but generally, fewer than one might expect. In the original PageRank paper [117], convergence on a graph with 322 million edges was reached in 52 iterations (see also Bianchini et al. [22] for additional discussion). On today's web, the answer is not very meaningful due to the adversarial nature of web search as previously discussed—the web is full of spam and populated with sites that are actively trying to "game" PageRank and related hyperlink-based metrics. As a result, running PageRank in its unmodified form presented here would yield unexpected and undesirable results. Of course, strategies developed by web search companies to combat link spam are proprietary (and closely guarded secrets, for obvious reasons)—but undoubtedly these algorithmic modifications impact convergence behavior. A full discussion of the escalating "arms race" between search engine companies and those that seek to promote their sites is beyond the scope of this book.[9]

5.4 ISSUES WITH GRAPH PROCESSING

The biggest difference between MapReduce graph algorithms and single-machine graph algorithms is that with the latter, it is usually possible to maintain global data structures in memory for fast, random access. For example, Dijkstra's algorithm uses a global priority queue that guides the expansion of nodes. This, of course, is not possible with MapReduce—the programming model does not provide any built-in mechanism for communicating global state. Since the most natural representation of large sparse graphs is with adjacency lists, communication can only occur from a node to the

---

[9]For the interested reader, the proceedings of a workshop series on Adversarial Information Retrieval (AIRWeb) provide great starting points into the literature.

nodes it links to, or to a node from nodes linked to it—in other words, passing information is only possible within the local graph structure.[10]

This restriction gives rise to the structure of many graph algorithms in MapReduce: local computation is performed on each node, the results of which are "passed" to its neighbors. With multiple iterations, convergence on the global graph is possible. The passing of partial results along a graph edge is accomplished by the shuffling and sorting provided by the MapReduce execution framework. The amount of intermediate data generated is on the order of the number of edges, which explains why all the algorithms we have discussed assume sparse graphs. For dense graphs, MapReduce running time would be dominated by copying intermediate data across the network, which in the worst case is $O(n^2)$ in the number of nodes in the graph. Since MapReduce clusters are designed around commodity networks (e.g., gigabit Ethernet), MapReduce algorithms are often impractical on large, dense graphs.

Combiners and the in-mapper combining pattern described in Section 3.1 can be used to decrease the running time of graph iterations. It is straightforward to use combiners for both parallel breadth-first search and PageRank since MIN and sum, used in the two algorithms, respectively, are both associative and commutative. However, combiners are only effective to the extent that there are opportunities for partial aggregation—unless there are nodes pointed to by multiple nodes being processed by an individual map task, combiners are not very useful. This implies that it would be desirable to partition large graphs into smaller components where there are many intra-component links and fewer inter-component links. This way, we can arrange the data such that nodes in the same component are handled by the same map task—thus maximizing opportunities for combiners to perform local aggregation.

Unfortunately, this sometimes creates a chicken-and-egg problem. It would be desirable to partition a large graph to facilitate efficient processing by MapReduce. But the graph may be so large that we can't partition it except with MapReduce algorithms! Fortunately, in many cases there are simple solutions around this problem in the form of "cheap" partitioning heuristics based on reordering the data [106]. For example, in a social network, we might sort nodes representing users by zip code, as opposed to by last name—based on the observation that friends tend to live close to each other. Sorting by an even more cohesive property such as school would be even better (if available): the probability of any two random students from the same school knowing each other is much higher than two random students from different schools. Another good example is to partition the web graph by the language of the page (since pages in one language tend to link mostly to other pages in that language) or by domain name (since inter-domain links are typically much denser than intra-domain links). Resorting records using MapReduce is both easy to do and a relatively cheap operation—however, whether the efficiencies gained by this crude form of partitioning are worth the extra time taken in performing the resort is an empirical question that will depend on the actual graph structure and algorithm.

---

[10]Of course, it is perfectly reasonable to compute derived graph structures in a pre-processing step. For example, if one wishes to propagate information from a node to all nodes that are within two links, one could process graph G to derive graph G', where there would exist a link from node n_i to n_j if n_j was reachable within two link traversals of n_i in the original graph G.

Finally, there is a practical consideration to keep in mind when implementing graph algorithms that estimate probability distributions over nodes (such as PageRank). For large graphs, the probability of any particular node is often so small that it underflows standard floating point representations. A very common solution to this problem is to represent probabilities using their logarithms. When probabilities are stored as logs, the product of two values is simply their sum. However, addition of probabilities is also necessary, for example, when summing PageRank contribution for a node. This can be implemented with reasonable precision as follows:

$$a \oplus b = \begin{cases} b + \log(1 + e^{a-b}) & a < b \\ a + \log(1 + e^{b-a}) & a \geq b \end{cases}$$

Furthermore, many math libraries include a `log1p` function which computes $\log(1 + x)$ with higher precision than the naïve implementation would have when x is very small (as is often the case when working with probabilities). Its use may further improve the accuracy of implementations that use log probabilities.

5.5   SUMMARY AND ADDITIONAL READINGS

This chapter covers graph algorithms in MapReduce, discussing in detail parallel breadth-first search and PageRank. Both are instances of a large class of iterative algorithms that share the following characteristics:

- The graph structure is represented with adjacency lists.

- Algorithms map over nodes and pass partial results to nodes on their adjacency lists. Partial results are aggregated for each node in the reducer.

- The graph structure itself is passed from the mapper to the reducer, such that the output is in the same form as the input.

- Algorithms are iterative and under the control of a non-MapReduce driver program, which checks for termination at the end of each iteration.

The MapReduce programming model does not provide a mechanism to maintain global data structures accessible and mutable by all the mappers and reducers.[11] One implication of this is that communication between pairs of arbitrary nodes is difficult to accomplish. Instead, information typically propagates along graph edges—which gives rise to the structure of algorithms discussed above.

Additional Readings.   The ubiquity of large graphs translates into substantial interest in scalable graph algorithms using MapReduce in industry, academia, and beyond. There is, of course, much beyond what has been covered in this chapter. For additional material, we refer readers to the

---

[11]However, maintaining globally-synchronized state may be possible with the assistance of other tools (e.g., a distributed database).

following: Kang et al. [80] presented an approach to estimating the diameter of large graphs using MapReduce and a library for graph mining [81]; Cohen [39] discussed a number of algorithms for processing undirected graphs, with social network analysis in mind; Rao and Yarowsky [128] described an implementation of label propagation, a standard algorithm for semi-supervised machine learning, on graphs derived from textual data; Schatz [132] tackled the problem of DNA sequence alignment and assembly with graph algorithms in MapReduce. Finally, it is easy to forget that parallel graph algorithms have been studied by computer scientists for several decades, particular in the PRAM model [60; 77]. It is not clear, however, to what extent well-known PRAM algorithms translate naturally into the MapReduce framework.

CHAPTER 6

EM Algorithms for Text Processing

Until the end of the 1980s, text processing systems tended to rely on large numbers of manually written rules to analyze, annotate, and transform text input, usually in a deterministic way. This rule-based approach can be appealing: a system's behavior can generally be understood and predicted precisely, and, when errors surface, they can be corrected by writing new rules or refining old ones. However, rule-based systems suffer from a number of serious problems. They are brittle with respect to the natural variation found in language, and developing systems that can deal with inputs from diverse domains is very labor intensive. Furthermore, when these systems fail, they often do so catastrophically, unable to offer even a "best guess" as to what the desired analysis of the input might be.

In the last 20 years, the rule-based approach has largely been abandoned in favor of more data-driven methods, where the "rules" for processing the input are inferred automatically from large corpora of examples, called *training data*. The basic strategy of the data-driven approach is to start with a processing algorithm capable of capturing how any instance of the *kinds* of inputs (e.g., sentences or emails) can relate to any instance of the kinds of outputs that the final system should produce (e.g., the syntactic structure of the sentence or a classification of the email as spam). At this stage, the system can be thought of as having the potential to produce any output for any input, but they are not distinguished in any way. Next, a *learning algorithm* is applied which refines this process based on the training data—generally attempting to make the model perform as well as possible at predicting the examples in the training data. The learning process, which often involves iterative algorithms, typically consists of activities like ranking rules, instantiating the content of rule templates, or determining parameter settings for a given model. This is known as *machine learning*, an active area of research.

Data-driven approaches have turned out to have several benefits over rule-based approaches to system development. Since data-driven systems can be trained using examples of the kind that they will eventually be used to process, they tend to deal with the complexities found in real data more robustly than rule-based systems do. Second, developing training data tends to be far less expensive than developing rules. For some applications, significant quantities of training data may even exist for independent reasons (e.g., translations of text into multiple languages are created by authors wishing to reach an audience speaking different languages, not because they are generating training data for a data-driven machine translation system). These advantages come at the cost of systems that often behave internally quite differently than a human-engineered system. As a result, correcting errors that the trained system makes can be quite challenging.

Data-driven information processing systems can be constructed using a variety of mathematical techniques, but in this chapter we focus on *statistical models*, which probabilistically relate inputs from an input set $\mathcal{X}$ (e.g., sentences, documents, etc.), which are always *observable*, to annotations from a set $\mathcal{Y}$, which is the space of possible annotations or analyses that the system should predict. This model may take the form of either a *joint model* $\Pr(x, y)$ which assigns a probability to every pair $\langle x, y \rangle \in \mathcal{X} \times \mathcal{Y}$ or a *conditional model* $\Pr(y|x)$, which assigns a probability to every $y \in \mathcal{Y}$, given an $x \in \mathcal{X}$. For example, to create a statistical spam detection system, we might have $\mathcal{Y} = \{\text{SPAM}, \text{NOTSPAM}\}$ and $\mathcal{X}$ be the set of all possible email messages. For machine translation, $\mathcal{X}$ might be the set of Arabic sentences and $\mathcal{Y}$ the set of English sentences.[1]

There are three closely related, but distinct, challenges in statistical text processing. The first is model selection. This entails selecting a representation of a joint or conditional distribution over the desired $\mathcal{X}$ and $\mathcal{Y}$. For a problem where $\mathcal{X}$ and $\mathcal{Y}$ are very small, one could imagine representing these probabilities in lookup tables. However, for something like email classification or machine translation, where the model space is infinite, the probabilities cannot be represented directly, and must be computed algorithmically. As an example of such models, we introduce *hidden Markov models* (HMMs), which define a joint distribution over sequences of inputs and sequences of annotations. The second challenge is *parameter estimation* or *learning*, which involves the application of an optimization algorithm and training criterion to select the parameters of the model to optimize the model's performance (with respect to the given training criterion) on the training data.[2] The parameters of a statistical model are the values used to compute the probability of some event described by the model. In this chapter we will focus on one particularly simple training criterion for parameter estimation, *maximum likelihood estimation*, which says to select the parameters that make the training data most probable under the model, and one learning algorithm that attempts to meet this criterion, called expectation maximization (EM). The final challenge for statistical modeling is the problem of *decoding*, or, given some x, using the model to select an annotation y. One very common strategy is to select y according to the following criterion:

$$y^* = \arg\max_{y \in \mathcal{Y}} \Pr(y|x)$$

In a conditional (or *direct*) model, this is a straightforward search for the best y under the model. In a joint model, the search is also straightforward, on account of the definition of conditional probability:

$$y^* = \arg\max_{y \in \mathcal{Y}} \Pr(y|x) = \arg\max_{y \in \mathcal{Y}} \frac{\Pr(x, y)}{\sum_{y'} \Pr(x, y')} = \arg\max_{y \in \mathcal{Y}} \Pr(x, y)$$

---

[1]In this chapter, we will consider discrete models only. They tend to be sufficient for text processing, and their presentation is simpler than models with continuous densities. It should be kept in mind that the sets $\mathcal{X}$ and $\mathcal{Y}$ may still be countably infinite.

[2]We restrict our discussion in this chapter to models with finite numbers of parameters and where the learning process refers to setting those parameters. Inference in and learning of so-called *nonparameteric models*, which have an infinite number of parameters and have become important statistical models for text processing in recent years, is beyond the scope of this chapter.

The specific form that the search takes will depend on how the model is represented. Our focus in this chapter will primarily be on the second problem: learning parameters for models, but we will touch on the third problem as well.

Machine learning is often categorized as either *supervised* or *unsupervised*. Supervised learning of statistical models simply means that the model parameters are estimated from training data consisting of pairs of inputs and annotations, that is $\mathcal{Z} = \langle \langle x_1, y_1 \rangle, \langle x_2, y_2 \rangle, \ldots \rangle$ where $\langle x_i, y_i \rangle \in \mathcal{X} \times \mathcal{Y}$ and y_i is the *gold standard* (i.e., correct) annotation of x_i. While supervised models often attain quite good performance, they are often uneconomical to use, since the training data requires each object that is to be classified (to pick a specific task), x_i to be paired with its correct label, y_i. In many cases, these gold standard training labels must be generated by a process of *expert annotation*, meaning that each x_i must be manually labeled by a trained individual. Even when the annotation task is quite simple for people to carry out (e.g., in the case of spam detection), the number of potential examples that could be classified (representing a subset of $\mathcal{X}$, which may of course be infinite in size) will far exceed the amount of data that can be annotated. As the annotation task becomes more complicated (e.g., when predicting more complex structures such as sequences of labels or when the annotation task requires specialized expertise), annotation becomes far more challenging.

Unsupervised learning, on the other hand, requires only that the training data consist of a representative collection of objects that should be annotated, that is $\mathcal{Z} = \langle x_1, x_2, \ldots \rangle$ where $x_i \in \mathcal{X}$, but *without* any example annotations. While it may at first seem counterintuitive that meaningful annotations can be learned without any examples of the desired annotations being given, the learning criteria and model structure (which crucially define the space of possible annotations $\mathcal{Y}$ and the process by which annotations relate to observable inputs) make it possible to induce annotations by relying on regularities in the unclassified training instances. While a thorough discussion of unsupervised learning is beyond the scope of this book, we focus on a particular class of algorithms—expectation maximization (EM) algorithms—that can be used to learn the parameters of a joint model $\Pr(x, y)$ from incomplete data (i.e., data where some of the variables in the model cannot be observed; in the case of unsupervised learning, the y_i's are unobserved). Expectation maximization algorithms fit naturally into the MapReduce paradigm, and are used to solve a number of problems of interest in text processing. Furthermore, these algorithms can be quite computationally expensive, since they generally require repeated evaluations of the training data. MapReduce therefore provides an opportunity not only to scale to larger amounts of data, but also to improve efficiency bottlenecks at scales where non-parallel solutions could be utilized.

This chapter is organized as follows. In Section 6.1, we describe maximum likelihood estimation for statistical models, show how this is generalized to models where not all variables are observable, and then introduce expectation maximization (EM). We describe hidden Markov models (HMMs) in Section 6.2, a very versatile class of models that uses EM for parameter estimation. Section 6.3 discusses how EM algorithms can be expressed in MapReduce, and then in Section 6.4 we look at a case study of word alignment for statistical machine translation. Section 6.5 examines similar algorithms that are appropriate for supervised learning tasks. This chapter concludes with a summary and pointers to additional readings.

6.1　EXPECTATION MAXIMIZATION

Expectation maximization (EM) algorithms [49] are a family of iterative optimization algorithms for learning probability distributions from incomplete data. They are extensively used in statistical natural language processing where one seeks to infer latent linguistic structure from unannotated text. To name just a few applications, EM algorithms have been used to find part-of-speech sequences, constituency and dependency trees, alignments between texts in different languages, alignments between acoustic signals and their transcriptions, as well as for numerous other clustering and structure discovery problems.

Expectation maximization generalizes the principle of maximum likelihood estimation to the case where the values of some variables are unobserved (specifically, those characterizing the latent structure that is sought).

6.1.1　MAXIMUM LIKELIHOOD ESTIMATION

Maximum likelihood estimation (MLE) is a criterion for fitting the parameters θ of a statistical model to some given data $\mathbf{x}$. Specifically, it says to select the parameter settings θ^* such that the likelihood of observing the training data given the model is maximized:

$$\theta^* = \arg\max_{\theta} \Pr(\mathbf{X} = \mathbf{x}; \theta) \qquad (6.1)$$

To illustrate, consider the simple marble game shown in Figure 6.1. In this game, a marble is released at the position indicated by the black dot, and it bounces down into one of the cups at the bottom of the board, being diverted to the left or right by the peg (indicated by a triangle) in the center. Our task is to construct a model that predicts which cup the ball will drop into. A "rule-based" approach might be to take exact measurements of the board and construct a physical model that we can use to predict the behavior of the ball. Given sophisticated enough measurements, this could certainly lead to a very accurate model. However, the construction of this model would be quite time consuming and difficult.

A statistical approach, on the other hand, might be to assume that the behavior of the marble in this game can be modeled using a Bernoulli random variable Y with parameter p. That is, the value of the random variable indicates whether path 0 or 1 is taken. We also define a random variable X whose value is the label of the cup that the marble ends up in; note that X is deterministically related to Y, so an observation of X is equivalent to an observation of Y.

To estimate the parameter p of the statistical model of our game, we need some *training data*, so we drop 10 marbles into the game which end up in cups $\mathbf{x} = \langle b, b, b, a, b, b, b, b, b, a \rangle$.

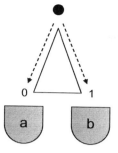

Figure 6.1: A simple marble game where a released marble takes one of two possible paths. This game can be modeled using a Bernoulli random variable with parameter p, which indicates the probability that the marble will go to the right when it hits the peg.

What is the maximum likelihood estimate of p given this data? By assuming that our samples are independent and identically distributed (i.i.d.), we can write the likelihood of our data as follows:[3]

$$
\begin{aligned}
\Pr(\mathbf{x}; p) &= \prod_{j=1}^{10} p^{\delta(x_j, a)}(1 - p)^{\delta(x_j, b)} \\
&= p^2 \cdot (1 - p)^8
\end{aligned}
$$

Since log is a monotonically increasing function, maximizing $\log \Pr(\mathbf{x}; p)$ will give us the desired result. We can do this differentiating with respect to p and finding where the resulting expression equals 0:

$$
\begin{aligned}
\frac{d \log \Pr(\mathbf{x}; p)}{dp} &= 0 \\
\frac{d[2 \cdot \log p + 8 \cdot \log(1 - p)]}{dp} &= 0 \\
\frac{2}{p} - \frac{8}{1 - p} &= 0
\end{aligned}
$$

Solving for p yields 0.2, which is the intuitive result. Furthermore, it is straightforward to show that in N trials where N_0 marbles followed path 0 to cup a, and N_1 marbles followed path 1 to cup b, the maximum likelihood estimate of p is $N_1/(N_0 + N_1)$.

While this model only makes use of an approximation of the true physical process at work when the marble interacts with the game board, it is an empirical question whether the model works well enough in practice to be useful. Additionally, while a Bernoulli trial is an extreme approximation of the physical process, if insufficient resources were invested in building a physical model,

---

[3]In this equation, δ is the Kroneker delta function which evaluates to 1 where its arguments are equal and 0 otherwise.

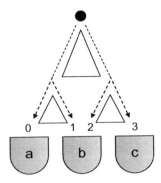

Figure 6.2: A more complicated marble game where the released marble takes one of four possible paths. We assume that we can only observe which cup the marble ends up in, not the specific path taken.

the approximation may perform better than the more complicated "rule-based" model. This sort of dynamic is found often in text processing problems: given enough data, astonishingly simple models can outperform complex knowledge-intensive models that attempt to simulate complicated processes.

6.1.2   A LATENT VARIABLE MARBLE GAME

To see where latent variables might come into play in modeling, consider a more complicated variant of our marble game shown in Figure 6.2. This version consists of three pegs that influence the marble's path, and the marble may end up in one of three cups. Note that both paths 1 and 2 lead to cup b.

To construct a statistical model of this game, we again assume that the behavior of a marble interacting with a peg can be modeled with a Bernoulli random variable. Since there are three pegs, we have three random variables with parameters $\theta = \langle p_0, p_1, p_2 \rangle$, corresponding to the probabilities that the marble will go to the right at the top, left, and right pegs. We further define a random variable X taking on values from $\{a, b, c\}$ indicating what cup the marble ends in, and Y, taking on values from $\{0, 1, 2, 3\}$ indicating which path was taken. Note that the full joint distribution $\Pr(X = x, Y = y)$ is determined by θ.

How should the parameters θ be estimated? If it were possible to observe the paths taken by marbles as they were dropped into the game, it would be trivial to estimate the parameters for our model using the maximum likelihood estimator—we would simply need to count the number of times the marble bounced left or right at each peg. If N_x counts the number of times a marble took path x in N trials, this is:

$$p_0 = \frac{N_2 + N_3}{N} \qquad p_1 = \frac{N_1}{N_0 + N_1} \qquad p_2 = \frac{N_3}{N_2 + N_3}$$

However, we wish to consider the case where the paths taken are *unobservable* (imagine an opaque sheet covering the center of the game board), but where we can see what cup a marble ends in. In other words, we want to consider the case where we have *partial* data. This is exactly the problem encountered in unsupervised learning: there is a statistical model describing the relationship between two sets of variables (X's and Y's), and there is data available from just one of them. Furthermore, such algorithms are quite useful in text processing, where latent variables may describe latent linguistic structures of the observed variables, such as parse trees or part-of-speech tags, or alignment structures relating sets of observed variables (see Section 6.4).

6.1.3 MLE WITH LATENT VARIABLES

Formally, we consider the problem of estimating parameters for statistical models of the form $\Pr(X, Y; \theta)$ which describe not only an observable variable X but a latent, or hidden, variable Y.

In these models, since only the values of the random variable X are observable, we define our optimization criterion to be the maximization of the *marginal* likelihood, that is, summing over all settings of the latent variable Y, which takes on values from set designated $\mathcal{Y}$:[4] Again, we assume that samples in the training data $\mathbf{x}$ are i.i.d.:

$$\Pr(X = x) = \sum_{y \in \mathcal{Y}} \Pr(X = x, Y = y; \theta)$$

For a vector of training observations $\mathbf{x} = \langle x_1, x_2, \ldots, x_\ell \rangle$, if we assume the samples are i.i.d.:

$$\Pr(\mathbf{x}; \theta) = \prod_{j=1}^{|\mathbf{x}|} \sum_{y \in \mathcal{Y}} \Pr(X = x_j, Y = y; \theta)$$

Thus, the maximum (marginal) likelihood estimate of the model parameters θ^* given a vector of i.i.d. observations $\mathbf{x}$ becomes:

$$\theta^* = \arg\max_{\theta} \prod_{j=1}^{|\mathbf{x}|} \sum_{y \in \mathcal{Y}} \Pr(X = x_j, Y = y; \theta)$$

Unfortunately, in many cases, this maximum cannot be computed analytically, but the iterative hill-climbing approach of expectation maximization can be used instead.

---

[4]For this description, we assume that the variables in our model take on discrete values. Not only does this simplify exposition, but discrete models are widely used in text processing.

6.1.4   EXPECTATION MAXIMIZATION

Expectation maximization (EM) is an iterative algorithm that finds a successive series of parameter estimates $\theta^{(0)}, \theta^{(1)}, \ldots$ that improve the marginal likelihood of the training data. That is, EM guarantees:

$$\prod_{j=1}^{|x|} \sum_{y \in \mathcal{Y}} \Pr(X = x_j, Y = y; \theta^{(i+1)}) \geq \prod_{j=1}^{|x|} \sum_{y \in \mathcal{Y}} \Pr(X = x_j, Y = y; \theta^{(i)})$$

The algorithm starts with some initial set of parameters $\theta^{(0)}$ and then updates them using two steps: expectation (E-step), which computes the posterior distribution over the latent variables given the observable data $\mathbf{x}$ and a set of parameters $\theta^{(i)}$,[5] and maximization (M-step), which computes new parameters $\theta^{(i+1)}$ maximizing the expected log likelihood of the joint distribution with respect to the distribution computed in the E-step. The process then repeats with these new parameters. The algorithm terminates when the likelihood remains unchanged.[6] In more detail, the steps are as follows:

E-step.   Compute the posterior probability of each possible hidden variable assignments $y \in \mathcal{Y}$ for each $x \in \mathcal{X}$ and the current parameter settings, weighted by the relative frequency with which x occurs in $\mathbf{x}$. Call this $q(X = x, Y = y; \theta^{(i)})$ and note that it defines a joint probability distribution over $\mathcal{X} \times \mathcal{Y}$ in that $\sum_{(x,y) \in \mathcal{X} \times \mathcal{Y}} q(x, y) = 1$.

$$q(x, y; \theta^{(i)}) = f(x|\mathbf{x}) \cdot \Pr(Y = y | X = x; \theta^{(i)}) = f(x|\mathbf{x}) \cdot \frac{\Pr(x, y; \theta^{(i)})}{\sum_{y'} \Pr(x, y'; \theta^{(i)})}$$

M-step.   Compute new parameter settings that maximize the expected log of the probability of the joint distribution under the q-distribution that was computed in the E-step:

$$
\begin{aligned}
\theta^{(i+1)} &= \arg \max_{\theta'} \mathbb{E}_{q(X=x, Y=y; \theta^{(i)})} \log \Pr(X = x, Y = y; \theta') \\
&= \arg \max_{\theta'} \sum_{(x,y) \in \mathcal{X} \times \mathcal{Y}} q(X = x, Y = y; \theta^{(i)}) \cdot \log \Pr(X = x, Y = y; \theta')
\end{aligned}
$$

We omit the proof that the model with parameters $\theta^{(i+1)}$ will have equal or greater marginal likelihood on the training data than the model with parameters $\theta^{(i)}$, but this is provably true [78].

Before continuing, we note that the effective application of expectation maximization requires that both the E-step and the M-step consist of tractable computations. Specifically, summing

---

[5]The term 'expectation' is used since the values computed in terms of the posterior distribution $\Pr(y|x; \theta^{(i)})$ that are required to solve the M-step have the form of an expectation (with respect to this distribution).

[6]The final solution is only guaranteed to be a *local maximum*, but if the model is fully convex, it will also be the global maximum.

over the space of hidden variable assignments must not be intractable. Depending on the independence assumptions made in the model, this may be achieved through techniques such as dynamic programming. However, some models may require intractable computations.

6.1.5   AN EM EXAMPLE

Let's look at how to estimate the parameters from our latent variable marble game from Section 6.1.2 using EM. We assume training data $\mathbf{x}$ consisting of $N = |\mathbf{x}|$ observations of X with N_a, N_b, and N_c indicating the number of marbles ending in cups a, b, and c. We start with some parameters $\theta^{(0)} = \langle p_0^{(0)}, p_1^{(0)}, p_2^{(0)} \rangle$ that have been randomly initialized to values between 0 and 1.

E-step.   We need to compute the distribution $q(X = x, Y = y; \theta^{(i)})$, as defined above. We first note that the relative frequency $f(x|\mathbf{x})$ is:

$$f(x|\mathbf{x}) = \frac{N_x}{N}$$

Next, we observe that $\Pr(Y = 0|X = a) = 1$ and $\Pr(Y = 3|X = c) = 1$ since cups a and c fully determine the value of the path variable Y. The posterior probability of paths 1 and 2 are only non-zero when X is b:

$$\Pr(1|b; \theta^{(i)}) = \frac{(1 - p_0^{(i)})p_1^{(i)}}{(1 - p_0^{(i)})p_1^{(i)} + p_0^{(i)}(1 - p_2^{(i)})} \qquad \Pr(2|b; \theta^{(i)}) = \frac{p_0^{(i)}(1 - p_2^{(i)})}{(1 - p_0^{(i)})p_1^{(i)} + p_0^{(i)}(1 - p_2^{(i)})}$$

Except for the four cases just described, $\Pr(Y = y|X = x)$ is zero for all other values of x and y (regardless of the value of the parameters).

M-step.   We now need to maximize the expectation of $\log \Pr(X, Y; \theta')$ (which will be a function in terms of the three parameter variables) under the q-distribution we computed in the E step. The non-zero terms in the expectation are as follows:

x	y	$q(X = x, Y = y; \theta^{(i)})$	$\log \Pr(X = x, Y = y; \theta')$
a	0	N_a/N	$\log(1 - p_0') + \log(1 - p_1')$
b	1	$N_b/N \cdot \Pr(1|b; \theta^{(i)})$	$\log(1 - p_0') + \log p_1'$
b	2	$N_b/N \cdot \Pr(2|b; \theta^{(i)})$	$\log p_0' + \log(1 - p_2')$
c	3	N_c/N	$\log p_0' + \log p_2'$

Multiplying across each row and adding from top to bottom yields the expectation we wish to maximize. Each parameter can be optimized independently using differentiation. The resulting optimal values are expressed in terms of the counts in $\mathbf{x}$ and $\theta^{(i)}$:

$$p_0 = \frac{\Pr(2|b; \theta^{(i)}) \cdot N_b + N_c}{N} \qquad p_1 = \frac{\Pr(1|b; \theta^{(i)}) \cdot N_b}{N_a + \Pr(1|b; \theta^{(i)}) \cdot N_b} \qquad p_2 = \frac{N_c}{\Pr(2|b; \theta^{(i)}) \cdot N_b + N_c}$$

It is worth noting that the form of these expressions is quite similar to the fully observed maximum likelihood estimate. However, rather than depending on *exact* path counts, the statistics used are the *expected* path counts, given $\mathbf{x}$ and parameters $\theta^{(i)}$.

Typically, the values computed at the end of the M-step would serve as new parameters for another iteration of EM. However, the example we have presented here is quite simple and the model converges to a global optimum after a single iteration. For most models, EM requires several iterations to converge, and it may not find a global optimum. And since EM only finds a locally optimal solution, the final parameter values depend on the values chose for $\theta^{(0)}$.

6.2 HIDDEN MARKOV MODELS

To give a more substantial and useful example of models whose parameters may be estimated using EM, we turn to hidden Markov models (HMMs). HMMs are models of data that are ordered *sequentially* (temporally, from left to right, etc.), such as words in a sentence, base pairs in a gene, or letters in a word. These simple but powerful models have been used in applications as diverse as speech recognition [78], information extraction [139], gene finding [143], part-of-speech tagging [44], stock market forecasting [70], text retrieval [108], and word alignment of parallel (translated) texts [150] (more in Section 6.4).

In an HMM, the data being modeled is posited to have been generated from an underlying *Markov process*, which is a stochastic process consisting of a finite set of states where the probability of entering a state at time $t + 1$ depends only on the state of the process at time t [130]. Alternatively, one can view a Markov process as a probabilistic variant of a finite state machine, where transitions are taken probabilistically. As another point of comparison, the PageRank algorithm considered in the previous chapter (Section 5.3) can be understood as a Markov process: the probability of following any link on a particular page is independent of the path taken to reach that page. The states of this Markov process are, however, not directly observable (i.e., *hidden*). Instead, at each time step, an observable token (e.g., a word, base pair, or letter) is emitted according to a probability distribution conditioned on the identity of the state that the underlying process is in.

A hidden Markov model $\mathcal{M}$ is defined as a tuple $\langle \mathcal{S}, \mathcal{O}, \theta \rangle$. $\mathcal{S}$ is a finite set of states, which generate symbols from a finite observation vocabulary $\mathcal{O}$. Following convention, we assume that variables q, r, and s refer to states in $\mathcal{S}$, and o refers to symbols in the observation vocabulary $\mathcal{O}$. This model is parameterized by the tuple $\theta = \langle A, B, \pi \rangle$ consisting of an $|\mathcal{S}| \times |\mathcal{S}|$ matrix A of *transition probabilities*, where $A_q(r)$ gives the probability of transitioning from state q to state r; an $|\mathcal{S}| \times |\mathcal{O}|$ matrix B of *emission probabilities*, where $B_q(o)$ gives the probability that symbol o will be emitted from state q; and an $|\mathcal{S}|$-dimensional vector π, where π_q is the probability that the process starts in state q.[7] These matrices may be dense, but for many applications sparse parameterizations

---

[7]This is only one possible definition of an HMM, but it is one that is useful for many text processing problems. In alternative definitions, initial and final states may be handled differently, observations may be emitted during the transition between states, or continuous-valued observations may be emitted (for example, from a Gaussian distribution).

are useful. We further stipulate that $A_q(r) \geq 0$, $B_q(o) \geq 0$, and $\pi_q \geq 0$ for all q, r, and o, as well as that:

$$\sum_{r \in \mathcal{S}} A_q(r) = 1 \; \forall q \qquad \sum_{o \in \mathcal{O}} B_q(o) = 1 \; \forall q \qquad \sum_{q \in \mathcal{S}} \pi_q = 1$$

A sequence of observations of length τ is generated as follows:

Step 0: let $t = 1$ and select an initial state q according to the distribution π.

Step 1: an observation symbol from $\mathcal{O}$ is emitted according to the distribution B_q.

Step 2: a new q is drawn according to the distribution A_q.

Step 3: t is incremented, and if $t \leq \tau$, the process repeats from Step 1.

Since all events generated by this process are conditionally independent, the joint probability of this sequence of observations and the state sequence used to generate it is the product of the individual event probabilities.

Figure 6.3 shows a simple example of a hidden Markov model for part-of-speech tagging, which is the task of assigning to each word in an input sentence its grammatical category (one of the first steps in analyzing textual content). States $\mathcal{S} = \{$DET, ADJ, NN, V $\}$ correspond to the parts of speech (determiner, adjective, noun, and verb), and observations $\mathcal{O} = \{$the, a, green, . . .$\}$ are a subset of English words. This example illustrates a key intuition behind many applications of HMMs: states correspond to equivalence classes or clustering of observations, and a single observation type may associated with several clusters (in this example, the word wash can be generated by an NN or V, since wash can either be a noun or a verb).

6.2.1 THREE QUESTIONS FOR HIDDEN MARKOV MODELS

There are three fundamental questions associated with hidden Markov models:[8]

1. Given a model $\mathcal{M} = \langle \mathcal{S}, \mathcal{O}, \theta \rangle$, and an observation sequence of symbols from $\mathcal{O}$, $\mathbf{x} = \langle x_1, x_2, \dots, x_\tau \rangle$, what is the probability that $\mathcal{M}$ generated the data (summing over all possible state sequences, $\mathcal{Y}$)?

$$\Pr(\mathbf{x}) = \sum_{y \in \mathcal{Y}} \Pr(\mathbf{x}, \mathbf{y}; \theta)$$

2. Given a model $\mathcal{M} = \langle \mathcal{S}, \mathcal{O}, \theta \rangle$ and an observation sequence $\mathbf{x}$, what is the most likely sequence of states that generated the data?

$$\mathbf{y}^* = \arg \max_{y \in \mathcal{Y}} \Pr(\mathbf{x}, \mathbf{y}; \theta)$$

---

[8]The organization of this section is based in part on ideas from Lawrence Rabiner's HMM tutorial [125].

Initial probabilities:

DET	ADJ	NN	V
0.5	0.1	0.3	0.1

Transition probabilities:

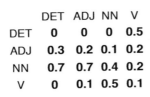

	DET	ADJ	NN	V
DET	0	0	0	0.5
ADJ	0.3	0.2	0.1	0.2
NN	0.7	0.7	0.4	0.2
V	0	0.1	0.5	0.1

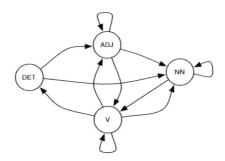

Emission probabilities:

DET		ADJ		NN		V	
the	0.7	green	0.1	book	0.3	might	0.2
a	0.3	big	0.4	plants	0.2	wash	0.3
		old	0.4	people	0.2	washes	0.2
		might	0.1	person	0.1	loves	0.1
				John	0.1	reads	0.19
				wash	0.1	books	0.01

Example outputs:

John might wash
NN   V   V

the big green person loves old plants
DET ADJ ADJ   NN   V   ADJ   NN

plants washes books books books
NN   V   V   NN   V

Figure 6.3: An example HMM that relates part-of-speech tags to vocabulary items in an English-like language. Possible (probability > 0) transitions for the Markov process are shown graphically. In the example outputs, the state sequences corresponding to the emissions are written beneath the emitted symbols.

3. Given a set of states $\mathcal{S}$, an observation vocabulary $\mathcal{O}$, and a series of ℓ i.i.d. observation sequences $\langle \mathbf{x}_1, \mathbf{x}_2, \ldots, \mathbf{x}_\ell \rangle$, what are the parameters $\theta = \langle A, B, \pi \rangle$ that maximize the likelihood of the training data?

$$\theta^* = \arg\max_\theta \prod_{i=1}^{\ell} \sum_{\mathbf{y} \in \mathcal{Y}} \Pr(\mathbf{x}_i, \mathbf{y}; \theta)$$

Using our definition of an HMM, the answers to the first two questions are in principle quite trivial to compute: by iterating over all state sequences $\mathcal{Y}$, the probability that each generated $\mathbf{x}$ can be computed by looking up and multiplying the relevant probabilities in A, B, and π, and then summing the result or taking the maximum. And, as we hinted at in the previous section, the third question can be answered using EM. Unfortunately, even with all the distributed computing power MapReduce makes available, we will quickly run into trouble if we try to use this naïve strategy since there are $|\mathcal{S}|^\tau$ distinct state sequences of length τ, making exhaustive enumeration computationally intractable. Fortunately, because the underlying model behaves exactly the same whenever it is in some state, regardless of how it got to that state, we can use dynamic programming algorithms to answer all of the above questions without summing over exponentially many sequences.

6.2.2 THE FORWARD ALGORITHM

Given some observation sequence, for example $\mathbf{x} = \langle \texttt{John}, \texttt{might}, \texttt{wash} \rangle$, Question 1 asks what is the probability that this sequence was generated by an HMM $\mathcal{M} = \langle \mathcal{S}, \mathcal{O}, \theta \rangle$. For the purposes of illustration, we assume that $\mathcal{M}$ is defined as shown in Figure 6.3.

There are two ways to compute the probability of $\mathbf{x}$ having been generated by $\mathcal{M}$. The first is to compute the sum over the joint probability of $\mathbf{x}$ and every possible labeling $\mathbf{y}' \in \{\langle$ DET , DET, DET$\rangle$, $\langle$DET , DET, NN$\rangle$, $\langle$DET, DET, V$\rangle$, $\ldots\}$. As indicated above, this is not feasible for most sequences, since the set of possible labels is exponential in the length of $\mathbf{x}$. The second, fortunately, is much more efficient.

We can make use of what is known as the *forward algorithm* to compute the desired probability in polynomial time. We assume a model $\mathcal{M} = \langle \mathcal{S}, \mathcal{O}, \theta \rangle$ as defined above. This algorithm works by recursively computing the answer to a related question: what is the probability that the process is in state q at time t and has generated $\langle x_1, x_2, \ldots, x_t \rangle$? Call this probability $\alpha_t(q)$. Thus, $\alpha_t(q)$ is a two dimensional matrix (of size $|\mathbf{x}| \times |\mathcal{S}|$), called a *trellis*. It is easy to see that the values of $\alpha_1(q)$ can be computed as the product of two independent probabilities: the probability of starting in state q and the probability of state q generating x_1:

$$\alpha_1(q) = \pi_q \cdot B_q(x_1)$$

From this, it's not hard to see that the values of $\alpha_2(r)$ for every r can be computed in terms of the $|\mathcal{S}|$ values in $\alpha_1(\cdot)$ and the observation x_2:

$$\alpha_2(r) = B_r(x_2) \cdot \sum_{q \in S} \alpha_1(q) \cdot A_q(r)$$

This works because there are $|S|$ different ways to get to state r at time $t = 2$: starting from state $1, 2, \ldots, |S|$ and transitioning to state r. Furthermore, because the behavior of a Markov process is determined only by the state it is in at some time (not by how it got to that state), $\alpha_t(r)$ can always be computed in terms of the $|S|$ values in $\alpha_{t-1}(\cdot)$ and the observation x_t:

$$\alpha_t(r) \quad = \quad B_r(x_t) \cdot \sum_{q \in S} \alpha_{t-1}(q) \cdot A_q(r)$$

We have now shown how to compute the probability of being in any state q at any time t, having generated $\langle x_1, x_2, \ldots, x_t \rangle$, with the forward algorithm. The probability of the full sequence is the probability of being in time $|\mathbf{x}|$ and in *any* state, so the answer to Question 1 can be computed simply by summing over α values at time $|\mathbf{x}|$ for all states:

$$\Pr(\mathbf{x}; \theta) = \sum_{q \in S} \alpha_{|\mathbf{x}|}(q)$$

In summary, there are two ways of computing the probability that a sequence of observations $\mathbf{x}$ was generated by $\mathcal{M}$: exhaustive enumeration with summing and the forward algorithm. Figure 6.4 illustrates the two possibilities. The upper panel shows the naïve exhaustive approach, enumerating all 4^3 possible labels $\mathbf{y}'$ of $\mathbf{x}$ and computing their joint probability $\Pr(\mathbf{x}, \mathbf{y}')$. Summing over all $\mathbf{y}'$, the marginal probability of $\mathbf{x}$ is found to be 0.00018. The lower panel shows the forward trellis, consisting of 4×3 cells. Summing over the final column also yields 0.00018, the same result.

6.2.3   THE VITERBI ALGORITHM

Given an observation sequence $\mathbf{x}$, the second question we might want to ask of $\mathcal{M}$ is: what is the most likely sequence of states that generated the observations? As with the previous question, the naïve approach to solving this problem is to enumerate all possible labels and find the one with the highest joint probability. Continuing with the example observation sequence $\mathbf{x} = \langle \texttt{John}, \texttt{might}, \texttt{wash} \rangle$, examining the chart of probabilities in the upper panel of Figure 6.4 shows that $\mathbf{y}^* = \langle \text{NN}, \text{V}, \text{V} \rangle$ is the most likely sequence of states under our example HMM.

However, a more efficient answer to Question 2 can be computed using the same intuition in the forward algorithm: determine the best state sequence for a short sequence and extend this to easily compute the best sequence for longer ones. This is known as the *Viterbi algorithm*. We define $\gamma_t(q)$, the Viterbi probability, to be the most probable sequence of states ending in state q at time t and generating observations $\langle x_1, x_2, \ldots, x_t \rangle$. Since we wish to be able to reconstruct the sequence

John	might	wash	p(x,y)	John	might	wash	p(x,y)	John	might	wash	p(x,y)	John	might	wash	p(x,y)
DET	DET	DET	0.0	ADJ	DET	DET	0.0	NN	DET	DET	0.0	V	DET	DET	0.0
DET	DET	ADJ	0.0	ADJ	DET	ADJ	0.0	NN	DET	ADJ	0.0	V	DET	ADJ	0.0
DET	DET	NN	0.0	ADJ	DET	NN	0.0	NN	DET	NN	0.0	V	DET	NN	0.0
DET	DET	V	0.0	ADJ	DET	V	0.0	NN	DET	V	0.0	V	DET	V	0.0
DET	ADJ	DET	0.0	ADJ	ADJ	DET	0.0	NN	ADJ	DET	0.0	V	ADJ	DET	0.0
DET	ADJ	ADJ	0.0	ADJ	ADJ	ADJ	0.0	NN	ADJ	ADJ	0.0	V	ADJ	ADJ	0.0
DET	ADJ	NN	0.0	ADJ	ADJ	NN	0.0	NN	ADJ	NN	0.000021	V	ADJ	NN	0.0
DET	ADJ	V	0.0	ADJ	ADJ	V	0.0	NN	ADJ	V	0.000009	V	ADJ	V	0.0
DET	NN	DET	0.0	ADJ	NN	DET	0.0	NN	NN	DET	0.0	V	NN	DET	0.0
DET	NN	ADJ	0.0	ADJ	NN	ADJ	0.0	NN	NN	ADJ	0.0	V	NN	ADJ	0.0
DET	NN	NN	0.0	ADJ	NN	NN	0.0	NN	NN	NN	0.0	V	NN	NN	0.0
DET	NN	V	0.0	ADJ	NN	V	0.0	NN	NN	V	0.0	V	NN	V	0.0
DET	V	DET	0.0	ADJ	V	DET	0.0	NN	V	DET	0.0	V	V	DET	0.0
DET	V	ADJ	0.0	ADJ	V	ADJ	0.0	NN	V	ADJ	0.0	V	V	ADJ	0.0
DET	V	NN	0.0	ADJ	V	NN	0.0	NN	V	NN	0.00006	V	V	NN	0.0
DET	V	V	0.0	ADJ	V	V	0.0	NN	V	V	0.00009	V	V	V	0.0

$$\Pr(\mathbf{x}) = \sum_{\mathbf{y} \in \mathcal{Y}} \Pr(\mathbf{x}, \mathbf{y}; \theta) = 0.00018$$

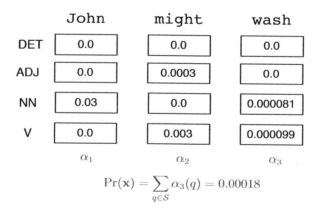

	John	might	wash
DET	0.0	0.0	0.0
ADJ	0.0	0.0003	0.0
NN	0.03	0.0	0.000081
V	0.0	0.003	0.000099
	α_1	α_2	α_3

$$\Pr(\mathbf{x}) = \sum_{q \in S} \alpha_3(q) = 0.00018$$

Figure 6.4: Computing the probability of the sequence ⟨John, might, wash⟩ under the HMM given in Figure 6.3 by explicitly summing over all possible sequence labels (upper panel) and using the forward algorithm (lower panel).

of states, we define $bp_t(q)$, the "backpointer", to be the state used in this sequence at time $t - 1$. The base case for the recursion is as follows (the state index of -1 is used as a placeholder since there is no previous best state at time $t = 1$):

$$\gamma_1(q) = \pi_q \cdot B_q(x_1)$$
$$bp_1(q) = -1$$

The recursion is similar to that of the forward algorithm, except rather than summing over previous states, the *maximum* value of all possible trajectories into state r at time t is computed. Note that the backpointer simply records the index of the originating state—a separate computation is not necessary.

$$\gamma_t(r) = \max_{q \in S} \gamma_{t-1}(q) \cdot A_q(r) \cdot B_r(x_t)$$
$$bp_t(r) = \arg\max_{q \in S} \gamma_{t-1}(q) \cdot A_q(r) \cdot B_r(x_t)$$

To compute the best sequence of states, $\mathbf{y}^*$, the state with the highest probability path at time $|\mathbf{x}|$ is selected, and then the backpointers are followed, recursively, to construct the rest of the sequence:

$$y_{|\mathbf{x}|}^* = \arg\max_{q \in S} \gamma_{|\mathbf{x}|}(q)$$
$$y_{t-1}^* = bp_t(y_t)$$

Figure 6.5 illustrates a Viterbi trellis, including backpointers that have been used to compute the most likely state sequence.

6.2.4   PARAMETER ESTIMATION FOR HMMS

We now turn to Question 3: given a set of states S and observation vocabulary O, what are the parameters $\theta^* = \langle A, B, \pi \rangle$ that maximize the likelihood of a set of training examples, $\langle \mathbf{x}_1, \mathbf{x}_2, \ldots, \mathbf{x}_\ell \rangle$?[9] Since our model is constructed in terms of variables whose values we cannot observe (the state sequence) in the training data, we may train it to optimize the marginal likelihood (summing over *all* state sequences) of $\mathbf{x}$ using EM. Deriving the EM update equations requires only the application of the techniques presented earlier in this chapter and some differential calculus. However, since the formalism is cumbersome, we will skip a detailed derivation, but readers interested in more information can find it in the relevant citations [78; 125].

In order to make the update equations as intuitive as possible, consider a fully observable HMM, that is, one where both the emissions and the state sequence are observable in all ℓ training instances. In this case, a training instance can be depicted as shown in Figure 6.6. When this is the

[9]Since an HMM models sequences, training data consist of a collection of example sequences.

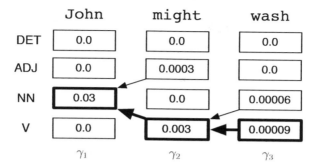

Figure 6.5: Computing the most likely state sequence that generated ⟨John, might, wash⟩ under the HMM given in Figure 6.3 using the Viterbi algorithm. The most likely state sequence is highlighted in bold and could be recovered programmatically by following backpointers from the maximal probability cell in the last column to the first column (thicker arrows).

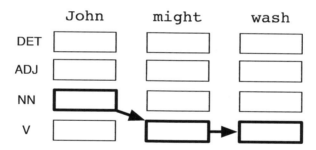

Figure 6.6: A "fully observable" HMM training instance. The output sequence is at the top of the figure, and the corresponding states and transitions are shown in the trellis below.

case, such as when we have a corpus of sentences in which all words have already been tagged with their parts of speech, the maximum likelihood estimate for the parameters can be computed in terms of the counts of the number of times the process transitions from state q to state r in all training instances, $T(q \rightarrow r)$; the number of times that state q emits symbol o, $O(q \uparrow o)$; and the number of times the process starts in state q, $I(q)$. In this example, the process starts in state NN; there is one NN→ v transition and one $v \rightarrow v$ transition. The NN state emits John in the first time step, and v state emits might and wash in the second and third time steps, respectively. We also define $N(q)$ to be the number of times the process enters state q. The maximum likelihood estimates of the parameters in the fully observable case are:

$$\pi_q = \frac{I(q)}{\ell = \sum_r I(r)} \qquad A_q(r) = \frac{T(q \to r)}{N(q) = \sum_{r'} T(q \to r')} \qquad B_q(o) = \frac{O(q \uparrow o)}{N(q) = \sum_{o'} O(q \uparrow o')} \tag{6.2}$$

For example, to compute the emission parameters from state NN, we simply need to keep track of the number of times the process is in state NN and what symbol it generated at each of these times. Transition probabilities are computed similarly: to compute, for example, the distribution $A_{\det}(\cdot)$, that is, the probabilities of transitioning away from state DET, we count the number of times the process is in state DET, and keep track of what state the process transitioned into at the next time step. This counting and normalizing be accomplished using the exact same counting and relative frequency algorithms that we described in Section 3.3. Thus, in the fully observable case, parameter estimation is not a new algorithm at all, but one we have seen before.

How should the model parameters be estimated when the state sequence is not provided? It turns out that the update equations have the satisfying form where the optimal parameter values for iteration $i + 1$ are expressed in terms of the *expectations* of the counts referenced in the fully observed case, according to the posterior distribution over the latent variables given the observations $\mathbf{x}$ and the parameters $\theta^{(i)}$:

$$\pi_q = \frac{\mathbb{E}[I(q)]}{\ell} \qquad A_q(r) = \frac{\mathbb{E}[T(q \to r)]}{\mathbb{E}[N(q)]} \qquad B_q(o) = \frac{\mathbb{E}[O(q \uparrow o)]}{\mathbb{E}[N(q)]} \tag{6.3}$$

Because of the independence assumptions made in the HMM, the update equations consist of $2 \cdot |\mathcal{S}| + 1$ independent optimization problems, just as was the case with the 'observable' HMM. Solving for the initial state distribution, π, is one problem; there are $|\mathcal{S}|$ solving for the transition distributions $A_q(\cdot)$ from each state q; and $|\mathcal{S}|$ solving for the emissions distributions $B_q(\cdot)$ from each state q. Furthermore, we note that the following must hold:

$$\mathbb{E}[N(q)] = \sum_{r \in \mathcal{S}} \mathbb{E}[T(q \to r)] = \sum_{o \in \mathcal{O}} \mathbb{E}[O(q \uparrow o)]$$

As a result, the optimization problems (i.e., Equations 6.2) require completely independent sets of statistics, which we will utilize later to facilitate efficient parallelization in MapReduce.

How can the expectations in Equation 6.3 be understood? In the fully observed training case, between every time step, there is exactly one transition taken and the source and destination states are observable. By progressing through the Markov chain, we can let each transition count as '1', and we can accumulate the total number of times each kind of transition was taken (by each kind, we simply mean the number of times that one state follows another, for example, the number of times NN follows DET). These statistics can then in turn be used to compute the MLE for an 'observable' HMM, as described above. However, when the transition sequence is not observable (as is most often the case), we can instead imagine that at each time step, *every* possible transition (there are $|\mathcal{S}|^2$ of them, and typically $|\mathcal{S}|$ is quite small) is taken, with a particular probability. The probability used is the *posterior probability* of the transition, given the model and an observation sequence (we describe how to compute this value below). By summing over all the time steps in the training data, and using this probability as the 'count' (rather than '1' as in the observable case), we compute the *expected count* of the number of times a particular transition was taken, given the training sequence. Furthermore, since the training instances are statistically independent, the value of the expectations can be computed by processing each training instance independently and summing the results.

Similarly for the necessary emission counts (the number of times each symbol in $\mathcal{O}$ was generated by each state in $\mathcal{S}$), we assume that any state could have generated the observation. We must therefore compute the probability of being in every state at each time point, which is then the size of the emission 'count'. By summing over all time steps we compute the expected count of the number of times that a particular state generated a particular symbol. These two sets of expectations, which are written formally here, are sufficient to execute the M-step.

$$\mathbb{E}[O(q \uparrow o)] \quad = \quad \sum_{i=1}^{|\mathbf{x}|} \Pr(y_i = q|\mathbf{x}; \theta) \cdot \delta(x_i, o) \tag{6.4}$$

$$\mathbb{E}[T(q \to r)] \quad = \quad \sum_{i=1}^{|\mathbf{x}|-1} \Pr(y_i = q, y_{i+1} = r|\mathbf{x}; \theta) \tag{6.5}$$

Posterior probabilities.   The expectations necessary for computing the M-step in HMM training are sums of probabilities that a particular transition is taken, given an observation sequence, and that some state emits some observation symbol, given an observation sequence. These are referred to as posterior probabilities, indicating that they are the probability of some event whose distribution we have a prior belief about, after addition evidence has been taken into consideration (here, the model parameters characterize our prior beliefs, and the observation sequence is the evidence). Both posterior probabilities can be computed by combining the forward probabilities, $\alpha_t(\cdot)$, which give the probability of reaching some state at time t, by any path, and generating the observations $\langle x_1, x_2, \ldots, x_t \rangle$, with *backward probabilities*, $\beta_t(\cdot)$, which give the probability of starting in some state at time t and generating the rest of the sequence $\langle x_{t+1}, x_{t+2}, \ldots, x_{|\mathbf{x}|} \rangle$, using any sequence of states to do so. The algorithm for computing the backward probabilities is given a bit later. Once the forward and backward probabilities have been computed, the state transition posterior probabilities and the emission posterior probabilities can be written as follows:

$$\Pr(y_i = q|\mathbf{x}; \theta) \quad = \quad \alpha_i(q) \cdot \beta_i(q) \tag{6.6}$$
$$\Pr(y_i = q, y_{i+1} = r|\mathbf{x}; \theta) \quad = \quad \alpha_i(q) \cdot A_q(r) \cdot B_r(x_{i+1}) \cdot \beta_{i+1}(r) \tag{6.7}$$

Equation 6.6 is the probability of being in state q at time i, given $\mathbf{x}$, and the correctness of the expression should be clear from the definitions of forward and backward probabilities. The intuition for Equation 6.7, the probability of taking a particular transition at a particular time, is also not complicated. It is the product of four conditionally independent probabilities: the probability of

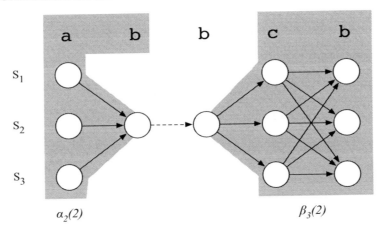

$$\alpha_2(2) \qquad\qquad\qquad\qquad\qquad \beta_3(2)$$

Figure 6.7: Using forward and backward probabilities to compute the posterior probability of the dashed transition, given the observation sequence a b b c b. The shaded area on the left corresponds to the forward probability $\alpha_2(s_2)$, and the shaded area on the right corresponds to the backward probability $\beta_3(s_2)$.

getting to state q at time i (having generated the first part of the sequence), the probability of taking transition $q \rightarrow r$ (which is specified in the parameters, θ), the probability of generating observation x_{i+1} from state r (also specified in θ), and the probability of generating the rest of the sequence, along any path. A visualization of the quantities used in computing this probability is shown in Figure 6.7. In this illustration, we assume an HMM with $\mathcal{S} = \{s_1, s_2, s_3\}$ and $\mathcal{O} = \{a, b, c\}$.

The backward algorithm.   Like the forward and Viterbi algorithms introduced above to answer Questions 1 and 2, the backward algorithm uses dynamic programming to incrementally compute $\beta_t(\cdot)$. Its base case starts at time $|\mathbf{x}|$, and is defined as follows:

$$\beta_{|\mathbf{x}|}(q) = 1$$

To understand the intuition of the base case, keep in mind that since the backward probabilities $\beta_t(\cdot)$ are the probability of generating the remainder of the sequence *after* time t (as well as being in some state), and since there is nothing left to generate after time $|\mathbf{x}|$, the probability must be 1. The recursion is defined as follows:

$$\beta_t(q) = \sum_{r \in \mathcal{S}} \beta_{t+1}(r) \cdot A_q(r) \cdot B_r(x_{t+1})$$

Unlike the forward and Viterbi algorithms, the backward algorithm is computed from right to left and makes no reference to the start probabilities, π.

6.2.5 FORWARD-BACKWARD TRAINING: SUMMARY

In the preceding section, we showed how to compute all quantities needed to find the parameter settings $\theta^{(i+1)}$ using EM training with a hidden Markov model $\mathcal{M} = \langle \mathcal{S}, \mathcal{O}, \theta^{(i)} \rangle$. To recap: each training instance $\mathbf{x}$ is processed independently, using the parameter settings of the current iteration, $\theta^{(i)}$. For each $\mathbf{x}$ in the training data, the forward and backward probabilities are computed using the algorithms given above (for this reason, this training algorithm is often referred to as the forward-backward algorithm). The forward and backward probabilities are in turn used to compute the expected number of times the underlying Markov process enters into each state, the number of times each state generates each output symbol type, and the number of times each state transitions into each other state. These expectations are summed over all training instances, completing the E-step. The M-step involves normalizing the expected counts computed in the E-step using the calculations in Equation 6.3, which yields $\theta^{(i+1)}$. The process then repeats from the E-step using the new parameters. The number of iterations required for convergence depends on the quality of the initial parameters, and the complexity of the model. For some applications, only a handful of iterations are necessary, whereas for others, hundreds may be required.

Finally, a few practical considerations: HMMs have a non-convex likelihood surface (meaning that it has the equivalent of many hills and valleys in the number of dimensions corresponding to the number of parameters in the model). EM training is only guaranteed to find a local maximum, and the quality of the learned model may vary considerably, depending on the initial parameters that are used. Strategies for optimal selection of initial parameters depend on the phenomena being modeled. Additionally, if some parameter is assigned a probability of 0 (either as an initial value or during one of the M-step parameter updates), EM will never change this in future iterations. This can be useful, since it provides a way of constraining the structures of the Markov model; however, one must be aware of this behavior.

Another pitfall to avoid when implementing HMMs is arithmetic underflow. HMMs typically define a massive number of sequences, and so the probability of any one of them is often vanishingly small—so small that they often underflow standard floating point representations. A very common solution to this problem is to represent probabilities using their logarithms. Note that expected counts do not typically have this problem and can be represented using normal floating point numbers. See Section 5.4 for additional discussion on working with log probabilities.

6.3 EM IN MAPREDUCE

Expectation maximization algorithms fit quite naturally into the MapReduce programming model. Although the model being optimized determines the details of the required computations, Map-Reduce implementations of EM algorithms share a number of characteristics:

- Each iteration of EM is one MapReduce job.

- A controlling process (i.e., driver program) spawns the MapReduce jobs and keeps track of the number of iterations and convergence criteria.

- Model parameters $\theta^{(i)}$, which are static for the duration of the MapReduce job, are loaded by each mapper from HDFS or other data provider (e.g., a distributed key-value store).

- Mappers map over independent training instances, computing partial latent variable posteriors (or summary statistics, such as expected counts).

- Reducers sum together the required training statistics *and* solve one or more of the M-step optimization problems.

- Combiners, which sum together the training statistics, are often quite effective at reducing the amount of data that must be shuffled across the network.

The degree of parallelization that can be attained depends on the statistical independence assumed in the model and in the derived quantities required to solve the optimization problems in the M-step. Since parameters are estimated from a collection of samples that are assumed to be i.i.d., the E-step can generally be parallelized effectively since every training instance can be processed independently of the others. In the limit, in fact, each independent training instance could be processed by a separate mapper![10]

Reducers, however, must aggregate the statistics necessary to solve the optimization problems as required by the model. The degree to which these may be solved independently depends on the structure of the model, and this constrains the number of reducers that may be used. Fortunately, many common models (such as HMMs) require solving several independent optimization problems in the M-step. In this situation, a number of reducers may be run in parallel. Still, it is possible that in the worst case, the M-step optimization problem will not decompose into independent subproblems, making it necessary to use a single reducer.

6.3.1 HMM TRAINING IN MAPREDUCE

As we would expect, the training of hidden Markov models parallelizes well in MapReduce. The process can be summarized as follows: in each iteration, mappers process training instances, emitting expected event counts computed using the forward-backward algorithm introduced in Section 6.2.4. Reducers aggregate the expected counts, completing the E-step, and then generate parameter estimates for the next iteration using the updates given in Equation 6.3.

This parallelization strategy is effective for several reasons. First, the majority of the computational effort in HMM training is the running of the forward and backward algorithms. Since there is no limit on the number of mappers that may be run, the full computational resources of a

---

[10]Although the wisdom of doing this is questionable, given that the startup costs associated with individual map tasks in Hadoop may be considerable.

cluster may be brought to bear to solve this problem. Second, since the M-step of an HMM training iteration with $|S|$ states in the model consists of $2 \cdot |S| + 1$ independent optimization problems that require non-overlapping sets of statistics, this may be exploited with as many as $2 \cdot |S| + 1$ reducers running in parallel. While the optimization problem is computationally trivial, being able to reduce in parallel helps avoid the data bottleneck that would limit performance if only a single reducer were used.

The statistics that are required to solve the M-step optimization problem are quite similar to the relative frequency estimation example discussed in Section 3.3; however, rather than counts of observed events, we aggregate *expected* counts of events. As a result of the similarity, we can employ the *stripes* representation for aggregating sets of related values, as described in Section 3.2. A *pairs* approach that requires less memory at the cost of slower performance is also feasible.

HMM training mapper. The pseudo-code for the HMM training mapper is given in Figure 6.8. The input consists of key-value pairs with a unique id as the key and a training instance (e.g., a sentence) as the value. For each training instance, $2n + 1$ stripes are emitted with unique keys, and every training instance emits the same set of keys. Each unique key corresponds to one of the independent optimization problems that will be solved in the M-step. The outputs are:

1. the probabilities that the unobserved Markov process begins in each state q, with a unique key designating that the values are initial state counts;

2. the expected number of times that state q generated each emission symbol o (the set of emission symbols included will be just those found in each training instance $\mathbf{x}$), with a key indicating that the associated value is a set of *emission* counts from state q; and

3. the expected number of times state q transitions to each state r, with a key indicating that the associated value is a set of *transition* counts from state q.

HMM training reducer. The reducer for one iteration of HMM training, shown together with an optional combiner in Figure 6.9, aggregates the count collections associated with each key by summing them. When the values for each key have been completely aggregated, the associative array contains all of the statistics necessary to compute a subset of the parameters for the next EM iteration. The optimal parameter settings for the following iteration are computed simply by computing the relative frequency of each event with respect to its expected count at the current iteration. The new computed parameters are emitted from the reducer and written to HDFS. Note that they will be spread across $2 \cdot |S| + 1$ keys, representing initial state probabilities π, transition probabilities A_q for each state q, and emission probabilities B_q for each state q.

```
1:  class MAPPER
2:      method INITIALIZE(integer iteration)
3:          ⟨S, O⟩ ←READMODEL
4:          θ ← ⟨A, B, π⟩ ←READMODELPARAMS(iteration)
5:      method MAP(sample id, sequence x)
6:          α ←FORWARD(x, θ)                                              ▷ cf. Section 6.2.2
7:          β ←BACKWARD(x, θ)                                            ▷ cf. Section 6.2.4
8:          I ← new ASSOCIATIVEARRAY                              ▷ Initial state expectations
9:          for all q ∈ S do                                              ▷ Loop over states
10:             I{q} ← α₁(q) · β₁(q)
11:         O ← new ASSOCIATIVEARRAY of ASSOCIATIVEARRAY                  ▷ Emissions
12:         for t = 1 to |x| do                                      ▷ Loop over observations
13:             for all q ∈ S do                                         ▷ Loop over states
14:                 O{q}{xₜ} ← O{q}{xₜ} + αₜ(q) · βₜ(q)
15:             t ← t + 1
16:         T ← new ASSOCIATIVEARRAY of ASSOCIATIVEARRAY                  ▷ Transitions
17:         for t = 1 to |x| − 1 do                                  ▷ Loop over observations
18:             for all q ∈ S do                                         ▷ Loop over states
19:                 for all r ∈ S do                                     ▷ Loop over states
20:                     T{q}{r} ← T{q}{r} + αₜ(q) · A_q(r) · B_r(x_{t+1}) · β_{t+1}(r)
21:             t ← t + 1
22:         EMIT(string 'initial', stripe I)
23:         for all q ∈ S do                                             ▷ Loop over states
24:             EMIT(string 'emit from' + q, stripe O{q})
25:             EMIT(string 'transit from' + q, stripe T{q})
```

Figure 6.8: Mapper pseudo-code for training hidden Markov models using EM. The mappers map over training instances (i.e., sequences of observations $\mathbf{x}_i$) and generate the expected counts of initial states, emissions, and transitions taken to generate the sequence.

```
1: class COMBINER
2:     method COMBINE(string t, stripes [C₁, C₂, . . .])
3:         C_f ← new ASSOCIATIVEARRAY
4:         for all stripe C ∈ stripes [C₁, C₂, . . .] do
5:             SUM(C_f, C)
6:         EMIT(string t, stripe C_f)
```

```
1: class REDUCER
2:     method REDUCE(string t, stripes [C₁, C₂, . . .])
3:         C_f ← new ASSOCIATIVEARRAY
4:         for all stripe C ∈ stripes [C₁, C₂, . . .] do
5:             SUM(C_f, C)
6:         z ← 0
7:         for all ⟨k, v⟩ ∈ C_f do
8:             z ← z + v
9:         P_f ← new ASSOCIATIVEARRAY                  ▷ Final parameters vector
10:        for all ⟨k, v⟩ ∈ C_f do
11:            P_f{k} ← v/z
12:        EMIT(string t, stripe P_f)
```

Figure 6.9: Combiner and reducer pseudo-code for training hidden Markov models using EM. The HMMs considered in this book are fully parameterized by multinomial distributions, so reducers do not require special logic to handle different types of model parameters (since they are all of the same type).

6.4   CASE STUDY: WORD ALIGNMENT FOR STATISTICAL MACHINE TRANSLATION

To illustrate the real-world benefits of expectation maximization algorithms using MapReduce, we turn to the problem of word alignment, which is an important task in statistical machine translation that is typically solved using models whose parameters are learned with EM.

We begin by giving a brief introduction to statistical machine translation and the phrase-based translation approach; for a more comprehensive introduction, refer to [85; 97]. Fully automated translation has been studied since the earliest days of electronic computers. After successes with code-breaking during World War II, there was considerable optimism that translation of human languages would be another soluble problem. In the early years, work on translation was dominated by manual attempts to encode linguistic knowledge into computers—another instance of the 'rule-based' approach we described in the introduction to this chapter. These early attempts failed to live up to the admittedly overly optimistic expectations. For a number of years, the idea of fully automated translation was viewed with skepticism. Not only was constructing a translation system labor intensive, but translation pairs had to be developed independently, meaning that improvements in a Russian-English translation system could not, for the most part, be leveraged to improve a French-English system.

After languishing for a number of years, the field was reinvigorated in the late 1980s when researchers at IBM pioneered the development of *statistical machine translation* (SMT), which took a data-driven approach to solving the problem of machine translation, attempting to improve both the quality of translation while reducing the cost of developing systems [29]. The core idea of SMT is to equip the computer to *learn* how to translate, using example translations which are produced for other purposes, and modeling the process as a statistical process with some parameters θ relating strings in a source language (typically denoted as $\mathbf{f}$) to strings in a target language (typically denoted as $\mathbf{e}$):

$$\mathbf{e}^* = \arg\max_{\mathbf{e}} \Pr(\mathbf{e}|\mathbf{f}; \theta)$$

With the statistical approach, translation systems can be developed cheaply and quickly for any language pair, as long as there is sufficient training data available. Furthermore, improvements in learning algorithms and statistical modeling can yield benefits in many translation pairs at once, rather than being specific to individual language pairs. Thus, SMT, like many other topics we are considering in this book, is an attempt to leverage the vast quantities of textual data that is available to solve problems that would otherwise require considerable manual effort to encode specialized knowledge. Since the advent of statistical approaches to translation, the field has grown tremendously and numerous statistical models of translation have been developed, with many incorporating quite specialized knowledge about the behavior of natural language as biases in their learning algorithms.

6.4.1   STATISTICAL PHRASE-BASED TRANSLATION

One approach to statistical translation that is simple yet powerful is called *phrase-based translation* [86]. We provide a rough outline of the process since it is representative of most state-of-the-art statistical translation systems, such as the one used inside Google Translate.[11] Phrase-based translation works by learning how strings of words, called *phrases*, translate between languages.[12] Example phrase pairs for Spanish-English translation might include ⟨*los estudiantes*, *the students*⟩, ⟨*los estudiantes*, *some students*⟩, and ⟨*soy*, *i am*⟩. From a few hundred thousand sentences of example translations, many millions of such phrase pairs may be automatically learned.

The starting point is typically a parallel corpus (also called *bitext*), which contains *pairs* of sentences in two languages that are translations of each other. Parallel corpora are frequently generated as the by-product of an organization's effort to disseminate information in multiple languages, for example, proceedings of the Canadian Parliament in French and English, and text generated by the United Nations in many different languages. The parallel corpus is then annotated with *word alignments*, which indicate which words in one language correspond to words in the other. By using these word alignments as a skeleton, phrases can be extracted from the sentence that is likely to preserve the meaning relationships represented by the word alignment. While an explanation of the process is not necessary here, we mention it as a motivation for learning word alignments, which we show below how to compute with EM. After phrase extraction, each phrase pair is associated with a number of scores which, taken together, are used to compute the phrase translation probability, a conditional probability that reflects how likely the source phrase translates into the target phrase. We briefly note that although EM could be utilized to learn the phrase translation probabilities, this is not typically done in practice since the maximum likelihood solution turns out to be quite bad for this problem. The collection of phrase pairs and their scores are referred to as the *translation model*. In addition to the translation model, phrase-based translation depends on a *language model*, which gives the probability of a string in the target language. The translation model attempts to preserve the meaning of the source language during the translation process, while the language model ensures that the output is fluent and grammatical in the target language. The phrase-based translation process is summarized in Figure 6.10.

A language model gives the probability that a string of words $\mathbf{w} = \langle w_1, w_2, \ldots, w_n \rangle$, written as w_1^n for short, is a string in the target language. By the chain rule of probability, we get:

$$\Pr(w_1^n) = \Pr(w_1)\Pr(w_2|w_1)\Pr(w_3|w_1^2)\ldots\Pr(w_n|w_1^{n-1}) = \prod_{k=1}^{n}\Pr(w_k|w_1^{k-1}) \qquad (6.8)$$

Due to the extremely large number of parameters involved in estimating such a model directly, it is customary to make the *Markov assumption*, that the sequence histories only depend on prior local

---

[11] http://translate.google.com

[12] Phrases are simply sequences of words; they are not required to correspond to the definition of a phrase in any linguistic theory.

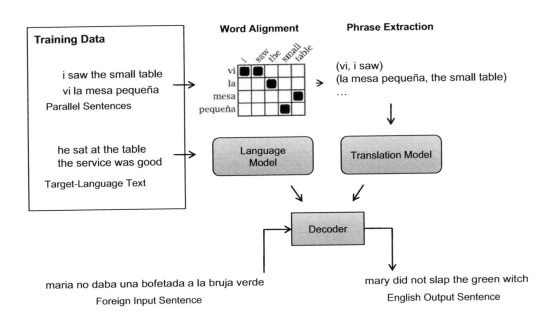

Figure 6.10: The standard phrase-based machine translation architecture. The translation model is constructed with phrases extracted from a word-aligned parallel corpus. The language model is estimated from a monolingual corpus. Both serve as input to the decoder, which performs the actual translation.

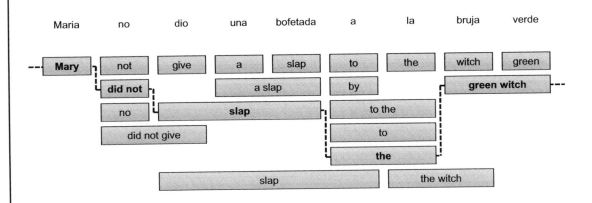

Figure 6.11: Translation coverage of the sentence *Maria no dio una bofetada a la bruja verde* by a phrase-based model. The best possible translation path is indicated with a dashed line.

context. That is, an n-gram language model is equivalent to a $(n-1)th$-order Markov model. Thus, we can approximate $P(w_k|w_1^{k-1})$ as follows:

$$\text{bigrams:} \quad P(w_k|w_1^{k-1}) \approx P(w_k|w_{k-1}) \tag{6.9}$$

$$\text{trigrams:} \quad P(w_k|w_1^{k-1}) \approx P(w_k|w_{k-1}w_{k-2}) \tag{6.10}$$

$$n\text{-grams:} \quad P(w_k|w_1^{k-1}) \approx P(w_k|w_{k-n+1}^{k-1}) \tag{6.11}$$

The probabilities used in computing $\Pr(w_1^n)$ based on an n-gram language model are generally estimated from a monolingual corpus of target language text. Since only target language text is necessary (without any additional annotation), language modeling has been well served by large-data approaches that take advantage of the vast quantities of text available on the web.

To translate an input sentence **f**, the phrase-based *decoder* creates a matrix of all translation possibilities of all substrings in the input string, as an example illustrates in Figure 6.11. A sequence of phrase pairs is selected such that each word in **f** is translated exactly once.[13] The decoder seeks to find the translation that maximizes the product of the translation probabilities of the phrases used and the language model probability of the resulting string in the target language. Because the phrase translation probabilities are independent of each other and the Markov assumption made in the language model, this may be done efficiently using dynamic programming. For a detailed introduction to phrase-based decoding, we refer the reader to a recent textbook by Koehn [85].

6.4.2 BRIEF DIGRESSION: LANGUAGE MODELING WITH MAPREDUCE

Statistical machine translation provides the context for a brief digression on distributed parameter estimation for language models using MapReduce, and provides another example illustrating the effectiveness of data-driven approaches in general. We briefly touched upon this work in Chapter 1. Even after making the Markov assumption, training n-gram language models still requires estimating an enormous number of parameters: potentially V^n, where V is the number of words in the vocabulary. For higher-order models (e.g., 5-grams) used in real-world applications, the number of parameters can easily exceed the number of words from which to estimate those parameters. In fact, most n-grams will never be observed in a corpus, no matter how large. To cope with this sparseness, researchers have developed a number of smoothing techniques [102], which all share the basic idea of moving probability mass from observed to unseen events in a principled manner. For many applications, a state-of-the-art approach is known as Kneser-Ney smoothing [35].

In 2007, Brants et al. [25] reported experimental results that answered an interesting question: given the availability of large corpora (i.e., the web), could a simpler smoothing strategy, applied to more text, beat Kneser-Ney in a machine translation task? It should come as no surprise that the answer is *yes*. Brants et al. introduced a technique known as "stupid backoff" that was exceedingly simple and so naïve that the resulting model didn't even define a valid probability distribution (it

---

[13]The phrases may not necessarily be selected in a strict left-to-right order. Being able to vary the order of the phrases used is necessary since languages may express the same ideas using different word orders.

assigned arbitrary scores as opposed to probabilities). The simplicity, however, afforded an extremely scalable implementations in MapReduce. With smaller corpora, stupid backoff didn't work as well as Kneser-Ney in generating accurate and fluent translations. However, as the amount of data increased, the gap between stupid backoff and Kneser-Ney narrowed, and eventually disappeared with sufficient data. Furthermore, with stupid backoff it was possible to train a language model on more data than was feasible with Kneser-Ney smoothing. Applying this language model to a machine translation task yielded better results than a (smaller) language model trained with Kneser-Ney smoothing.

The role of the language model in statistical machine translation is to select fluent, grammatical translations from a large hypothesis space: the more training data a language model has access to, the better its description of relevant language phenomena and hence its ability to select good translations. Once again, large data triumphs! For more information about estimating language models using MapReduce, we refer the reader to a forthcoming book from Morgan & Claypool [26].

6.4.3   WORD ALIGNMENT

Word alignments, which are necessary for building phrase-based translation models (as well as many other more sophisticated translation models), can be learned automatically using EM. In this section, we introduce a popular alignment model based on HMMs.

In the statistical model of word alignment considered here, the observable variables are the words in the source and target sentences (conventionally written using the variables $\mathbf{f}$ and $\mathbf{e}$, respectively), and their alignment is the latent variable. To make this model tractable, it is assumed that words are translated independently of one another, which means that the model's parameters include the probability of any word in the source language translating to any word in the target language. While this independence assumption is problematic in many ways, it results in a simple model structure that admits efficient inference yet produces reasonable alignments. Alignment models that make this assumption generate a string $\mathbf{e}$ in the target language by selecting words in the source language according to a lexical translation distribution. The indices of the words in $\mathbf{f}$ used to generate each word in $\mathbf{e}$ are stored in an alignment variable, $\mathbf{a}$.[14] This means that the variable a_i indicates the source word position of the ith target word generated, and $|\mathbf{a}| = |\mathbf{e}|$. Using these assumptions, the probability of an alignment and translation can be written as follows:

$$\Pr(\mathbf{e}, \mathbf{a}|\mathbf{f}) = \underbrace{\Pr(\mathbf{a}|\mathbf{f}, \mathbf{e})}_{\text{Alignment probability}} \times \underbrace{\prod_{i=1}^{|\mathbf{e}|} \Pr(e_i|f_{a_i})}_{\text{Lexical probability}}$$

Since we have parallel corpora consisting of only $\langle \mathbf{f}, \mathbf{e} \rangle$ pairs, we can learn the parameters for this model using EM and treating $\mathbf{a}$ as a latent variable. However, to combat data sparsity in the alignment

---

[14]In the original presentation of statistical lexical translation models, a special null word is added to the source sentences, which permits words to be inserted 'out of nowhere'. Since this does not change any of the important details of training, we omit it from our presentation for simplicity.

probability, we must make some further simplifying assumptions. By letting the probability of an alignment depend only on the position of the previous aligned word we capture a valuable insight (namely, words that are nearby in the source language will tend to be nearby in the target language), and our model acquires the structure of an HMM [150]:

$$\Pr(\mathbf{e}, \mathbf{a}|\mathbf{f}) \quad = \quad \underbrace{\prod_{i=1}^{|\mathbf{e}|} \Pr(a_i|a_{i-1})}_{\text{Transition probability}} \times \underbrace{\prod_{i=1}^{|\mathbf{e}|} \Pr(e_i|f_{a_i})}_{\text{Emission probability}}$$

This model can be trained using the forward-backward algorithm described in the previous section, summing over all settings of $\mathbf{a}$, and the best alignment for a sentence pair can be found using the Viterbi algorithm.

To properly initialize this HMM, it is conventional to further simplify the alignment probability model, and use this simpler model to learn initial lexical translation (emission) parameters for the HMM. The favored simplification is to assert that all alignments are uniformly probable:

$$\Pr(\mathbf{e}, \mathbf{a}|\mathbf{f}) \quad = \quad \frac{1}{|\mathbf{f}|^{|\mathbf{e}|}} \times \prod_{i=1}^{|\mathbf{e}|} \Pr(e_i|f_{a_i})$$

This model is known as IBM Model 1. It is attractive for initialization because it is convex everywhere, and therefore EM will learn the same solution regardless of initialization. Finally, while the forward-backward algorithm could be used to compute the expected counts necessary for training this model by setting $A_q(r)$ to be a constant value for all q and r, the uniformity assumption means that the expected emission counts can be estimated in time $O(|\mathbf{e}| \cdot |\mathbf{f}|)$, rather than time $O(|\mathbf{e}| \cdot |\mathbf{f}|^2)$ required by the forward-backward algorithm.

6.4.4   EXPERIMENTS

How well does a MapReduce word aligner for statistical machine translation perform? We describe previously published results [54] that compared a Java-based Hadoop implementation against a highly optimized word aligner called Giza++ [112], which was written in C++ and designed to run efficiently on a single core. We compared the training time of Giza++ and our aligner on a Hadoop cluster with 19 slave nodes, each with two single-core processors and two disks (38 cores total).

Figure 6.12 shows the performance of Giza++ in terms of the running time of a single EM iteration for both Model 1 and the HMM alignment model as a function of the number of training pairs. Both axes in the figure are on a log scale, but the ticks on the y-axis are aligned with 'meaningful' time intervals rather than exact orders of magnitude. There are three things to note. First, the running time scales linearly with the size of the training data. Second, the HMM is a constant factor slower than Model 1. Third, the alignment process is quite slow as the size of the training data grows—

at one million sentences, a single iteration takes over three hours to complete! Five iterations are generally necessary to train the models, which means that full training takes the better part of a day.

In Figure 6.13 we plot the running time of our MapReduce implementation running on the 38-core cluster described above. For reference, we plot points indicating what 1/38 of the running time of the Giza++ iterations would be at each data size, which gives a rough indication of what an 'ideal' parallelization could achieve, assuming that there was no overhead associated with distributing computation across these machines. Three things may be observed in the results. First, as the amount of data increases, the relative cost of the overhead associated with distributing data, marshaling and aggregating counts, decreases. At one million sentence pairs of training data, the HMM alignment iterations begin to approach optimal runtime efficiency. Second, Model 1, which we observe is light on computation, does not approach the theoretical performance of an ideal parallelization, and in fact, has almost the same running time as the HMM alignment algorithm. We conclude that the overhead associated with distributing and aggregating data is significant compared to the Model 1 computations, although a comparison with Figure 6.12 indicates that the MapReduce implementation is still substantially faster than the single core implementation, at least once a certain training data size is reached. Finally, we note that, in comparison to the running times of the single-core implementation, at large data sizes, there is a significant advantage to using the distributed implementation, even of Model 1.

Although these results do confound several variables (Java vs. C++ performance, memory usage patterns), it is reasonable to expect that the confounds would tend to make the single-core system's performance appear relatively *better* than the MapReduce system (which is, of course, the opposite pattern from what we actually observe). Furthermore, these results show that when computation is distributed over a cluster of many machines, even an unsophisticated implementation of the HMM aligner could compete favorably with a highly optimized single-core system whose performance is well-known to many people in the MT research community.

Why are these results important? Perhaps the most significant reason is that the quantity of parallel data that is available to train statistical machine translation models is ever increasing, and as is the case with so many problems we have encountered, more data lead to improvements in translation quality [54]. Recently, a corpus of one billion words of French-English data was mined automatically from the web and released publicly [33].[15] Single-core solutions to model construction simply cannot keep pace with the amount of translated data that is constantly being produced. Fortunately, several independent researchers have shown that existing modeling algorithms can be expressed naturally and effectively using MapReduce, which means that we can take advantage of this data. Furthermore, the results presented here show that even at data sizes that may be tractable on single machines, significant performance improvements are attainable using MapReduce implementations. This improvement reduces experimental turnaround times, which allows researchers to more quickly explore the solution space—which will, we hope, lead to rapid new developments in statistical machine translation.

---

[15]http://www.statmt.org/wmt10/translation-task.html

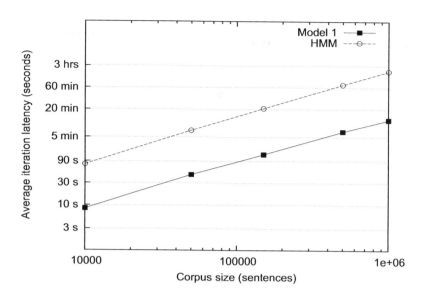

Figure 6.12: Running times of Giza++ (baseline single-core system) for Model 1 and HMM training iterations at various corpus sizes.

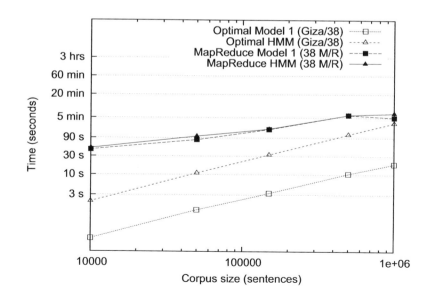

Figure 6.13: Running times of our MapReduce implementation of Model 1 and HMM training iterations at various corpus sizes. For reference, 1/38 running times of the Giza++ models are shown.

For the reader interested in statistical machine translation, there is an open source Hadoop-based MapReduce implementation of a training pipeline for phrase-based translation that includes word alignment, phrase extraction, and phrase scoring [56].

6.5 EM-LIKE ALGORITHMS

This chapter has focused on expectation maximization algorithms and their implementation in the MapReduce programming framework. These important algorithms are indispensable for learning models with latent structure from unannotated data, and they can be implemented quite naturally in MapReduce. We now explore some related learning algorithms that are similar to EM but can be used to solve more general problems, and discuss their implementation.

In this section we focus on *gradient-based optimization*, which refers to a class of techniques used to optimize any objective function, provided it is differentiable with respect to the parameters being optimized. Gradient-based optimization is particularly useful in the learning of maximum entropy (maxent) models [110] and conditional random fields (CRF) [87] that have an exponential form and are trained to maximize conditional likelihood. In addition to being widely used supervised classification models in text processing (meaning that during training, both the data and their annotations must be observable), their gradients take the form of expectations. As a result, some of the previously introduced techniques are also applicable for optimizing these models.

6.5.1 GRADIENT-BASED OPTIMIZATION AND LOG-LINEAR MODELS

Gradient-based optimization refers to a class of iterative optimization algorithms that use the derivatives of a function to find the parameters that yield a minimal or maximal value of that function. Obviously, these algorithms are only applicable in cases where a useful objective exists, is differentiable, and its derivatives can be efficiently evaluated. Fortunately, this is the case for many important problems of interest in text processing. For the purposes of this discussion, we will give examples in terms of minimizing functions.

Assume that we have some real-valued function $F(\theta)$ where θ is a k-dimensional vector and that F is differentiable with respect to θ. Its gradient is defined as:

$$\nabla F(\theta) = \left\langle \frac{\partial F}{\partial \theta_1}(\theta), \frac{\partial F}{\partial \theta_2}(\theta), \ldots, \frac{\partial F}{\partial \theta_k}(\theta) \right\rangle$$

The gradient has two crucial properties that are exploited in gradient-based optimization. First, the gradient ∇F is a vector field that points in the direction of the greatest increase of F and whose magnitude indicates the rate of increase. Second, if θ^* is a (local) minimum of F, then the following is true:

$$\nabla F(\theta^*) = 0$$

An extremely simple gradient-based minimization algorithm produces a series of parameter estimates $\theta^{(1)}, \theta^{(2)}, \ldots$ by starting with some initial parameter settings $\theta^{(1)}$ and updating parameters through successive iterations according to the following rule:

$$\theta^{(i+1)} = \theta^{(i)} - \eta^{(i)} \nabla F(\theta^{(i)}) \tag{6.12}$$

The parameter $\eta^{(i)} > 0$ is a learning rate which indicates how quickly the algorithm moves along the gradient during iteration i. Provided this value is small enough that F decreases, this strategy will find a local minimum of F. However, while simple, this update strategy may converge slowly, and proper selection of η is non-trivial. More sophisticated algorithms perform updates that are informed by approximations of the second derivative, which are estimated by successive evaluations of $\nabla F(\theta)$, and can converge much more rapidly [96].

Gradient-based optimization in MapReduce. Gradient-based optimization algorithms can often be implemented effectively in MapReduce. Like EM, where the structure of the model determines the specifics of the realization, the details of the function being optimized determines how it should best be implemented, and not every function optimization problem will be a good fit for MapReduce. Nevertheless, MapReduce implementations of gradient-based optimization tend to have the following characteristics:

- Each optimization iteration is one MapReduce job.

- The objective should decompose linearly across training instances. This implies that the gradient also decomposes linearly, and therefore mappers can process input data in parallel. The values they emit are pairs $\langle F(\theta), \nabla F(\theta) \rangle$, which are linear components of the objective and gradient.

- Evaluations of the function and its gradient are often computationally expensive because they require processing lots of data. This make parallelization with MapReduce worthwhile.

- Whether more than one reducer can run in parallel depends on the specific optimization algorithm being used. Some, like the trivial algorithm of Equation 6.12 treat the dimensions of θ independently, whereas many are sensitive to global properties of $\nabla F(\theta)$. In the latter case, parallelization across multiple reducers is non-trivial.

- Reducer(s) sum the component objective/gradient pairs, compute the total objective and gradient, run the optimization algorithm, and emit $\theta^{(i+1)}$.

- Many optimization algorithms are stateful and must persist their state between optimization iterations. This may either be emitted together with $\theta^{(i+1)}$ or written to the distributed file system as a side effect of the reducer. Such external side effects must be handled carefully; refer to Section 2.2 for a discussion.

Parameter learning for log-linear models. Gradient-based optimization techniques can be quite effectively used to learn the parameters of probabilistic models with a log-linear parameterization [100]. While a comprehensive introduction to these models is beyond the scope of this book, such models are used extensively in text processing applications, and their training using gradient-based optimization, which may otherwise be computationally expensive, can be implemented effectively using MapReduce. We therefore include a brief summary.

Log-linear models are particularly useful for supervised learning (unlike the unsupervised models learned with EM), where an annotation $\mathbf{y} \in \mathcal{Y}$ is available for every $\mathbf{x} \in \mathcal{X}$ in the training data. In this case, it is possible to directly model the conditional distribution of label given input:

$$\Pr(\mathbf{y}|\mathbf{x}; \theta) = \frac{\exp \sum_i \theta_i \cdot H_i(\mathbf{x}, \mathbf{y})}{\sum_{\mathbf{y}'} \exp \sum_i \theta_i \cdot H_i(\mathbf{x}, \mathbf{y}')}$$

In this expression, H_i are real-valued functions sensitive to features of the input and labeling. The parameters of the model is selected so as to minimize the negative conditional log likelihood of a set of training instances $\langle \langle \mathbf{x}, \mathbf{y} \rangle_1, \langle \mathbf{x}, \mathbf{y} \rangle_2, \ldots \rangle$, which we assume to be i.i.d.:

$$F(\theta) \quad = \quad \sum_{\langle \mathbf{x}, \mathbf{y} \rangle} - \log \Pr(\mathbf{y}|\mathbf{x}; \theta) \tag{6.13}$$

$$\theta^* \quad = \quad \arg \min_{\theta} F(\theta) \tag{6.14}$$

As Equation 6.13 makes clear, the objective decomposes linearly across training instances, meaning it can be optimized quite well in MapReduce. The gradient derivative of F with respect to θ_i can be shown to have the following form [141]:[16]

$$\frac{\partial F}{\partial \theta_i}(\theta) = \sum_{\langle \mathbf{x}, \mathbf{y} \rangle} \left[H_i(\mathbf{x}, \mathbf{y}) - \mathbb{E}_{\Pr(\mathbf{y}'|\mathbf{x}; \theta)}[H_i(\mathbf{x}, \mathbf{y}')] \right]$$

The expectation in the second part of the gradient's expression can be computed using a variety of techniques. However, as we saw with EM, when very large event spaces are being modeled, as is the case with sequence labeling, enumerating all possible values $\mathbf{y}$ can become computationally intractable. And, as was the case with HMMs, independence assumptions can be used to enable efficient computation using dynamic programming. In fact, the forward-backward algorithm introduced in Section 6.2.4 can, with only minimal modification, be used to compute the expectation $\mathbb{E}_{\Pr(\mathbf{y}'|\mathbf{x}; \theta)}[H_i(\mathbf{x}, \mathbf{y}')]$ needed in CRF sequence models, as long as the feature functions respect the same Markov assumption that is made in HMMs. For more information about inference in CRFs using the forward-backward algorithm, we refer the reader to Sha et al. [140].

As we saw in the previous section, MapReduce offers significant speedups when training iterations require running the forward-backward algorithm. The same pattern of results holds when training linear CRFs.

---

[16]This assumes that when $\langle \mathbf{x}, \mathbf{y} \rangle$ is present the model is fully observed (i.e., there are no additional latent variables).

6.6   SUMMARY AND ADDITIONAL READINGS

This chapter focused on learning the parameters of statistical models from data, using expectation maximization algorithms or gradient-based optimization techniques. We focused especially on EM algorithms for three reasons. First, these algorithms can be expressed naturally in the MapReduce programming model, making them a good example of how to express a commonly used algorithm in this new framework. Second, many models, such as the widely used hidden Markov model (HMM) trained using EM, make independence assumptions that permit an high degree of parallelism in both the E- and M-steps. Thus, they are particularly well positioned to take advantage of large clusters. Finally, EM algorithms are unsupervised learning algorithms, which means that they have access to far more training data than comparable supervised approaches. This is quite important. In Chapter 1, when we hailed large data as the "rising tide that lifts all boats" to yield more effective algorithms, we were mostly referring to unsupervised approaches, given that the manual effort required to generate annotated data remains a bottleneck in many supervised approaches. Data acquisition for unsupervised algorithms is often as simple as crawling specific web sources, given the enormous quantities of data available "for free". This, combined with the ability of MapReduce to process large datasets in parallel, provides researchers with an effective strategy for developing increasingly effective applications.

Since EM algorithms are relatively computationally expensive, even for small amounts of data, this led us to consider how related supervised learning models (which typically have much less training data available), can also be implemented in MapReduce. The discussion demonstrates that not only does MapReduce provide a means for coping with ever-increasing amounts of data, but it is also useful for parallelizing expensive computations. Although MapReduce has been designed with mostly data-intensive applications in mind, the ability to leverage clusters of commodity hardware to parallelize computationally expensive algorithms is an important use case.

Additional Readings.   Because of its ability to leverage large amounts of training data, machine learning is an attractive problem for MapReduce and an area of active research. Chu et al. [37] presented general formulations of a variety of machine learning problems, focusing on a normal form for expressing a variety of machine learning algorithms in MapReduce. The Apache Mahout project is an open-source implementation of these and other learning algorithms,[17] and it is also the subject of a forthcoming book [116]. Issues associated with a MapReduce implementation of latent Dirichlet allocation (LDA), which is another important unsupervised learning technique, with certain similarities to EM, have been explored by Wang et al. [151].

---

[17]http://lucene.apache.org/mahout/

CHAPTER 7

Closing Remarks

The need to process enormous quantities of data has never been greater. Not only are terabyte- and petabyte-scale datasets rapidly becoming commonplace, but there is consensus that great value lies buried in them, waiting to be unlocked by the right computational tools. In the commercial sphere, business intelligence—driven by the ability to gather data from a dizzying array of sources—promises to help organizations better understand their customers and the marketplace, hopefully leading to better business decisions and competitive advantages. For engineers building information processing tools and applications, larger datasets lead to more effective algorithms for a wide range of tasks, from machine translation to spam detection. In the natural and physical sciences, the ability to analyze massive amounts of data may provide the key to unlocking the secrets of the cosmos or the mysteries of life.

In the preceding chapters, we have shown how MapReduce can be exploited to solve a variety of problems related to text processing at scales that would have been unthinkable a few years ago. However, no tool—no matter how powerful or flexible—can be perfectly adapted to every task, so it is only fair to discuss the limitations of the MapReduce programming model and survey alternatives. Section 7.1 covers *online learning algorithms* and *Monte Carlo simulations*, which are examples of algorithms that require maintaining global state. As we have seen, this is difficult to accomplish in MapReduce. Section 7.2 discusses alternative programming models, and the book concludes in Section 7.3.

7.1 LIMITATIONS OF MAPREDUCE

As we have seen throughout this book, solutions to many interesting problems in text processing do not require global synchronization. As a result, they can be expressed naturally in MapReduce, since map and reduce tasks run independently and in isolation. However, there are many examples of algorithms that depend crucially on the existence of shared global state during processing, making them difficult to implement in MapReduce (since the single opportunity for global synchronization in MapReduce is the barrier between the map and reduce phases of processing).

The first example is *online learning*. Recall from Chapter 6 the concept of learning as the setting of parameters in a statistical model. Both EM and the gradient-based learning algorithms we described are instances of what are known as *batch* learning algorithms. This simply means that the full "batch" of training data is processed before any updates to the model parameters are made. On one hand, this is quite reasonable: updates are not made until the full evidence of the training data has been weighed against the model. An earlier update would seem, in some sense, to be hasty.

However, it is generally the case that more frequent updates can lead to *more* rapid convergence of the model (in terms of number of training instances processed), even if those updates are made by considering *less* data [24]. Thinking in terms of gradient optimization (see Section 6.5), online learning algorithms can be understood as computing an approximation of the true gradient, using only a few training instances. Although only an approximation, the gradient computed from a small subset of training instances is often quite reasonable, and the aggregate behavior of multiple updates tends to even out errors that are made. In the limit, updates can be made after *every* training instance.

Unfortunately, implementing online learning algorithms in MapReduce is problematic. The model parameters in a learning algorithm can be viewed as shared global state, which must be updated as the model is evaluated against training data. All processes performing the evaluation (presumably the mappers) must have access to this state. In a batch learner, where updates occur in one or more reducers (or, alternatively, in the driver code), synchronization of this resource is enforced by the MapReduce framework. However, with online learning, these updates must occur after processing smaller numbers of instances. This means that the framework must be altered to support faster processing of smaller datasets, which goes against the design choices of most existing MapReduce implementations. Since MapReduce was specifically optimized for batch operations over large amounts of data, such a style of computation would likely result in inefficient use of resources. In Hadoop, for example, map and reduce tasks have considerable startup costs. This is acceptable because in most circumstances, this cost is amortized over the processing of many key-value pairs. However, for small datasets, these high startup costs become intolerable. An alternative is to abandon shared global state and run independent instances of the training algorithm in parallel (on different portions of the data). A final solution is then arrived at by merging individual results. Experiments, however, show that the merged solution is inferior to the output of running the training algorithm on the entire dataset [52].

A related difficulty occurs when running what are called *Monte Carlo simulations*, which are used to perform inference in probabilistic models where evaluating or representing the model exactly is impossible. The basic idea is quite simple: samples are drawn from the random variables in the model to simulate its behavior, and then simple frequency statistics are computed over the samples. This sort of inference is particularly useful when dealing with so-called *nonparametric models*, which are models whose structure is not specified in advance, but is rather inferred from training data. For an illustration, imagine learning a hidden Markov model, but inferring the number of states, rather than having them specified. Being able to parallelize Monte Carlo simulations would be tremendously valuable, particularly for unsupervised learning applications where they have been found to be far more effective than EM-based learning (which requires specifying the model). Although recent work [10] has shown that the delays in synchronizing sample statistics due to parallel implementations do not necessarily damage the inference, MapReduce offers no natural mechanism for managing the global shared state that would be required for such an implementation.

The problem of global state is sufficiently pervasive that there has been substantial work on solutions. One approach is to build a distributed datastore capable of maintaining the global state.

However, such a system would need to be highly scalable to be used in conjunction with MapReduce. Google's Bigtable [34], which is a sparse, distributed, persistent multidimensional sorted map built on top of GFS, fits the bill, and has been used in exactly this manner. Amazon's Dynamo [48], which is a distributed key-value store (with a very different architecture), might also be useful in this respect, although it wasn't originally designed with such an application in mind. Unfortunately, it is unclear if the open-source implementations of these two systems (HBase and Cassandra, respectively) are sufficiently mature to handle the low-latency and high-throughput demands of maintaining global state in the context of massively distributed processing (but recent benchmarks are encouraging [40]).

7.2   ALTERNATIVE COMPUTING PARADIGMS

Streaming algorithms [3] represent an alternative programming model for dealing with large volumes of data with limited computational and storage resources. This model assumes that data are presented to the algorithm as one or more *streams* of inputs that are processed in order, and only once. The model is agnostic with respect to the source of these streams, which could be files in a distributed file system, but more interestingly, data from an "external" source or some other data gathering device. Stream processing is very attractive for working with time-series data (news feeds, tweets, sensor readings, etc.), which is difficult in MapReduce (once again, given its batch-oriented design). Furthermore, since streaming algorithms are comparatively simple (because there is only so much that can be done with a particular training instance), they can often take advantage of modern GPUs, which have a large number of (relatively simple) functional units [104]. In the context of text processing, streaming algorithms have been applied to language modeling [90], translation modeling [89], and detecting the first mention of news event in a stream [121].

The idea of stream processing has been generalized in the Dryad framework as arbitrary dataflow graphs [75; 159]. A Dryad job is a directed acyclic graph where each vertex represents developer-specified computations and edges represent data channels that capture dependencies. The dataflow graph is a logical computation graph that is automatically mapped onto physical resources by the framework. At runtime, channels are used to transport partial results between vertices, and can be realized using files, TCP pipes, or shared memory.

Another system worth mentioning is Pregel [98], which implements a programming model inspired by Valiant's Bulk Synchronous Parallel (BSP) model [148]. Pregel was specifically designed for large-scale graph algorithms, but unfortunately there are few published details at present. However, a longer description is anticipated in a forthcoming paper [99].

What is the significance of these developments? The power of MapReduce derives from providing an abstraction that allows developers to harness the power of large clusters. As anyone who has taken an introductory computer science course would know, abstractions manage complexity by hiding details and presenting well-defined behaviors to users of those abstractions. This process makes certain tasks easier, but others more difficult, if not impossible. MapReduce is certainly no exception to this generalization, and one of the goals of this book has been to give the reader a better understanding of what's easy to do in MapReduce and what its limitations are. But of course, this begs the obvious question: What other abstractions are available in the massively distributed datacenter environment? Are there more appropriate computational models that would allow us to tackle classes of problems that are difficult for MapReduce?

Dryad and Pregel are alternative answers to these questions. They share in providing an abstraction for large-scale distributed computations, separating the *what* from the *how* of computation and isolating the developer from the details of concurrent programming. They differ, however, in how distributed computations are conceptualized: functional-style programming, arbitrary dataflows, or BSP. These conceptions represent different trade offs between simplicity and expressivity: for example, Dryad is more flexible than MapReduce, and in fact, MapReduce can be trivially implemented in Dryad. However, it remains unclear, at least at present, which approach is more appropriate for different classes of applications. Looking forward, we can certainly expect the development of new models and a better understanding of existing ones. MapReduce is not the end, and perhaps not even the best. It is merely the first of many approaches to harness large-scaled distributed computing resources.

Even within the Hadoop/MapReduce ecosystem, we have already observed the development of alternative approaches for expressing distributed computations. For example, there is a proposal to add a third *merge* phase after map and reduce to better support relational operations [36]. Pig [114], which was inspired by Google's Sawzall [122], can be described as a data analytics platform that provides a lightweight scripting language for manipulating large datasets. Although Pig scripts (in a language called *Pig Latin*) are ultimately converted into Hadoop jobs by Pig's execution engine, constructs in the language allow developers to specify data transformations (filtering, joining, grouping, etc.) at a much higher level. Similarly, Hive [68], another open-source project, provides an abstraction on top of Hadoop that allows users to issue SQL queries against large relational datasets stored in HDFS. Hive queries (in HiveQL) "compile down" to Hadoop jobs by the Hive query engine. Therefore, the system provides a data analysis tool for users who are already comfortable with relational databases, while simultaneously taking advantage of Hadoop's data processing capabilities.

7.3   MAPREDUCE AND BEYOND

The capabilities necessary to tackle large-data problems are already within reach by many and will continue to become more accessible over time. By scaling "out" with commodity servers, we have been able to economically bring large clusters of machines to bear on problems of interest. But this has only been possible with corresponding innovations in software and how computations are organized on a massive scale. Important ideas include: moving processing to the data, as opposed to the other way around; also, emphasizing throughput over latency for batch tasks by sequential scans through data, avoiding random seeks. Most important of all, however, is the development of new abstractions that hide system-level details from the application developer. These abstractions are at the level of entire datacenters, and provide a model using which programmers can reason about computations at a massive scale without being distracted by fine-grained concurrency management, fault tolerance, error recovery, and a host of other issues in distributed computing. This, in turn, paves the way for innovations in scalable algorithms that can run on petabyte-scale datasets.

None of these points are new or particularly earth shattering—computer scientists have known about these principles for decades. However, MapReduce is unique in that, for the first time, all these ideas came together and were demonstrated on practical problems at scales unseen before, both in terms of computational resources and the impact on the daily lives of millions. The engineers at Google deserve a tremendous amount of credit for that, and also for sharing their insights with the rest of the world. Furthermore, the engineers and executives at Yahoo deserve a lot of credit for starting the open-source Hadoop project, which has made MapReduce accessible to everyone and created the vibrant software ecosystem that flourishes today. Add to that the advent of utility computing, which eliminates capital investments associated with cluster infrastructure, large-data processing capabilities are now available "to the masses" with a relatively low barrier to entry.

The golden age of massively distributed computing is *finally* upon us.

Bibliography

[1] Azza Abouzeid, Kamil Bajda-Pawlikowski, Daniel Abadi, Avi Silberschatz, and Alexander Rasin. HadoopDB: An architectural hybrid of MapReduce and DBMS technologies for analytical workloads. In *Proceedings of the 35th International Conference on Very Large Data Base (VLDB 2009)*, pages 922–933, Lyon, France, 2009. 59

[2] Réka Albert and Albert-László Barabási. Statistical mechanics of complex networks. *Reviews of Modern Physics*, 74:47–97, 2002. DOI: 10.1103/RevModPhys.74.47 92

[3] Noga Alon, Yossi Matias, and Mario Szegedy. The space complexity of approximating the frequency moments. In *Proceedings of the 28th Annual ACM Symposium on Theory of Computing (STOC '96)*, pages 20–29, Philadelphia, Pennsylvania, 1996. DOI: 10.1145/237814.237823 145

[4] Peter Alvaro, Tyson Condie, Neil Conway, Khaled Elmeleegy, Joseph M. Hellerstein, and Russell C. Sears. BOOM: Data-centric programming in the datacenter. Technical Report UCB/EECS-2009-98, Electrical Engineering and Computer Sciences, University of California at Berkeley, 2009. 32

[5] Gene Amdahl. Validity of the single processor approach to achieving large-scale computing capabilities. In *Proceedings of the AFIPS Spring Joint Computer Conference*, pages 483–485, 1967. DOI: 10.1145/1465482.1465560 17

[6] Rajagopal Ananthanarayanan, Karan Gupta, Prashant Pandey, Himabindu Pucha, Prasenjit Sarkar, Mansi Shah, and Renu Tewari. Cloud analytics: Do we *really* need to reinvent the storage stack? In *Proceedings of the 2009 Workshop on Hot Topics in Cloud Computing (HotCloud 09)*, San Diego, California, 2009. 29

[7] Thomas Anderson, Michael Dahlin, Jeanna Neefe, David Patterson, Drew Roselli, and Randolph Wang. Serverless network file systems. In *Proceedings of the 15th ACM Symposium on Operating Systems Principles (SOSP 1995)*, pages 109–126, Copper Mountain Resort, Colorado, 1995. DOI: 10.1145/224056.224066 29

[8] Vo Ngoc Anh and Alistair Moffat. Inverted index compression using word-aligned binary codes. *Information Retrieval*, 8(1):151–166, 2005. DOI: 10.1023/B:INRT.0000048490.99518.5c 76

[9] Michael Armbrust, Armando Fox, Rean Griffith, Anthony D. Joseph, Randy H. Katz, Andrew Konwinski, Gunho Lee, David A. Patterson, Ariel Rabkin, Ion Stoica, and Matei Zaharia. Above the clouds: A Berkeley view of cloud computing. Technical Report UCB/EECS-2009-28, Electrical Engineering and Computer Sciences, University of California at Berkeley, 2009. 6

[10] Arthur Asuncion, Padhraic Smyth, and Max Welling. Asynchronous distributed learning of topic models. In *Advances in Neural Information Processing Systems 21 (NIPS 2008)*, pages 81–88, Vancouver, British Columbia, Canada, 2008. 144

[11] Ricardo Baeza-Yates, Carlos Castillo, Flavio Junqueira, Vassilis Plachouras, and Fabrizio Silvestri. Challenges on distributed web retrieval. In *Proceedings of the IEEE 23rd International Conference on Data Engineering (ICDE 2007)*, pages 6–20, Istanbul, Turkey, 2007. DOI: 10.1109/ICDE.2007.367846 83

[12] Ricardo Baeza-Yates, Carlos Castillo, and Vicente López. PageRank increase under different collusion topologies. In *Proceedings of the First International Workshop on Adversarial Information Retrieval on the Web (AIRWeb 2005)*, pages 17–24, Chiba, Japan, 2005. 96

[13] Ricardo Baeza-Yates, Aristides Gionis, Flavio Junqueira, Vanessa Murdock, Vassilis Plachouras, and Fabrizio Silvestri. The impact of caching on search engines. In *Proceedings of the 30th Annual International ACM SIGIR Conference on Research and Development in Information Retrieval (SIGIR 2007)*, pages 183–190, Amsterdam, The Netherlands, 2007. DOI: 10.1145/1277741.1277775 82

[14] Michele Banko and Eric Brill. Scaling to very very large corpora for natural language disambiguation. In *Proceedings of the 39th Annual Meeting of the Association for Computational Linguistics (ACL 2001)*, pages 26–33, Toulouse, France, 2001. DOI: 10.3115/1073012.1073017 4

[15] Paul Barham, Boris Dragovic, Keir Fraser, Steven Hand, Tim Harris, Alex Ho, Rolf Neugebauer, Ian Pratt, and Andrew Warfield. Xen and the art of virtualization. In *Proceedings of the 19th ACM Symposium on Operating Systems Principles (SOSP 2003)*, pages 164–177, Bolton Landing, New York, 2003. DOI: 10.1145/945445.945462 6

[16] Luiz André Barroso, Jeffrey Dean, and Urs Hölzle. Web search for a planet: The Google cluster architecture. *IEEE Micro*, 23(2):22–28, 2003. DOI: 10.1109/MM.2003.1196112 82

[17] Luiz André Barroso and Urs Hölzle. The case for energy-proportional computing. *Computer*, 40(12):33–37, 2007. DOI: 10.1109/MC.2007.443 9

[18] Luiz André Barroso and Urs Hölzle. *The Datacenter as a Computer: An Introduction to the Design of Warehouse-Scale Machines*. Morgan & Claypool Publishers, 2009. DOI: 10.2200/S00193ED1V01Y200905CAC006 8, 9, 10, 14

[19] Jacek Becla, Andrew Hanushevsky, Sergei Nikolaev, Ghaleb Abdulla, Alex Szalay, Maria Nieto-Santisteban, Ani Thakar, and Jim Gray. Designing a multi-petabyte database for LSST. SLAC Publications SLAC-PUB-12292, Stanford Linear Accelerator Center, May 2006. 2

[20] Jacek Becla and Daniel L. Wang. Lessons learned from managing a petabyte. In *Proceedings of the Second Biennial Conference on Innovative Data Systems Research (CIDR 2005)*, Asilomar, California, 2005. 2

[21] Gordon Bell, Tony Hey, and Alex Szalay. Beyond the data deluge. *Science*, 323(5919):1297–1298, 2009. 2

[22] Monica Bianchini, Marco Gori, and Franco Scarselli. Inside PageRank. *ACM Transactions on Internet Technology*, 5(1):92–128, 2005. DOI: 10.1145/1052934.1052938 98, 100

[23] Jorge Luis Borges. *Collected Fictions (translated by Andrew Hurley)*. Penguin, 1999. 5

[24] Léon Bottou. Stochastic learning. In Olivier Bousquet and Ulrike von Luxburg, editors, *Advanced Lectures on Machine Learning*, Lecture Notes in Artificial Intelligence, LNAI 3176, pages 146–168. Springer Verlag, Berlin, 2004. DOI: 10.1007/b100712 144

[25] Thorsten Brants, Ashok C. Popat, Peng Xu, Franz J. Och, and Jeffrey Dean. Large language models in machine translation. In *Proceedings of the 2007 Joint Conference on Empirical Methods in Natural Language Processing and Computational Natural Language Learning*, pages 858–867, Prague, Czech Republic, 2007. 4, 5, 133

[26] Thorsten Brants and Peng Xu. *Distributed Language Models*. Morgan & Claypool Publishers, 2010. 134

[27] Eric Brill, Jimmy Lin, Michele Banko, Susan Dumais, and Andrew Ng. Data-intensive question answering. In *Proceedings of the Tenth Text REtrieval Conference (TREC 2001)*, pages 393–400, Gaithersburg, Maryland, 2001. 4

[28] Frederick P. Brooks. *The Mythical Man-Month: Essays on Software Engineering, Anniversary Edition*. Addison-Wesley, Reading, Massachusetts, 1995. 12

[29] Peter F. Brown, Vincent J. Della Pietra, Stephen A. Della Pietra, and Robert L. Mercer. The mathematics of statistical machine translation: Parameter estimation. *Computational Linguistics*, 19(2):263–311, 1993. 130

[30] Stefan Büttcher, Charles L. A. Clarke, and Gordon V. Cormack. *Information Retrieval: Implementing and Evaluating Search Engines*. MIT Press, Cambridge, Massachusetts, 2010. 78, 83

[31] Rajkumar Buyya, Chee Shin Yeo, Srikumar Venugopal, James Broberg, and Ivona Brandic. Cloud computing and emerging IT platforms: Vision, hype, and reality for delivering computing as the 5th utility. *Future Generation Computer Systems*, 25(6):599–616, 2009. DOI: 10.1016/j.future.2008.12.001 6

[32] Luis-Felipe Cabrera and Darrell D. E. Long. Swift: Using distributed disk striping to provide high I/O data rates. *Computer Systems*, 4(4):405–436, 1991. 29

[33] Chris Callison-Burch, Philipp Koehn, Christof Monz, and Josh Schroeder. Findings of the 2009 workshop on statistical machine translation. In *Proceedings of the Fourth Workshop on Statistical Machine Translation (StatMT '09)*, pages 1–28, Athens, Greece, 2009. 136

[34] Fay Chang, Jeffrey Dean, Sanjay Ghemawat, Wilson C. Hsieh, Deborah A. Wallach, Michael Burrows, Tushar Chandra, Andrew Fikes, and Robert Gruber. Bigtable: A distributed storage system for structured data. In *Proceedings of the 7th Symposium on Operating System Design and Implementation (OSDI 2006)*, pages 205–218, Seattle, Washington, 2006. 24, 145

[35] Stanley F. Chen and Joshua Goodman. An empirical study of smoothing techniques for language modeling. In *Proceedings of the 34th Annual Meeting of the Association for Computational Linguistics (ACL 1996)*, pages 310–318, Santa Cruz, California, 1996. DOI: 10.3115/981863.981904 5, 133

[36] Hung chih Yang, Ali Dasdan, Ruey-Lung Hsiao, and D. Stott Parker. Map-Reduce-Merge: Simplified relational data processing on large clusters. In *Proceedings of the 2007 ACM SIGMOD International Conference on Management of Data*, pages 1029–1040, Beijing, China, 2007. DOI: 10.1145/1247480.1247602 146

[37] Cheng-Tao Chu, Sang Kyun Kim, Yi-An Lin, Yuan Yuan Yu, Gary Bradski, Andrew Ng, and Kunle Olukotun. Map-Reduce for machine learning on multicore. In *Advances in Neural Information Processing Systems 19 (NIPS 2006)*, pages 281–288, Vancouver, British Columbia, Canada, 2006. 141

[38] Kenneth W. Church and Patrick Hanks. Word association norms, mutual information, and lexicography. *Computational Linguistics*, 16(1):22–29, 1990. 48

[39] Jonathan Cohen. Graph twiddling in a MapReduce world. *Computing in Science and Engineering*, 11(4):29–41, 2009. DOI: 10.1109/MCSE.2009.120 103

[40] Brian F. Cooper, Adam Silberstein, Erwin Tam, Raghu Ramakrishnan, and Russell Sears. Benchmarking cloud serving systems with YCSB. In *Proceedings of the First ACM Symposium on Cloud Computing (ACM SOCC 2010)*, Indianapolis, Indiana, 2010. 145

[41] Thomas H. Cormen, Charles E. Leiserson, and Ronald L. Rivest. *Introduction to Algorithms*. MIT Press, Cambridge, Massachusetts, 1990. 88

[42] W. Bruce Croft, Donald Meztler, and Trevor Strohman. *Search Engines: Information Retrieval in Practice*. Addison-Wesley, Reading, Massachusetts, 2009. 83

[43] David Culler, Richard Karp, David Patterson, Abhijit Sahay, Klaus Erik Schauser, Eunice Santos, Ramesh Subramonian, and Thorsten von Eicken. LogP: Towards a realistic model of parallel computation. *ACM SIGPLAN Notices*, 28(7):1–12, 1993. DOI: 10.1145/173284.155333 15

[44] Doug Cutting, Julian Kupiec, Jan Pedersen, and Penelope Sibun. A practical part-of-speech tagger. In *Proceedings of the Third Conference on Applied Natural Language Processing*, pages 133–140, Trento, Italy, 1992. DOI: 10.3115/974499.974523 114

[45] Jeffrey Dean and Sanjay Ghemawat. MapReduce: Simplified data processing on large clusters. In *Proceedings of the 6th Symposium on Operating System Design and Implementation (OSDI 2004)*, pages 137–150, San Francisco, California, 2004. 1, 24, 25

[46] Jeffrey Dean and Sanjay Ghemawat. MapReduce: Simplified data processing on large clusters. *Communications of the ACM*, 51(1):107–113, 2008. DOI: 10.1145/1327452.1327492 2

[47] Jeffrey Dean and Sanjay Ghemawat. MapReduce: A flexible data processing tool. *Communications of the ACM*, 53(1):72–77, 2010. DOI: 10.1145/1629175.1629198 59

[48] Giuseppe DeCandia, Deniz Hastorun, Madan Jampani, Gunavardhan Kakulapati, Avinash Lakshman, Alex Pilchin, Swami Sivasubramanian, Peter Vosshall, and Werner Vogels. Dynamo: Amazon's highly available key-value store. In *Proceedings of the 21st ACM Symposium on Operating Systems Principles (SOSP 2007)*, pages 205–220, Stevenson, Washington, 2007. 145

[49] Arthur P. Dempster, Nan M. Laird, and Donald B. Rubin. Maximum likelihood from incomplete data via the EM algorithm. *Journal of the Royal Statistical Society. Series B (Methodological)*, 39(1):1–38, 1977. 108

[50] David J. DeWitt and Jim Gray. Parallel database systems: The future of high performance database systems. *Communications of the ACM*, 35(6):85–98, 1992. DOI: 10.1145/129888.129894 12

[51] David J. DeWitt, Randy H. Katz, Frank Olken, Leonard D. Shapiro, Michael R. Stonebraker, and David Wood. Implementation techniques for main memory database systems. *ACM SIGMOD Record*, 14(2):1–8, 1984. DOI: 10.1145/971697.602261 63

[52] Mark Dredze, Alex Kulesza, and Koby Crammer. Multi-domain learning by confidence-weighted parameter combination. *Machine Learning*, 79:123–149, 2010. DOI: 10.1007/s10994-009-5148-0 144

[53] Susan Dumais, Michele Banko, Eric Brill, Jimmy Lin, and Andrew Ng. Web question answering: Is more always better? In *Proceedings of the 25th Annual International ACM SIGIR Conference on Research and Development in Information Retrieval (SIGIR 2002)*, pages 291–298, Tampere, Finland, 2002. DOI: 10.1145/564376.564428 4

[54] Chris Dyer, Aaron Cordova, Alex Mont, and Jimmy Lin. Fast, easy, and cheap: Construction of statistical machine translation models with MapReduce. In *Proceedings of the Third Workshop on Statistical Machine Translation at ACL 2008*, pages 199–207, Columbus, Ohio, 2008. 47, 135, 136

[55] John R. Firth. A synopsis of linguistic theory 1930–55. In *Studies in Linguistic Analysis, Special Volume of the Philological Society*, pages 1–32. Blackwell, Oxford, 1957. 48

[56] Qin Gao and Stephan Vogel. Training phrase-based machine translation models on the cloud: Open source machine translation toolkit Chaski. *The Prague Bulletin of Mathematical Linguistics*, 93:37–46, 2010. DOI: 10.2478/v10108-010-0004-8 138

[57] Sanjay Ghemawat, Howard Gobioff, and Shun-Tak Leung. The Google File System. In *Proceedings of the 19th ACM Symposium on Operating Systems Principles (SOSP 2003)*, pages 29–43, Bolton Landing, New York, 2003. DOI: 10.1145/945445.945450 29

[58] Seth Gilbert and Nancy Lynch. Brewer's Conjecture and the feasibility of consistent, available, partition-tolerant web services. *ACM SIGACT News*, 33(2):51–59, 2002. DOI: 10.1145/564585.564601 32

[59] Michelle Girvan and Mark E. J. Newman. Community structure in social and biological networks. *Proceedings of the National Academy of Science*, 99(12):7821–7826, 2002. DOI: 10.1073/pnas.122653799 85

[60] Ananth Grama, Anshul Gupta, George Karypis, and Vipin Kumar. *Introduction to Parallel Computing*. Addison-Wesley, Reading, Massachusetts, 2003. 14, 103

[61] Mark S. Granovetter. The strength of weak ties. *The American Journal of Sociology*, 78(6):1360–1380, 1973. DOI: 10.1086/225469 92

[62] Mark S. Granovetter. The strength of weak ties: A network theory revisited. *Sociological Theory*, 1:201–233, 1983. DOI: 10.2307/202051 92

[63] Zoltán Gyöngyi and Hector Garcia-Molina. Web spam taxonomy. In *Proceedings of the First International Workshop on Adversarial Information Retrieval on the Web (AIRWeb 2005)*, pages 39–47, Chiba, Japan, 2005. 96

[64] Per Hage and Frank Harary. *Island Networks: Communication, Kinship, and Classification Structures in Oceania*. Cambridge University Press, Cambridge, England, 1996. 86

[65] Alon Halevy, Peter Norvig, and Fernando Pereira. The unreasonable effectiveness of data. *Communications of the ACM*, 24(2):8–12, 2009. DOI: 10.1109/MIS.2009.36 5

[66] James Hamilton. On designing and deploying Internet-scale services. In *Proceedings of the 21st Large Installation System Administration Conference (LISA '07)*, pages 233–244, Dallas, Texas, 2007. 10

[67] James Hamilton. Cooperative Expendable Micro-Slice Servers (CEMS): Low cost, low power servers for Internet-scale services. In *Proceedings of the Fourth Biennial Conference on Innovative Data Systems Research (CIDR 2009)*, Asilomar, California, 2009. 9, 10

[68] Jeff Hammerbacher. Information platforms and the rise of the data scientist. In Toby Segaran and Jeff Hammerbacher, editors, *Beautiful Data*, pages 73–84. O'Reilly, Sebastopol, California, 2009. 6, 59, 146

[69] Zelig S. Harris. *Mathematical Structures of Language*. Wiley, New York, 1968. 48

[70] Md. Rafiul Hassan and Baikunth Nath. Stock market forecasting using hidden Markov models: A new approach. In *Proceedings of the 5th International Conference on Intelligent Systems Design and Applications (ISDA '05)*, pages 192–196, Wroclaw, Poland, 2005. DOI: 10.1109/ISDA.2005.85 114

[71] Bingsheng He, Wenbin Fang, Qiong Luo, Naga K. Govindaraju, and Tuyong Wang. Mars: A MapReduce framework on graphics processors. In *Proceedings of the 17th International Conference on Parallel Architectures and Compilation Techniques (PACT 2008)*, pages 260–269, Toronto, Ontario, Canada, 2008. DOI: 10.1145/1454115.1454152 20

[72] Tony Hey, Stewart Tansley, and Kristin Tolle. *The Fourth Paradigm: Data-Intensive Scientific Discovery*. Microsoft Research, Redmond, Washington, 2009. 3

[73] Tony Hey, Stewart Tansley, and Kristin Tolle. Jim Gray on eScience: A transformed scientific method. In Tony Hey, Stewart Tansley, and Kristin Tolle, editors, *The Fourth Paradigm: Data-Intensive Scientific Discovery*. Microsoft Research, Redmond, Washington, 2009. 3

[74] John Howard, Michael Kazar, Sherri Menees, David Nichols, Mahadev Satyanarayanan, Robert Sidebotham, and Michael West. Scale and performance in a distributed file system. *ACM Transactions on Computer Systems*, 6(1):51–81, 1988. DOI: 10.1145/35037.35059 29

[75] Michael Isard, Mihai Budiu, Yuan Yu, Andrew Birrell, and Dennis Fetterly. Dryad: Distributed data-parallel programs from sequential building blocks. In *Proceedings of the ACM SIGOPS/EuroSys European Conference on Computer Systems 2007 (EuroSys 2007)*, pages 59–72, Lisbon, Portugal, 2007. DOI: 10.1145/1272998.1273005 145

[76] Adam Jacobs. The pathologies of big data. *ACM Queue*, 7(6), 2009. DOI: 10.1145/1563821.1563874 11

[77] Joseph JaJa. *An Introduction to Parallel Algorithms*. Addison-Wesley, Reading, Massachusetts, 1992. 14, 103

[78] Frederick Jelinek. *Statistical methods for speech recognition*. MIT Press, Cambridge, Massachusetts, 1997. 112, 114, 120

[79] Daniel Jurafsky and James H. Martin. *Speech and Language Processing*. Pearson, Upper Saddle River, New Jersey, 2009. 5

[80] U Kang, Charalampos Tsourakakis, Ana Paula Appel, Christos Faloutsos, and Jure Leskovec. HADI: Fast diameter estimation and mining in massive graphs with Hadoop. Technical Report CMU-ML-08-117, School of Computer Science, Carnegie Mellon University, 2008. 103

[81] U Kang, Charalampos E. Tsourakakis, and Christos Faloutsos. PEGASUS: A peta-scale graph mining system—implementation and observations. In *Proceedings of the 2009 Ninth IEEE International Conference on Data Mining (ICDM 2009)*, pages 229–238, Miami, Floria, 2009. DOI: 10.1109/ICDM.2009.14 103

[82] Howard Karloff, Siddharth Suri, and Sergei Vassilvitskii. A model of computation for Map-Reduce. In *Proceedings of the 21st Annual ACM-SIAM Symposium on Discrete Algorithms (SODA 2010)*, Austin, Texas, 2010. 15

[83] Aaron Kimball, Sierra Michels-Slettvet, and Christophe Bisciglia. Cluster computing for Web-scale data processing. In *Proceedings of the 39th ACM Technical Symposium on Computer Science Education (SIGCSE 2008)*, pages 116–120, Portland, Oregon, 2008. DOI: 10.1145/1352135.1352177 71

[84] Jon M. Kleinberg. Authoritative sources in a hyperlinked environment. *Journal of the ACM*, 46(5):604–632, 1999. DOI: 10.1145/324133.324140 65, 95

[85] Philipp Koehn. *Statistical Machine Translation*. Cambridge University Press, Cambridge, England, 2010. 130, 133

[86] Philipp Koehn, Franz J. Och, and Daniel Marcu. Statistical phrase-based translation. In *Proceedings of the 2003 Human Language Technology Conference of the North American Chapter of the Association for Computational Linguistics (HLT/NAACL 2003)*, pages 48–54, Edmonton, Alberta, Canada, 2003. DOI: 10.3115/1073445.1073462 131

[87] John D. Lafferty, Andrew McCallum, and Fernando Pereira. Conditional random fields: Probabilistic models for segmenting and labeling sequence data. In *Proceedings of the Eighteenth International Conference on Machine Learning (ICML '01)*, pages 282–289, San Francisco, California, 2001. 138

[88] Ronny Lempel and Shlomo Moran.   SALSA: The Stochastic Approach for Link-Structure Analysis. *ACM Transactions on Information Systems*, 19(2):131–160, 2001. DOI: 10.1145/382979.383041 65, 95

[89] Abby Levenberg, Chris Callison-Burch, and Miles Osborne. Stream-based translation models for statistical machine translation. In *Proceedings of the 11th Annual Conference of the North American Chapter of the Association for Computational Linguistics (NAACL HLT 2010)*, Los Angeles, California, 2010. 145

[90] Abby Levenberg and Miles Osborne. Stream-based randomised language models for SMT. In *Proceedings of the 2009 Conference on Empirical Methods in Natural Language Processing*, pages 756–764, Singapore, 2009. 145

[91] Adam Leventhal.   Triple-parity RAID and beyond.   *ACM Queue*, 7(11), 2009. DOI: 10.1145/1661785.1670144 2

[92] Jimmy Lin.   An exploration of the principles underlying redundancy-based factoid question answering.   *ACM Transactions on Information Systems*, 27(2):1–55, 2007. DOI: 10.1145/1229179.1229180 4

[93] Jimmy Lin. Exploring large-data issues in the curriculum: A case study with MapReduce. In *Proceedings of the Third Workshop on Issues in Teaching Computational Linguistics (TeachCL-08) at ACL 2008*, pages 54–61, Columbus, Ohio, 2008. 71

[94] Jimmy Lin. Scalable language processing algorithms for the masses: A case study in computing word co-occurrence matrices with MapReduce. In *Proceedings of the 2008 Conference on Empirical Methods in Natural Language Processing (EMNLP 2008)*, pages 419–428, Honolulu, Hawaii, 2008. 47, 51

[95] Jimmy Lin, Anand Bahety, Shravya Konda, and Samantha Mahindrakar. Low-latency, high-throughput access to static global resources within the Hadoop framework. Technical Report HCIL-2009-01, University of Maryland, College Park, Maryland, January 2009. 63

[96] Dong C. Liu, Jorge Nocedal, Dong C. Liu, and Jorge Nocedal. On the limited memory BFGS method for large scale optimization. *Mathematical Programming B*, 45(3):503–528, 1989. DOI: 10.1007/BF01589116 139

[97] Adam Lopez. Statistical machine translation. *ACM Computing Surveys*, 40(3):1–49, 2008. DOI: 10.1145/1380584.1380586 130

[98] Grzegorz Malewicz, Matthew H. Austern, Aart J. C. Bik, James C. Dehnert, Ilan Horn, Naty Leiser, and Grzegorz Czajkowski. Pregel: A system for large-scale graph processing. In *Proceedings of the 28th ACM Symposium on Principles of Distributed Computing (PODC 2009)*, page 6, Calgary, Alberta, Canada, 2009. DOI: 10.1145/1583991.1584010 86, 145

[99] Grzegorz Malewicz, Matthew H. Austern, Aart J. C. Bik, James C. Dehnert, Ilan Horn, Naty Leiser, and Grzegorz Czajkowski. Pregel: A system for large-scale graph processing. In *Proceedings of the 2010 ACM SIGMOD International Conference on Management of Data*, Indianapolis, Indiana, 2010. DOI: 10.1145/1582716.1582723 86, 145

[100] Robert Malouf. A comparison of algorithms for maximum entropy parameter estimation. In *Proceedings of the Sixth Conference on Natural Language Learning (CoNLL-2002)*, pages 49–55, Taipei, Taiwan, 2002. DOI: 10.3115/1118853.1118871 140

[101] Christopher D. Manning, Prabhakar Raghavan, and Hinrich Schütze. *An Introduction to Information Retrieval*. Cambridge University Press, Cambridge, England, 2008. 42, 83

[102] Christopher D. Manning and Hinrich Schütze. *Foundations of Statistical Natural Language Processing*. MIT Press, Cambridge, Massachusetts, 1999. 5, 133

[103] Elaine R. Mardis. The impact of next-generation sequencing technology on genetics. *Trends in Genetics*, 24(3):133–141, 2008. DOI: 10.1016/j.tig.2007.12.007 2

[104] Michael D. McCool. Scalable programming models for massively multicore processors. *Proceedings of the IEEE*, 96(5):816–831, 2008. DOI: 10.1109/JPROC.2008.917731 13, 145

[105] Marshall K. McKusick and Sean Quinlan. GFS: Evolution on fast-forward. *ACM Queue*, 7(7), 2009. DOI: 10.1145/1594204.1594206 32

[106] John Mellor-Crummey, David Whalley, and Ken Kennedy. Improving memory hierarchy performance for irregular applications using data and computation reorderings. *International Journal of Parallel Programming*, 29(3):217–247, 2001. DOI: 10.1023/A:1011119519789 101

[107] Donald Metzler, Jasmine Novak, Hang Cui, and Srihari Reddy. Building enriched document representations using aggregated anchor text. In *Proceedings of the 32nd Annual International ACM SIGIR Conference on Research and Development in Information Retrieval (SIGIR 2009)*, pages 219–226, 2009. DOI: 10.1145/1571941.1571981 68, 88

[108] David R. H. Miller, Tim Leek, and Richard M. Schwartz. A hidden Markov model information retrieval system. In *Proceedings of the 22nd Annual International ACM SIGIR Conference on Research and Development in Information Retrieval (SIGIR 1999)*, pages 214–221, Berkeley, California, 1999. DOI: 10.1145/312624.312680 114

[109] Alistair Moffat, William Webber, and Justin Zobel. Load balancing for term-distributed parallel retrieval. In *Proceedings of the 29th Annual International ACM SIGIR Conference on Research and Development in Information Retrieval (SIGIR 2006)*, pages 348–355, Seattle, Washington, 2006. DOI: 10.1145/1148170.1148232 82

[110] Kamal Nigam, John Lafferty, and Andrew McCallum. Using maximum entropy for text classification. In *Proceedings of the IJCAI-99 Workshop on Machine Learning for Information Filtering*, pages 61–67, Stockholm, Sweden, 1999. 138

[111] Daniel Nurmi, Rich Wolski, Chris Grzegorczyk, Graziano Obertelli, Sunil Soman, Lamia Youseff, and Dmitrii Zagorodnov. The Eucalyptus open-source cloud-computing system. In *Proceedings of the 9th IEEE/ACM International Symposium on Cluster Computing and the Grid*, pages 124–131, Washington, D.C., 2009. DOI: 10.1109/CCGRID.2009.93 7

[112] Franz J. Och and Hermann Ney. A systematic comparison of various statistical alignment models. *Computational Linguistics*, 29(1):19–51, 2003. DOI: 10.1162/089120103321337421 135

[113] Christopher Olston and Marc Najork. Web crawling. *Foundations and Trends in Information Retrieval*, 4(3):175–246, 2010. DOI: 10.1561/1500000017 67

[114] Christopher Olston, Benjamin Reed, Utkarsh Srivastava, Ravi Kumar, and Andrew Tomkins. Pig Latin: A not-so-foreign language for data processing. In *Proceedings of the 2008 ACM SIGMOD International Conference on Management of Data*, pages 1099–1110, Vancouver, British Columbia, Canada, 2008. DOI: 10.1145/1376616.1376726 59, 146

[115] Kunle Olukotun and Lance Hammond. The future of microprocessors. *ACM Queue*, 3(7):27–34, 2005. DOI: 10.1145/1095408.1095418 13

[116] Sean Owen and Robin Anil. *Mahout in Action*. Manning Publications Co., Greenwich, Connecticut, 2010. 141

[117] Lawrence Page, Sergey Brin, Rajeev Motwani, and Terry Winograd. The PageRank citation ranking: Bringing order to the Web. Stanford Digital Library Working Paper SIDL-WP-1999-0120, Stanford University, 1999. 65, 95, 100

[118] Bo Pang and Lillian Lee. Opinion mining and sentiment analysis. *Foundations and Trends in Information Retrieval*, 2(1–2):1–135, 2008. DOI: 10.1561/1500000011 3

[119] David A. Patterson. The data center is the computer. *Communications of the ACM*, 52(1):105, 2008. 14

[120] Andrew Pavlo, Erik Paulson, Alexander Rasin, Daniel J. Abadi, David J. DeWitt, Samuel Madden, and Michael Stonebraker. A comparison of approaches to large-scale data analysis. In *Proceedings of the 35th ACM SIGMOD International Conference on Management of Data*, pages 165–178, Providence, Rhode Island, 2009. DOI: 10.1145/1559845.1559865 59

[121] Sasa Petrovic, Miles Osborne, and Victor Lavrenko. Streaming first story detection with application to Twitter. In *Proceedings of the 11th Annual Conference of the North American*

Chapter of the Association for Computational Linguistics (NAACL HLT 2010), Los Angeles, California, 2010. 145

[122] Rob Pike, Sean Dorward, Robert Griesemer, and Sean Quinlan. Interpreting the data: Parallel analysis with Sawzall. *Scientific Programming Journal*, 13(4):277–298, 2005. 146

[123] Eduardo Pinheiro, Wolf-Dietrich Weber, and Luiz André Barroso. Failure trends in a large disk drive population. In *Proceedings of the 5th USENIX Conference on File and Storage Technologies (FAST 2007)*, San Jose, California, 2008. 10, 26

[124] Xiaoguang Qi and Brian D. Davison. Web page classification: Features and algorithms. *ACM Computing Surveys*, 41(2), 2009. DOI: 10.1145/1459352.1459357 82

[125] Lawrence R. Rabiner. A tutorial on hidden Markov models and selected applications in speech recognition. In *Readings in Speech Recognition*, pages 267–296. Morgan Kaufmann Publishers, San Francisco, California, 1990. DOI: 10.1109/5.18626 115, 120

[126] M. Mustafa Rafique, Benjamin Rose, Ali R. Butt, and Dimitrios S. Nikolopoulos. Supporting MapReduce on large-scale asymmetric multi-core clusters. *ACM Operating Systems Review*, 43(2):25–34, 2009. DOI: 10.1145/1531793.1531800 20

[127] Colby Ranger, Ramanan Raghuraman, Arun Penmetsa, Gary Bradski, and Christos Kozyrakis. Evaluating MapReduce for multi-core and multiprocessor systems. In *Proceedings of the 13th International Symposium on High-Performance Computer Architecture (HPCA 2007)*, pages 205–218, Phoenix, Arizona, 2007. DOI: 10.1109/HPCA.2007.346181 20

[128] Delip Rao and David Yarowsky. Ranking and semi-supervised classification on large scale graphs using Map-Reduce. In *Proceedings of the ACL/IJCNLP 2009 Workshop on Graph-Based Methods for Natural Language Processing (TextGraphs-4)*, Singapore, 2009. 103

[129] Michael A. Rappa. The utility business model and the future of computing services. *IBM Systems Journal*, 34(1):32–42, 2004. DOI: 10.1147/sj.431.0032 6

[130] Sheldon M. Ross. *Stochastic processes*. Wiley, New York, 1996. 114

[131] Thomas Sandholm and Kevin Lai. MapReduce optimization using regulated dynamic prioritization. In *Proceedings of the Eleventh International Joint Conference on Measurement and Modeling of Computer Systems (SIGMETRICS '09)*, pages 299–310, Seattle, Washington, 2009. DOI: 10.1145/1555349.1555384 25

[132] Michael Schatz. *High Performance Computing for DNA Sequence Alignment and Assembly*. PhD thesis, University of Maryland, College Park, 2010. 103

[133] Frank Schmuck and Roger Haskin. GPFS: A shared-disk file system for large computing clusters. In *Proceedings of the First USENIX Conference on File and Storage Technologies*, pages 231–244, Monterey, California, 2002. 29

[134] Donovan A. Schneider and David J. DeWitt. A performance evaluation of four parallel join algorithms in a shared-nothing multiprocessor environment. In *Proceedings of the 1989 ACM SIGMOD International Conference on Management of Data*, pages 110–121, Portland, Oregon, 1989. DOI: 10.1145/67544.66937 60

[135] Bianca Schroeder, Eduardo Pinheiro, and Wolf-Dietrich Weber. DRAM errors in the wild: A large-scale field study. In *Proceedings of the Eleventh International Joint Conference on Measurement and Modeling of Computer Systems (SIGMETRICS '09)*, pages 193–204, Seattle, Washington, 2009. DOI: 10.1145/1555349.1555372 10, 26

[136] Hinrich Schütze. Automatic word sense discrimination. *Computational Linguistics*, 24(1):97–123, 1998. 48

[137] Hinrich Schütze and Jan O. Pedersen. A cooccurrence-based thesaurus and two applications to information retrieval. *Information Processing and Management*, 33(3):307–318, 1998. DOI: 10.1016/S0306-4573(96)00068-4 48

[138] Satoshi Sekine and Elisabete Ranchhod. *Named Entities: Recognition, Classification and Use*. John Benjamins, Amsterdam, The Netherlands, 2009. 3

[139] Kristie Seymore, Andrew Mccallum, and Ronald Rosenfeld. Learning hidden Markov model structure for information extraction. In *Proceedings of the AAAI-99 Workshop on Machine Learning for Information Extraction*, pages 37–42, Orlando, Florida, 1999. 114

[140] Fei Sha and Fernando Pereira. Shallow parsing with conditional random fields. In *Proceedings of the 2003 Human Language Technology Conference of the North American Chapter of the Association for Computational Linguistics (HLT/NAACL 2003)*, pages 134–141, Edmonton, Alberta, Canada, 2003. DOI: 10.3115/1073445.1073473 140

[141] Noah Smith. Log-linear models. `http://www.cs.cmu.edu/~nasmith/papers/smith.tut04.pdf`, 2004. 140

[142] Christopher Southan and Graham Cameron. Beyond the tsunami: Developing the infrastructure to deal with life sciences data. In Tony Hey, Stewart Tansley, and Kristin Tolle, editors, *The Fourth Paradigm: Data-Intensive Scientific Discovery*. Microsoft Research, Redmond, Washington, 2009. 2

[143] Mario Stanke and Stephan Waack. Gene prediction with a hidden Markov model and a new intron submodel. *Bioinformatics*, 19 Suppl 2:ii215–225, October 2003. DOI: 10.1093/bioinformatics/btg1080 114

[144] Michael Stonebraker, Daniel Abadi, David J. DeWitt, Sam Madden, Erik Paulson, Andrew Pavlo, and Alexander Rasin. MapReduce and parallel DBMSs: Friends or foes? *Communications of the ACM*, 53(1):64–71, 2010. DOI: 10.1145/1629175.1629197 59

[145] Alexander S. Szalay, Peter Z. Kunszt, Ani Thakar, Jim Gray, Don Slutz, and Robert J. Brunner. Designing and mining multi-terabyte astronomy archives: The Sloan Digital Sky Survey. *SIGMOD Record*, 29(2):451–462, 2000. DOI: 10.1145/335191.335439 2

[146] Wittawat Tantisiriroj, Swapnil Patil, and Garth Gibson. Data-intensive file systems for Internet services: A rose by any other name.... Technical Report CMU-PDL-08-114, Parallel Data Laboratory, Carnegie Mellon University, 2008. 29

[147] Chandramohan A. Thekkath, Timothy Mann, and Edward K. Lee. Frangipani: A scalable distributed file system. In *Proceedings of the 16th ACM Symposium on Operating Systems Principles (SOSP 1997)*, pages 224–237, Saint-Malo, France, 1997. DOI: 10.1145/268998.266694 29

[148] Leslie G. Valiant. A bridging model for parallel computation. *Communications of the ACM*, 33(8):103–111, 1990. DOI: 10.1145/79173.79181 13, 14, 15, 86, 145

[149] Luis M. Vaquero, Luis Rodero-Merino, Juan Caceres, and Maik Lindner. A break in the clouds: Towards a cloud definition. *ACM SIGCOMM Computer Communication Review*, 39(1):50–55, 2009. DOI: 10.1145/1496091.1496100 6

[150] Stephan Vogel, Hermann Ney, and Christoph Tillmann. HMM-based word alignment in statistical translation. In *Proceedings of the 16th International Conference on Computational Linguistics (COLING 1996)*, pages 836–841, Copenhagen, Denmark, 1996. DOI: 10.3115/993268.993313 114, 135

[151] Yi Wang, Hongjie Bai, Matt Stanton, Wen-Yen Chen, and Edward Y. Chang. PLDA: Parallel latent Dirichlet allocation for large-scale applications. In *Proceedings of the Fifth International Conference on Algorithmic Aspects in Information and Management (AAIM 2009)*, pages 301–314, San Francisco, California, 2009. DOI: 10.1007/978-3-642-02158-9_26 141

[152] Duncan J. Watts and Steven H. Strogatz. Collective dynamics of 'small-world' networks. *Nature*, 393:440–442, 1998. DOI: 10.1038/30918 92

[153] Xingzhi Wen and Uzi Vishkin. FPGA-based prototype of a PRAM-On-Chip processor. In *Proceedings of the 5th Conference on Computing Frontiers*, pages 55–66, Ischia, Italy, 2008. DOI: 10.1145/1366230.1366240 14

[154] Tom White. *Hadoop: The Definitive Guide*. O'Reilly, Sebastopol, California, 2009. 15, 23

[155] Eugene Wigner. The unreasonable effectiveness of mathematics in the natural sciences. *Communications in Pure and Applied Mathematics*, 13(1):1–14, 1960. DOI: 10.1002/cpa.3160130102 5

[156] Ian H. Witten, Alistair Moffat, and Timothy C. Bell. *Managing Gigabytes: Compressing and Indexing Documents and Images.* Morgan Kaufmann Publishing, San Francisco, California, 1999. DOI: 10.1023/A:1011472308196 69, 77, 78, 83

[157] Jinxi Xu and W. Bruce Croft. Corpus-based stemming using cooccurrence of word variants. *ACM Transactions on Information Systems*, 16(1):61–81, 1998. DOI: 10.1145/267954.267957 48

[158] Rui Xu and Donald Wunsch II. Survey of clustering algorithms. *IEEE Transactions on Neural Networks*, 16(3):645–678, 2005. DOI: 10.1109/TNN.2005.845141 86

[159] Yuan Yu, Michael Isard, Dennis Fetterly, Mihai Budiu, Úlfar Erlingsson, Pradeep Kumar Gunda, and Jon Currey. DryadLINQ: A system for general-purpose distributed data-parallel computing using a high-level language. In *Proceedings of the 8th Symposium on Operating System Design and Implementation (OSDI 2008)*, pages 1–14, San Diego, California, 2008. 145

[160] Matei Zaharia, Dhruba Borthakur, Joydeep Sen Sarma, Khaled Elmeleegy, Scott Shenker, and Ion Stoica. Job scheduling for multi-user MapReduce clusters. Technical Report UCB/EECS-2009-55, Electrical Engineering and Computer Sciences, University of California at Berkeley, 2009. 25

[161] Matei Zaharia, Andy Konwinski, Anthony D. Joseph, Randy Katz, and Ion Stoica. Improving MapReduce performance in heterogeneous environments. In *Proceedings of the 8th Symposium on Operating System Design and Implementation (OSDI 2008)*, pages 29–42, San Diego, California, 2008. 25

[162] Justin Zobel and Alistair Moffat. Inverted files for text search engines. *ACM Computing Surveys*, 38(6):1–56, 2006. 78, 83

Authors' Biographies

JIMMY LIN

Jimmy Lin is an Associate Professor in the iSchool (College of Information Studies) at the University of Maryland, College Park. He directs the recently-formed Cloud Computing Center, an interdisciplinary group that explores the many aspects of cloud computing as it impacts technology, people, and society. Lin's research lies at the intersection of natural language processing and information retrieval, with a recent emphasis on scalable algorithms and large-data processing. He received his Ph.D. from MIT in Electrical Engineering and Computer Science in 2004.

CHRIS DYER

Chris Dyer is graduating with a Ph.D. in Linguistics from the University of Maryland, College Park in June, 2010 and will be joining the Language Technologies Institute at Carnegie Mellon University as a postdoctoral researcher. His research interests include statistical machine translation and machine learning, and he has served as a reviewer for numerous conferences and journals in the areas of natural language processing and computational linguistics. He first became acquainted with MapReduce in 2007 using Hadoop, version 0.13.0, and gained further experience with MapReduce during an internship with Google Research in 2008.

Made in the USA
Lexington, KY
23 June 2010